D0805928

PASTORAL CARE

Heinemann Organization in Schools Series

HEAD OF DEPARTMENT
Michael Marland

THE ENVIRONMENT OF LEARNING
Elizabeth Richardson

PASTORAL CARE
Michael Marland

THE TUTOR
Keith Blackburn

COMPREHENSIVE VALUES
Pat Daunt

ORGANIZING RESOURCES, SIX CASE STUDIES
Norman Beswick

Other Heinemann Books and Editions by the same Author

ENGLISH FOR THE INDIVIDUAL
(with Denys Thompson)

PETER GRIMES
(a dramatization of Crabbe's poem)

THE WIDOWING OF MRS HOLROYD
and THE DAUGHTER-IN-LAW
(an edition of two plays by D. H. Lawrence)

Pastoral Care

organizing the care and guidance of
the individual pupil in a comprehensive school

MICHAEL MARLAND
Headmaster
Woodberry Down School
London

with contributions by

C. JAMES GILL
BOB GROVE
DENIS INCE
PATRICK MCGEENEY
and
CHARLES STUART-JERVIS

225965

HEINEMANN EDUCATIONAL BOOKS
LONDON

Heinemann Educational Books Ltd
LONDON EDINBURGH MELBOURNE AUCKLAND TORONTO
SINGAPORE HONG KONG KUALA LUMPUR
IBADAN NAIROBI JOHANNESBURG
LUSAKA NEW DELHI

ISBN 0 435 80574 6

Introduction and Chapters 3, 4, 5, 9, 11 and 12
© Michael Marland 1974
Chapter 2 © Charles Stuart-Jervis 1974
Chapter 6 © Bob Grove 1974
Chapter 7 © C. James Gill 1974
Chapter 8 © Patrick McGeeney 1974
Chapter 10 © Denis Ince 1974
First published 1974
Reprinted 1975

Published by
Heinemann Educational Books Ltd
48 Charles Street, London W1X 8AH
Printed Offset Litho and bound in Great Britain by
Cox & Wyman Ltd, London, Fakenham and Reading

Contents

Contents

for Rose,
who understands

Preface

This book, as the title-page makes clear, is one of a series devoted to exploring against a theoretical background the practical possibilities of organization in the secondary school, especially the comprehensive secondary school. The series has been planned as a whole so that the major aspects of secondary-school organization are methodically covered. However, each book is also written to stand on its own. Inevitably this means some overlapping between the volumes, for certain topics (such as a school's relationship with its parents) are covered in a number of books, though with varying degrees of detail and from different points of view.

The justification for the entire series is a simple one, and it is one that is widely felt: it is no longer acceptable for a school merely to organize by default and to plan by inertia: changing social conditions, the introduction of non-selective schools, the growth of various forms of organization other than the 11–18 pattern, and, above all it seems to me, the markedly greater *ambition* of education have all led us to question what we know about ways of organizing schools so that the educational experience can be as rich and as profitable for all as is possible. In considering our planning, we have rescued the word 'organization' from the perjorative limbo to which it had been consigned – perhaps by those with memories of wartime service 'admin'. We see that administration is a creative process, not a dry and sterile chore; we see that it involves working mainly with people, not with paper; we see that it requires thought, not mere repetition; we sense that it is collaborative, not hierarchial. Finally, we realize that the administrators need to be able to deploy a range of knowledge: merely to choose between a couple of alternatives, when in fact there are many other possibilities that could be considered, is not really to choose at all.

In this context, the job of the outside adviser, the course, the conference, or the book is to survey the needs, study the factors available to the school for variation, note as wide a range of strategies and details as possible. It is very definitely not the job of such a book as this to attempt to lay down a would-be 'ideal' pattern – there is no such thing. On one occasion when

I was speaking to a large audience of teachers on an aspect of organizing pastoral care, an enthusiastic teacher came up to me the night before, clutching a blank postcard. She explained that she would unfortunately have to leave before my talk. Would I, she asked, pencil poised, be kind enough just to tell before the evening meal (only a few minutes off) what 'the answer is'. Would I, she asked, 'be recommending the horizontal or the vertical?' Merely to recount such an incident is to reveal the too easily accepted fallacy. There is no 'answer'; there is no single pattern which can be universally applied and which holds an optimum balance of advantages and difficulties. What, though, is valuable for schools is a description of various models, with as objective as possible an assessment of their strengths and weaknesses. Thus readers will not find a 'What I do in my school' account in this book. I have resisted also the temptation to describe in positive and clear tones 'the job of a housemaster' or 'how an attendance system can be organized'. Instead I have attempted a survey of the problems and possibilities, with a number of case studies to illustrate them.

Underpinning, I hope, the entire book is reference to such research as is relevant. The traditional reluctance of the teacher to refer to research, and to regard it as anything other than an eccentric hobby of unrealistic escapers from the real problems, is fading away as important and significant findings have been shown to be valuable to work in schools. At the same time, research reports are becoming more accessible both in written style and publication format. The subject of this book is one that has been illuminated in a number of ways by recent research. I hope that most of the available work has been explored and introduced at the appropriate moments. School decisions need the triple perspective: theoretical understanding, knowledge of what is done elsewhere, and a scrutiny of the particular pattern of the school at that time.

I have had a number of readers in mind throughout the book: in the first place the head teacher, or any of his or her senior colleagues, who is surveying the pastoral organization of a school, or contemplating the organization or re-organization of one. Secondly I have also considered the needs of the pastoral heads (head of year, housemaster, senior mistress, senior master, and so on) and those experienced teachers aspiring to such a post. There is little or nothing in print to help them prepare for their tasks, tasks which need the full power that comes only from professional knowledge as well as personal strength. On the other hand, my emphasis is not on the techniques of those posts themselves so much as on the working context that the school organization must create for the individual. This is not, then, a book for the newer teacher who has only limited influence over major policy. Such a teacher would, I hope, also find it interesting for an understanding of secondary-school organization, but there is little direct advice for him or her in it. (*The Tutor*, by Keith Blackburn, also in this series, has been written precisely with the needs of such a teacher in mind.) Lastly, I very much hope that the many workers in related fields outside schools – psychologists, social workers, welfare workers, and LEA administrators – will find the book helpful in their work.

The structure of the book may be found unusual, but I hope not awkward. I should describe it as a semi-symposium, and in devising it I have had in mind what I take to be the twin faults of many books on aspects of schools: the book by a single author can be well shaped, but usually is either written from afar and tends to lack personal involvement, or is written from within and thus becomes over-personal. On the other hand I must admit to considerable dissatisfaction with many symposia – including ones to which I have myself contributed: it is extremely difficult for one editor to create complete coherence.

In this book I have tried to keep the coherence of a single-author book, but to draw on the special experiences, knowledge, and convictions of five important contributors, each giving the reader his special expertise where what I hope is the logic of the book requires it. I have not tried to avoid all overlapping. To have done so not only would have limited the contributors, but also would have given the impression that the field could be firmly divided when in fact it is closely intermeshed. The question of home-visiting, for instance, relates to many aspects of the subject, and references to it will be found in several different parts of the book.

I am myself responsible for the overall shape, for all the unsigned sections, and for the commissioning and placing of the contributors' pieces. Should there be any error of fact, judgement, or emphasis, the fault is thus mine. On the other hand I hope readers will find the structure clear and practical, and the semi-symposium form which I have devised satisfactory. (Together with my contributors, I must point out that, as would be expected, the views we express are our own, and do not necessarily coincide with those of the Authorities for whom we work.)

I am very grateful to a large number of colleagues in three comprehensive schools who have discussed the aims, difficulties, and possible methods of looking after pupils with me, both in general terms and in the cases of particular pupils. Amongst the particularly knowledgeable individuals with whom I have not worked, but have had detailed and lengthy discussions and whose ideas and formulations have helped me a great deal are Pat Daunt, John Hipkin, Catherine Avent, Geoffrey Petter, and Denys John. Of course, none of those are in any way responsible for any errors of judgement or fact which I may have made.

I have also benefited from the questions, ideas, and suggestions of many course members on LEA and DES courses on which I have spoken on aspects of comprehensive-school organization. In particular I should like to thank those who attended the large Advisory Centre for Education courses which I directed at Churchill College, Cambridge, in 1971 and 1972. Their accumulated experience and wisdom was very impressive. I am eager also to make special mention of the headteachers and senior staff of a number of schools to which I was welcomed to study their pastoral organization and methods. I am grateful to Shirley Hase for permission to include an excerpt from her valuable research on page 208. My task has been considerably helped by the bibliographical skills of the Woodberry Down school librarian, Mrs J. Cumming. Finally I should like to thank Jean Hardy, who typed and retyped the various drafts of the book with patience and the ability to unravel the most complex MS.

I owe a considerable debt to a small but growing number of valuable books on school organization. When I started work on the companion volume to this, *Head of Department*, only a few years ago, there were almost no detailed books in this field. The Simon-Benn volume and the NFER publications listed on pages 231-2 have notably remedied this, and surely no practical school head or senior staff could work without a close study of these – particularly B. M. Moore's *Guidance in Comprehensive Schools* (NFER, 1970), an excellent study which I think of as necessary background reading to this volume.

On the other hand I have aimed at something rather different from those books. While definitely wanting to avoid a merely personal account of the particular school for which I

am responsible, I have wanted to keep closer to the pressure
of daily reality than those writers. I have wanted to keep the
particular always in the forefront, and to highlight detail. There
is an endless fascination in the details of schools; indeed in the
huge challenge of making the current educational generalities
actually operational, detailed examples are vital. Just because
there is so much in common between various British schools, so
there is all the more fascination in the differences that there
are. Being part of the leadership of a secondary school today
is an exhilarating and challenging task. It is, though, one
which cannot be tolerably attempted, I suggest, without knowledge of these differences, and thus of the possibilities of real
planning.

1 Introduction

The Pastoral Need

One serious disadvantage of the title for this book is that it could be seen as accepting that school life must divide into two sides, the pastoral and the academic. It is important to stress that at the heart of the matter there can be no pastoral/academic split. The secondary school (whatever its precise age-organization) is the experience which our civilization has chosen to use to bring adolescents through what the psychologist Erik H. Erikson so potently called 'the crisis of identity'[1]: 'What do I want to make of myself, and what do I have to work with?'[2] Here is the core of the pastoral need. The crisis involves a search of considerable subtlety and possible difficulty, all the more fraught in twentieth-century Western civilization. The nature of the essentially pastoral work of a school is illuminated by Erikson's points about the effect of the division of labour:

> In pre-literate people much is learned from adults who become teachers by acclamation rather than by appointment, and much is learned from older children, but the knowledge gained is related to the basic skills of simple technologies which can be understood the moment the child gets ready to handle utensils, the tools, and the weapons (or facsimiles thereof) used by the big people. He enters the technology of his tribe very gradually but also very directly. More literate people, with more specialized careers, must prepare the child by teaching him things which first of all make him literate. He is then given the widest possible basic education for the greatest number of possible careers. The greater the specialization, the more indistinct the goal of initiative becomes, the more complicated the social reality, and the vaguer the father's and mother's role in it. Between childhood and adulthood, then, our children go to school, and school skill seems to many to be a world all by itself, with its own goals and limitations, its achievements and disappointments.

The force of this passage, which like the section from which it comes[3] seems to me extraordinarily rich in its implications, lies in the penultimate sentence: '... the more indistinct the goal of initiative becomes, the more complicated the social reality ...' Erikson is reminding us that school learning, however intrinsically interesting we may endeavour to make it, is an inevitable but perhaps regrettable layer which we have had to insert between the child and his adult life. It is a layer necessarily preliminary and necessarily obscure. As Erikson stresses, it therefore develops 'its own goals and limitations, its achieve-

---

[1] This idea is elaborated in a book of great importance: *Identity, Youth and Crisis* (Faber, 1968; paper 1971).
[2] Ibid., 1971 edition, p. 314.
[3] 'School Age and Task Identification', ibid., p. 122.

ments and disappointments'. To help re-focus the experience, and to relate it to later life (which has come to be thought of as 'real life') is a pastoral need for twentieth-century youth, and one which cannot be accomplished by 'pure' teaching. As the range of jobs has increased so immensely, the range of beliefs on offer has also increased, social and geographical mobility have accelerated, cultural experiences have diversified, and the question 'Who am I?' has become less and less simple to answer. Indeed, as Western culture has been less dominated by the insistent and optionless demands of the immediate and local work-market, the question has become even more complex. Erikson again pinpoints this:

> The majority of men have always consolidated their identity needs around their technical and occupational capacities, leaving it to special groups (special by birth, by choice or election, and by giftedness) to establish and preserve those 'higher' institutions without which man's daily work has always seemed an inadequate self-expression, if not a mere grind or even a kind of curse. It may be for that very reason that the identity problem in our time becomes both psychiatrically and historically relevant. For as man can leave some of the grind and curse to machines, he can visualize a greater freedom of identity for a larger segment of mankind.[1]

If that trend is true of the century, how additionally sharp is the problem today, because of the shape and texture of our post-war, post-austerity society. In Chapter 3 I trace some of the influences on today's world and our young people in it which are significant for pastoral care. For the time being I shall merely state my belief that pupils who have been coming into secondary schools, especially in urban areas, since about 1964 have been notably different from their predecessors as a result of their upbringing. This has intensified the pastoral need in a number of ways. As Pat Daunt observes in another volume in this series,[2] 'The rate at which the media are diseducating children in obedience is far greater than that at which schools are educating them in any alternatives', and in Chapter 3 I have elaborated this thesis also. Daunt sees the alternative as 'responsible autonomy'. However, a mere 'teaching' organization requires simple obedience if it is to function. Further, it has little or no power to mould that obedience if the demands of the teaching situation are not met. If the expectation of obedience

[1] Ibid., pp. 127–128.
[2] *Comprehensive Values* (Heinemann, 1975).

is frustrated, the demand can merely be intensified. If it is still frustrated, the system has to admit its impotence by resigning or asking for the recalcitrant pupil to be removed. Pastoral care involves recognizing the truth of Pat Daunt's analysis not merely as a ghastly fact of the age to be regretted, but as a challenge to further work. The development of 'responsible autonomy' is an urgent pastoral need of today's adolescent, but one that can be met only in an ordered community.

Simultaneously, social, economic, and political pressures (some of them, such as the reduced availability of work in many areas, closely related to the causes of the changes) have kept more of the young in school for longer than ever. The tradition of secondary education with which we confronted them was peculiarly unsuited for extending to the whole range of age, ability, and background in the way in which we were attempting to do so. It assumed that humane non-vocational learning is the summit of human activity, and that this learning is justified for its own sake and without requiring social dividends. Secondly, it regarded the peak achievement in learning as being realized within a study in depth.[1] Never before have we attempted to assist the generality of young people through schools, and thus never before has the perhaps inevitable artificiality of school life been lit up so clearly. The efforts of recent years to adapt have been largely directed to reforming the *curriculum*. This has been especially true of the ROSLA schemes, and such reform is institutionalized in the terms of reference and constitution of the Schools Council. This curriculum development has been essential, but in no respect is the artificiality of schools clearer than in the realm of pastoral care. It is here that the need for careful thought is greatest.

Even the reform of the curriculum, however, illustrates from another point of view that there can be no pastoral/academic split: there is rarely any curricular reality unless there is reciprocity between teachers and learner; and where there is reciprocity – wherever there is human relationship – then there is 'pastoral' work in the important sense. As the late Derek Morell put it:

In curriculum we are concerned with human beings whose feelings and aspirations are far more real and immediately important to them than the cognitive development which is the educator's main stock in

[1] I have taken this formulation from Hopkinson, David, 'The 16–18 Question', *Trends in Education*, 20 (October 1970), p. 5.

trade. . . . It is a waste of time to fuss about what we think the children should learn if we do not understand how to organize a system of
pupil–teacher relationships which is productive of our intended
learnings.[1]

Yet even in the narrower curricular sense, some schools are
organized to do more pastorally than others. For instance, a
school with a first year of two periods of geography, one period
RE, two history, etc., inevitably has more impersonal teaching
and less reciprocity than one with, say, eight periods of humanities. However, by whatever ingenuities the curricular work is
made to fit the personal needs of the pupils, sufficient human
support, control, and enrichment cannot be accomplished
merely through the curriculum. Admittedly, it is prime for two
reasons: inevitably it takes the bulk of school time, and secondly it offers a medium for contact – something outside the
pupil which can be talked about. It is to 'pastoral care', though,
that a school looks for the wider completing of the process of
meeting pupils' needs.

The acceptance of such a responsibility has always been
enshrined in the *ideal* of the British school. 'Boy!' thundered a
famous early nineteenth-century public school headmaster to a
weeping new entrant, 'The school is your father! Boy! the
school is your mother . . . and all your other relatives too!'[2]
This all-embracing concern was especially typical of the isolated public boarding school, many of whose pupils had parents
abroad. The British state day school has been seen as taking
on the strengths of the boarding public school. This is not the
place to analyse that institution, nor to assess with what degree
of faith the state day school really did borrow from it. A careful
scrutiny would, I suspect, reveal that far less than has been
imagined was actually taken over, and that those elements
which were taken were seriously changed in the process of
transference. What is certain, though, is that this ideal picture
of the school was essentially of a community which is concerned
with the total welfare of the young person – a caring community.

To this extent at least the concept of pastoral care is not at all
new. However, the growth of comprehensive schools has given

[1] Talk to Anglo–American Education Association, reprinted in *The
Times Educational Supplement* (19 December 1969).
[2] The Reverend Boyer, Headmaster of Christ's Hospital, in 1800,
quoted in Morpurgo, J., *The Christ's Hospital Book* (Hamish Hamilton,
1953), page xi.

it new and extended life. They have two important features which have strong implications for the welfare of the individual pupil: size and diversity. These have led to new forms of organization, and, a most important point, to a development of more vigorous and detailed style of care than had been the tradition in even the best schools of the past. Early heads and planners of comprehensive schools saw their problem as one of finding ways in the larger school, of which the nation was so nervous, of 'preserving' the social life and individual care thought to exist in the smaller separate school.[1] Their efforts and vision were repaid by schools where the individual clearly had a place. It is no criticism, though, of the pioneers of comprehensive schools to say that they apparently did not foresee that the pastoral care systems which they were forging would rapidly establish not merely a new version of the old smaller school in the larger community, but a different kind, one that was infinitely more ambitious, more detailed, more personal, and thus more caring. What was originally seen merely as a way of *coping* with the size and diversity of the new schools, proved to be a tool for achieving more. (I shall explore this further in Chapter 5.)

Further, this first main phase of comprehensive schools co-incided with, and, indeed, partially prompted, a series of curricular changes. Amongst the least discussed[2] was the shift away from timetable patterns which gave secondary-modern pupils perhaps two-thirds of the week with 'form teachers'. The growth of the comprehensive school, building strong subject departments and developing teaching approaches through those subject teams, marked the end of the 'General Subjects' form teacher. Later moves towards fewer subjects and at least some integrated areas have seemed to reverse the process by putting the curricular teaching in fewer teachers' hands and by making the teaching group more often the same as the pastoral group. However, even the most advanced of these schemes are essentially *specialist* arrangements, which cannot function with 'General Subjects' teachers. These specialist teams often moved the school towards pupil-grouping arrange-ments, whether setting for mathematics or team-taught blocks for humanities, which fractured the basic teaching group. Not

[1] cf. especially the historically interesting account by H. R. Chetwynd in Chapter X of *Comprehensive School: Woodberry Down* (Routledge and Kegan Paul, 1959).

[2] But see Chapter 2 of Walton, Jack, *The Secondary School Timetable* (Ward Lock Educational, 1972), for a good historical analysis.

only had the form teacher disappeared, but even the form had gone also. Schools looking at themselves during these processes naturally turned to deliberate ways of injecting alternative pastoral arrangements. These would at least make up for what had been lost with the partial break-up of the form and the diminution of the role of its form teacher, who previously taught them for a substantial period of time. Again, the alternative approaches, which were devised as replacements, I should suggest proved more potent than their predecessors.

There was another influence, however. The period of the development of the first phase of comprehensive schools coincided, of course, with the growth of sociological studies of the effects of education and its constraints in the community. Despite the almost pathological resistance within the education system to the conscious study of research results, the overwhelming weight of the research studies has now been felt deeply by schools. The massive *National Child Development Study*, which is following a complete cohort of children born in one week in March 1958, had not reported on the children's secondary years by the time I was working on this book. However, the conclusions in the report of the first seven years is a culmination of the gradually massing weight of diverse evidence from other research on the social correlation: 'equality of educational opportunity cannot be achieved solely by improving our educational institutions.'[1] The implications of that statement lie well beyond the scope of this book, but the conviction gradually grew that this was indeed true. This growing belief influenced comprehensive schools in the 'sixties, and the schools tried progressively to cope with the realization by strengthening their pastoral care. The harsh analysis of sociological data had shown how relatively powerless schools are to overcome extra-school factors. But all the more effort was clearly required at least to mitigate them by sharpening what power the schools have. From the Crowther Report[2] onwards, the evidence was accumulating more and more clearly: factors outside the classroom have massive classroom implications. It became harder and harder for any teacher to define his or her task as 'merely' teaching. There are, of course, still those in the

[1] Davies, Ronald, *et al.*, *From Birth to Seven* (Longman, 1972), p. 190.
[2] Ministry of Education: Central Advisory Council for Education (England), *15 to 18*: volume I, report; volume II, surveys (HMSO, 1959, 1960).

profession who expect the school organization to serve up
manageable groups of pupils to receive instruction in their particular subject, who would dispense this instruction with
generosity and sympathy, but who would reject the notion that
any learning failures should be followed up in wider contexts.
Certainly, there is wisdom in realizing that schools cannot
take on the whole range of social ills single-handed. It may be,
as a DES paper put it in 1970, 'that some schools, in attempting to remedy social deprivation, venture beyond their prov-
ince and that other professional workers could perform some
of the time-consuming tasks which are performed with varying
efficiency by teachers'.[1]

Nevertheless, the personal and social needs of pupils have
achieved prominence in teachers' minds, at least as important
factors in effective learning, by a combination of the acceptance of research findings and of the new school structures
which were making action necessary and possible. What is even
more encouraging is that in this situation teachers have found
a great personal reward in the new work, and many have
begun to see 'pastoral care', as it now became called, not
merely as a way of supporting the academic work, but as
having a central educative purpose in itself.[2] That is the view
which this book takes of pastoral care.

Education uses a number of strange metaphors. There is a
thesis to be written on the growth and influence of terms like
'streaming', 'catchment area', 'throwing up an intake', and
'house'. Of all of them, 'pastoral care' is perhaps the oddest. Its
associations with pasture and shepherds are barely appropriate. The use of the term in religious communities certainly
does give an indication of its nature. Some definition is still
necessary.

'Pastoral care' is not an exact term. Negatively one can say
that the phrase covers all aspects of work with pupils in a school
other than pure teaching. One of the themes of this book,
though, is that the line where 'pastoral care' becomes 'teaching'
is necessarily ill-defined. All pastoral care has a teaching
element, and the converse is equally true: you cannot 'teach'
at all effectively without establishing some form of relationship. The pedagogic concern inevitably has a personal element.
In this book 'pastoral care' means looking after the total wel-

---

[1] Smart, P. F., *Social and Pastoral Organisation in Comprehensive Schools*,
COSMOS Paper 2, 70 (DES duplicated circulation, 1970).
[2] cf. Charles Stuart-Jervis in Chapter 2.

fare of the pupil. I should describe the overall aims of secondary education as to help the individual to be true to the best of himself; to develop his talents to the full; to learn the basis of understanding himself, his family, his community, and the world; and to do all this while developing respect for the beliefs, characters, and talents of others. These are various ways in which one can look at the needs of young people moving through the adolescent years. I find the following formulation in which W. D. Wall, now Dean of the University of London Institute of Education, explores the needs of adolescence, both convincing and helpful. He suggests that the road to maturity lies through the construction of what he calls 'a series of four selves – Social, Sexual, Vocational and Philosophic':

> Between say 13 and 25, the growing boy or girl has to develop a social self, oriented to others, aware of a place in society, of duties as well as of privileges, and in general emancipated from egocentric dependence on parents or indeed on others. A sexual self too must be shaped, capable of a range of feeling from friendly indifference to deep involvement with a member of the opposite sex, adequate adjustment in marriage and the ability to found and care for a family. For the boy, and increasingly for the girl, vocational adjustment, a working self, is also essential, not only to economic independence but as a basis of self-respect and self knowledge. This aspect is complex and consists both of a certain satisfaction derived from work and of a sense of being needed, and of being something more than a replaceable unit. Finally, however simple it may be, most of us need an interpretation of life, philosophic, religious, political, vaguely or clearly formulated, something by reference to which major decisions can be taken and the behaviour and attitudes of others understood.

In as far as a school can assist this 'construction of a series of four selves', I suggest that it is, broadly interpreted, a *pastoral* task. This is seen very clearly in a later passage from the same chapter:

> Wise choice in almost any matter of importance implies self-knowledge. Schools and their teachers in a variety of ways are always feeding back to pupils judgements and evaluations. Some of these are direct – marks for work done, comments on personality and behaviour; others are indirect and unconscious – the acceptance or rejection which may be implied by being placed in the A or D stream, the conceding or withholding of responsibility and trust. All of them contribute to build up a self-image. In a society of rising expectations, the objectivity and reasonableness of this self-image and the adjustment between level of capacity and level of aspiration in the individual are of immense importance to personal happiness and personal effectiveness, and are even more important to the stability of the whole social framework. The

[1] Wall, W. D., *Adolescents in Schools and Society* (NFER, 1968), p. 13.

school is preeminently the place where boys and girls should be able
to get reasonably unemotional and balanced answers to the questions
with which many become increasingly concerned: 'What sort of
person am I? What sort of person do I hope to become? What do
others really think of me?'[1]

Again, this is clearly a pastoral need, and the help towards
answering it a pastoral task. I therefore see the pastoral under-
taking as the central one. Of course, there are important sections of school work which because of their complexity could
become almost independent. Development of physical skills is
possibly one. But far from 'pastoral care' being primarily a prop
for the 'real' business of academic teaching, I see the concern
for knowledge as only a part of the greater need. After all, we
persuade or encourage young people to learn the discipline
of science, say, for *their* good, not primarily for the good of the
subject. The overall good of the young person is thus wider
than the subject teaching. Clearly the school is not going to be,
nor would it want to be, so pervasive as to speak for the whole
of the young person's life. Nevertheless the young person's
growing needs must be diagnosed, felt, and met by a caring
pastoral organization, which can call on a range of specialized
service within and without the school.

The broad area of 'pastoral care' can be broken down into
complementary separate aims:

  (i) to assist the individual to enrich his personal life;
  (ii) to help prepare the young person for educational choice;
  (iii) to offer guidance or counselling, helping young people to make
       their own decisions – by question and focus, and by information
       where appropriate;
  (iv) to support the 'subject' teaching;
  (v) to assist the individual to develop his or her own life-style and to
       respect that of others;
  (vi) to maintain an orderly atmosphere in which all this is possible.

In some ways and at some times the individual pupil might
have to be protected *against* the pressures of the overall school
organization.[2] Certainly the pupil will have to be helped
through the education system with its inevitable complexities and
discontinuities. Elizabeth Richardson puts it unfashionably but
clearly: 'Discontinuities in experience are part of the reality of
living. The real educational problem is not to eliminate the
discontinuities but to decide where the major ones occur and to

[1] ibid., pp. 15–16.
[2] cf. Bob Grove on page 118.

manage them in such a way that pupils can be helped to cope with them.'[1]

A school accepting something along the lines of the argument of this section will obviously need to structure itself to make this recognition operational. Clearly the pastoral focus is wide, and it is wider than mere learning. Thus, as I see it, the school *is* its pastoral organization. This has important practical implications. Some schools seem to set up 'a pastoral system' within, or even, as it were, beside the main structure – rather like the plumbing system in a building. This ultimately proves unsatisfactory, because it is not the main structure, and there is a 'dis-location' between the teaching and the caring.

It is really a truism of school planning that what you want to happen must be institutionalized. It is not enough to rely on goodwill, dedication, hard work, personality, and so on. Relationships are encouraged or inhibited by the institutionalized structure. Very few schools have been truly free to devise their own patterns as they believe they would work best. Most schools have had a cargo of the past in the form of traditions, staff, amalgamation remnants, or past procedures – and it is this cargo which always has to be used as the basis for further building. (I should also suggest that lack of knowledge has often been a further hidden constraint. Only when we know the fullest possible range of ideas, small or large, can we truly say that we have chosen.) These difficulties, though, must not be used as a reason for avoiding the structural challenge of working to institutionalize the relationships which you want, and I thus believe that the school organization is an embodiment of its care commitment, and can substantially encourage or inhibit the quality of that care.

There are those today who see the death of the school as we know it. I take my stand on the value of schools, and their adaptability to current needs. As Jerome Bruner says:

> There will always be a need, not for the school, but a school. You need this vehicle to hand on the culture when you've got a society of such complexity that the divisions of labour can't be understood in a local context.[2]

The vehicle is indeed needed, but it will not achieve that handing on and will come under strenuous attack if it does not help

[1] Richardson, Elizabeth, *The Teacher, The School, and the Task of Management* (Heinemann, 1973) p. 21.
[2] Bruner, J. S., interviewed for the *Times Educational Supplement* (15 September 1972).

the individual pupil to find himself, and find meaning for his
studies and his life. To do this, the central task of the school, its
pastoral work, must be sensitive, warm, human, efficient, realistic, and thorough. The core of a school's work is the disciplinary, educational, vocational, and personal guidance; and the
pupils' real situation must contribute to the formulation of
school policy. This is the pastoral need.

2 The Teacher and the Task of the School

by Charles Stuart-Jervis

There are few certainties in teaching and few conclusions to be reached at the end of the day which we can say with any degree of confidence will endure. Schools which have developed new courses and new techniques after months of discussion and soul-searching find that a change in the environment or in the social constitution of the area has necessitated a thorough re-examination of the assumptions on which the courses and techniques were based. No area of school life is so liable to change or so in need of a truly flexible approach as that which is concerned with caring for the needs of individual pupils. It is from an understanding of the individual pupil in his academic or social life that the successful operation of a number of school systems will flow. The patterns of care outlined elsewhere in this book depend upon the willingness of teachers to become deeply involved with pupils who will themselves exhibit from day to day a bewildering variety of moods and behaviour, which may largely be the result of the many interactions that occur between home and school, parents and children, teachers and pupils, and so on.

There are still, sadly, teachers capable of excellent teaching in one sense who are unable to operate satisfactorily outside a classroom or a pure teaching situation. There is quite enough to do, they will argue, without all this emphasis on knowing the child and his home background. Though one may not agree with this attitude one can understand it. There are still teachers in the schools who were not trained in the application of pastoral techniques and who find grave difficulty in accepting a much wider responsibility for children than had been envisaged when they first entered the profession.

However, it is precisely these additional problems that underline the all too real complexities that face schools, children and parents. Schools stand at the very centre of society. They 'educate' children for industry, for university, for living. Behind the children stand their parents, so many of whom are bewildered and upset and confused by the changing patterns and expectations of society, much more so than are their children, and parents have been led by the real or imagined benefits of education to believe that the school will produce young people with a considerably higher standard of literacy and numeracy than they themselves have attained. Industry needs and demands a more capable recruit than heretofore, and industry does not concern itself so much with what the schools are doing and thinking as with established criteria by which they can compare what is with what has gone before. Industry, indeed, is dissatisfied and critical when it discovers that overall educational standards are not what it would like.

The pressures on children, therefore, are great and children are suffering. Established social patterns are collapsing and it is not only poverty that creates the problem child. The academic and welfare needs of boys and girls are inseparable, and there are so many types of 'care' that may need to be provided that the proper establishment of care facilities is, in itself, a major systems and operational problem.

Quite properly, one may argue, the emphasis in society today is falling upon the need to individualize. The danger that the individual may become lost in the crowd has led in turn to the questioning of the very bases of authority by students, and in some cases by Authority itself. The belief that the individual has a right to stand up for himself and to ask why such and such an action has been taken in his name and on his behalf or for his good is beginning to pose new and increasingly awkward problems within schools.

It is for this reason, among others, that schools constantly need to examine the relationships that exist between teachers and pupils, indeed within the school as a whole, and ask some, or all, of the following questions: Is it possible in today's climate of opinion to continue operating on an authoritarian basis? Can discipline be maintained in a situation where there is little day-to-day social commerce between students and teachers, and where relationships are based, not upon mutual trust and understanding, but upon a 'Do as I say and argue afterwards' approach? Can we, indeed, pursue the line of argument which says that sanctions must loom very large in any argument on school discipline? Should we not instead be looking at a system which relieves tension and improves communications? How much effort are we making to understand the pressures under which children are operating (or failing to operate)? What, come to think of it, do we mean by discipline, anyway? How far is it possible to open lines of communication in such a way as to admit the possibility of children being outspokenly and fiercely critical of what is happening in their own school?

Those teachers who are committed pastorally are painfully aware of the near impossibility of laying down rules of conduct that will apply equally to all children, and staff who have been involved in the endless and fruitless arguments that rage

about difficult and obstreperous children will have realized
themselves how difficult it is to begin to codify standards of
conduct that are acceptable in a variety of different situations.

For this and other reasons it is essential that teachers concerned with the pastoral side of life in schools appreciate that
care systems, whatever their final form, are brought into
being by the existence of various sets of problems. Some of
these problems may be peculiar to the school and some may be
experienced in all schools. The recognition of the problems and
their causes is of the first importance, and the solutions are
found quickly, or slowly, or not at all according to the availability of staff of the right calibre, the provision of materials
and bases, and the beliefs and preoccupations of the staff
themselves. Because of this, the care system may well be in
need of a radical overhaul within a year if, for example, there
is a sudden influx of immigrants into the neighbourhood, a
policy of slum clearance is being pursued by the local council,
the middle-class element in the locality increases, there is an
exodus of staff, or there is a fundamental change in the goals,
objectives and direction of a school.

There are, too, some inherent dangers in care systems, however well-intentioned. Some may become overlaid with a
phoney sentimentality, a false feeling that care is all, that
concern is enough. There needs to be a rigorous intellectualism,
a solid core of hard thought about the aims and objectives of
any system of care obtaining within a school. Indeed a school,
having made what it considers to be the necessary provision
for the pastoral welfare of its pupils, may say, 'There now, the
system is in operation, leave it to function.' But all systems need
regular maintenance and review. No matter how good the
machinery or plant when it is installed, wear creates its own
problems, and some of the difficulties that schools face might
well be avoided by ensuring that built into the system is a
machinery that will from time to time question the assumptions
upon which the original system was based.

Primarily, however, the concern must be with the child and
the way or ways in which any child lives and moves within the
school. The pastoral ideal is, one presumes, that the pupil
functions happily and efficiently within the school, that his
social relationships are easy, and that his functioning within the
peer group is sound. But in large schools it is necessary to spread
the net wide in order to catch all children. It is not so much
the child whose relationships are sound and satisfactory with

whom we are mostly concerned but with those who have some-how failed to establish contact or maintain good relationships with others. Indeed it is often the child presenting the fewest problems who may, paradoxically, constitute the greatest prob-lem. The extrovert child who can maintain his equilibrium by aggressively anti-social behaviour may be reached: he has established his claim for attention. The shy, introverted child who retreats from contact is more difficult, more reserved, more suspicious of friendly overtures.

The success of any pastoral system will depend to a very large extent upon the ability of the system to draw in and involve all manner of children, and this, in its turn, will de-pend upon the availability of a variety of resources, chiefly human. The form teacher or group tutor may well be friendly, open, and approachable, but he may not be the problem child's type, and somewhere there should be another teacher who *is* his type and to whom he can talk. The argument in favour of school counselling developed in Chapter 7 is central to any argument in favour of school pastoral systems.

Because a primary need for the problem or socially dis-advantaged child is the provision of someone to whom he can turn, the *availability* of staff is vital. The teacher is not, nor can he ever be, available for personal contact in the classroom teaching situation. Similarly he is not readily available in the tutorial period, however hard he may try to approach each of his tutor group individually. The teacher is only truly avail-able to the child in a non-stress situation, in predominantly social contexts or on those occasions when he is not in an authoritarian posture. Out-of-school activities, clubs and socie-ties, occasions when staff and children are together in a situa-tion that is mutually satisfying, when trust and friendship are implicit, when they are enjoying something together, when conversation is easy and relaxed, are the truly available moments in the school day when contacts may be made and the otherwise unapproachable child may be drawn into a social situation which will allow him to make overtures or to reveal himself.

There is little point in teachers believing that an expressed desire to help, to guide and to advise will be accepted at its face value by today's child. The teacher has to prove himself through a period of apprenticeship, during which time he will be assessed by the children themselves. If, during this time, he reveals a genuine, as opposed to an expressed, interest he will eventually be accepted in both a tutorial and perhaps a counselling role.

I admit to a personal doubt as to whether any teacher will be accepted in a counselling role if he has not at some time or other joined regularly in some activity involving prolonged contact with children in a social setting. Children are not making an outrageous demand in this respect. Few of us give our trust merely because someone invites us to do so. It is unreasonable of teachers to expect children to extend their trust and friendship to those who are not prepared to make an effort to meet them on neutral ground.

Once a child has committed his trust there is a further need to create situations where, if necessary, the teacher may make himself available to children in a private capacity, as a friend, when he may be talked to alone and in confidence. In the ideal situation where children are bringing their problems to staff, new problems, new difficulties occur. Tutors sometimes become the unwilling recipients of scraps of information that are socially dangerous. How, if one is told in complete confidence, does one deal with repeated complaints made against colleagues, or with the news that an under-age girl is having sexual relations with a senior boy?

Yet these are situations to be welcomed by schools which value the co-operation of children and their parents, because it must be apparent that faith is implicit in the honesty and integrity of the teachers concerned and perhaps in the wider total situation of the school. All close contact is risky and all personal relationships need careful and sympathetic handling. But better by far that children should be willing to come forward and talk than that they should allow their resentments to fester and their sorrows to multiply. How many children might have been saved days, weeks or years of unhappiness had there been someone near who had listened and perhaps advised without censure, rancour or blame? Perhaps as important, how many schools would have avoided the acute disciplinary problems that occur when faith and trust are lacking in the day-to-day relationships that exist between teachers and taught?

But the pressures on teachers today are considerable, especially since their sphere of operations has increased to include the individual welfare of all children in form or tutor groups. Unfortunately it is hard to see how tutors can become tutors in the real sense of the word unless they are prepared to become deeply involved (though not so involved as to be unable to be dispassionate and clear-sighted) in the interests and preoccupations of the children. This can only be achieved by time given out of school. The teacher's preparedness to accept the heavy responsibility inherent in the term 'tutor', as discussed in Chapter 5, will determine whether or not part or all of the school's pastoral system works. To fill the position satisfactorily implies a desire to know the child's background and his family history, and it implies also a respect for the child as he *is*, and not as we would like him to be.

Not all staff are able to fill this position satisfactorily, often through no fault of their own, so safeguards such as school counsellors must be built into the system which will allow the child to be reached by somebody. For this to be acceptable all staff, in whatever capacity, must acknowledge the principle of interdependence, i.e. that no single system in any school can be independent of any other, whether academic or social. One dearly held tenet of the teacher's creed is at risk here, i.e. the belief that within his own form-room he is king. Clearly, this cannot be acceptable for obvious reasons. The principle of interdependence suggests that there are colleagues in the classroom and in the staff-room who will operate more satisfactorily in certain spheres than one does oneself. What is essential is that this is seen not as failure but as an acceptance of the fact that all staff have limitations in certain areas of school life. We are aiming for co-operation in order to be more efficient in our dealings with other people, and there is no implication that Mr Y is a failure merely because Mr Z does that particular thing better.

The leadership qualities of the head of house or year, which are explored in Chapter 5, are clearly of paramount importance in this context. If the head of house can accept that there are younger and less experienced members of staff who can do certain things better than he there will be a much greater willingness on the part of house staff to participate and contribute. Hierarchical concepts can be seriously detrimental in the pastoral context. Younger and junior staff are frequently better able than seniors to communicate with children, maybe because of their nearness to them in age, or because the young teacher is not tinged with awesome authority in the eyes of the children. Whatever the reason, a really successful pastoral system will depend on channels of communication being kept well open, with a constant information flow being directed to where the information will be most useful. Indeed, the most successful

head of house or year will not be the one who does everything himself, but the one who is most aware of shifts of emphasis and atmosphere within the house, and who knows which
member of his house staff is most likely to be effective in a
given situation. The ability to utilize resources fully, to control
and direct the effectiveness of staff, is the hallmark of the leader.
Perhaps, too, housemasters should constantly reassess their own
roles in schools, ensuring that their house staff participate in
house activities and share fully in the decision-making process.
This is not merely to ask that staff do their share: it is part of
the professional development that should be expected of all
staff, and it is a major part of the housemaster's task to see that
staff, especially young teachers, share an opportunity to develop
fully. Where the house is failing to provide such opportunities
for staff and pupils to meet and communicate socially it is
emasculating itself in so far as pastoral care is concerned. No
amount of formal meetings, sharing of house points, and inter-
house and inter-year competitions can compensate for the lack
of social contact in informal situations. It is important for
children to develop their own social potential. Social graces and
social awareness do not come from sitting with others and
listening to lectures; they are the result of good social interaction, of group activity, of communication, of shared experience.

Indeed, for many young teachers the difficulties involved in
communicating with children come not from a lack of desire,
but rather from having no initial point of contact, and the
house system that brings young staff into contact with children
for the express purpose of giving both a point of communication
gained from shared experience is well on the way to solving
many of the disciplinary problems that spring from a lack of
understanding between teachers and children. Too often the
house or year system is seen purely as a useful administrative
unit within the large school. No one would deny that administration is a large part of its function. But just as departments
need to define their aims and objectives, so pastoral systems
need to know clearly what they are endeavouring to do, and
why, and one of the aims must be to bridge the gap that so
often exists between children and school. The house programme
must somewhere include a recognition of the need experienced
by young people for a satisfactory self-picture, and it should
surely structure many of its activities towards this end. Where
this is successful it is obvious that the school, house, department
or whatever is likely to receive a much greater degree of co-

operation than would otherwise have been the case. Children and school both benefit.

Where there are a large number of social problems facing a school it is also plain that the pastoral system needs to clear out of the way the minor problems that so often impair clear vision. The major problems are those which are occasioned by children who are facing severe difficulties in adjusting to society and school, and in some cases to their families as well. The deep-rooted problems may not be cleared away by the creation of a climate of help and discussion within the system, but they may well be alleviated, and certainly there is a much greater possibility of good contact being made.

There remain, however, the turbulent and withdrawn children. And who knows, or ever can know, how deeply they are affected by school and home situations? A drinking father, an unsympathetic teacher, chronic illness within the family, an incompetent mother, over-ambitious parents, brutality, fear of failure, submerged school-phobia, and chronic anxiety are but a few of the factors that may seriously impair a child's performance at school or in the wider social setting. The argument that schools should not have to deal with the children who present serious behaviour problems is to beg the question. Besides which, many of these children need only the help and understanding that a sympathetic school situation can give them. The school that is alert and sensitive to the needs of the children, a school that is neither too critical nor too permissive, that will make allowances based on understanding, that will accept the shortcomings of its environment, is well on the way to creating an atmosphere of friendly co-operation between staff, parents and children.

Against this background it seems hardly right therefore to consider the application of sanctions, whatever they may be, to disruptive and turbulent children. It is always more realistic to examine the relationships that exist within schools, and through the establishment of good lines of communication and a helpful and constructive system of care to hope and work for a healthy co-operation. It is odd that so many teachers who rightly maintain that it is better to encourage and help children and to gain their co-operation should, when difficulties arise, be so ready to reach for the detention book or some form of punishment in a way that argues that coercion will succeed where reason and goodwill have failed. There are, no doubt, occasions when, with a healthy and averagely naughty child, it is understandable that some sanction or other should be imposed for the sort of conduct that one associates with normal naughtiness or for conduct that brings the school into disrepute or others into danger. But for those children who are already facing quite considerable personal handicaps it is clearly the responsibility of the pastoral system within the school to support and guide. The best discipline always comes from good personal relationships, and among the inherent dangers that attend upon the imposition of sanctions, however well-intentioned, is the damage that can be done to staff and children in terms of mistrust and misunderstanding. Good discipline is achieved only through time taken to appreciate the problems, through the desire to discover why children behave as they do, and only rarely should it be necessary to have recourse to a system of penalties.

Care in all its forms is at once the great responsibility and the great strength of teachers. If care and concern for others is seen to be a desirable human trait the teachers in the schools must be seen to exercise it. We are not only hoping to help, we are seeking also to change attitudes that will, eventually, pass from one generation to the next.

3 The Pupils in their Times

There are two legitimate attitudes among teachers, providing, I suppose, the motivation for *three* sections of the teaching profession. One wing argues that education must react to the trends of society, and must take the pupil as he is. This wing would adjust the educational experience to match up with the social experience as far as possible. The opposite wing argues rather that it is the job of normal education to stand back from the world and *complement* its tendencies by an educational experience based on what would be best in an ideal society. The first group, to take an example, might wish pupils to come to school in entirely their own choice of clothes. The second, on the other hand, would argue that whereas their own choice, heavily influenced as it will be by current fashions, is excellent for out-of-school time, it is the task of the school to stand outside such fashions and to insist on timeless, objective 'standards of dress'.

I mentioned *three* groups. The large third group are those who dither. They feel that the experience of school must in many respects at least be moulded to the shape of the age, that is, really to reinforce it. On the other hand, there are some aspects of the age which clearly require counterbalancing. To that extent, they feel the school should compensate for social trends, and should organize itself to work against them.

In looking at the organization of pastoral care in a secondary school, both these attitudes are needed. The starting point must be the pupils in their times. Efforts must be made to understand the secondary-age pupils through pastoral contact in the first place – and some pastoral systems are peculiarly badly constructed to encourage such personal knowledge. More than that, though, the skills of physiology, psychology, sociology, and artistic response must be brought to bear to produce a sympathetic analysis of our pupils and their times. We can then formulate procedures that take cognizance of our findings, both to fit ourselves better to our pupils and to fit them for their world better. In some aspects we shall be, as it were, conceding points to society; in others we shall be compensating for society, creating a 'complementary environment'.

Only through knowledge can we do either. Yet in my experience schools very rarely debate the society in which we live in anything but the most perfunctory of ways. In many schools, I fancy that such a debate would seem a diversion. I would suggest it is a necessary starting point. This chapter is an attempt to look at a picture of our times for those aspects which are of especial significance to the organizing of pastoral care. Obviously it is a difficult section to write, and obviously it will be in many ways superficial and to some seem arbitrarily selective. However, the picture must be attempted. Clearly each school would need to build on this, especially by a detailed study of its locality.

* * * * *

Ours is the age of eclecticism. Never before has the individual felt able to choose to such an extent the separate items that will go to make up his life-style. There is a popular journalistic theory, based on only part of the evidence, that ours is essentially a *standardized* society, and that mass-production has led to central domination, bureaucracy, and 'massification'. But, as Frank Musgrove has argued, 'The facts of contemporary society do not show a shift towards bureaucracy. . . . Despite accusations of massification, this never was less so . . . What we have is not a massed standardized society.'[1] In fact minority tastes, and a freedom not only to choose, but to choose personal *combinations* of items towards a life-style, are flourishing as never before.

It may be argued that in certain respects and for certain individuals the range of choice is more apparent than real. Even the seeming range, though, is a highly significant element in the lives of our pupils. The eclecticism of the second half of the twentieth century seems to me one of the dominant influences on the young, but it contrasts forcibly with the implicit pattern of schooling. Schools have a tendency to build an ideal single picture of society and the individual. Society, however, is in fact continuing to diversify.

For me this can be symbolized in the fact that Beethoven never once heard Bach's Mass in B Minor. This is relevant, for today it is inconceivable that any composer would not have access to a major work by a major predecessor. Two complementary factors have changed the situation since Beethoven's day: technological devices have made available really rather faithful and comparatively cheap reproductions. The disc, the tape, lithographic printing, and photographic processes – even more recently and on a small scale three-dimensional modelling copies such as the British Museum Replicas – have all combined to make it physically possible for a range of art-forms and the

[1] 'The Decline of Deference, the Problem of Dignity, and the Loss of the Stable State', transcript of opening address to 1973 ACE Conference.

trappings of a range of life-styles to be more-or-less authenti-
cally available.

More important, though, there has been a cultural change,
a change in aesthetics, in readiness for experience. Because of the
frequent changes of aspects of fashion in clothing particularly,
it is common to think of ours as an age dominated by fashion.
However, the very speed and force of the fashions have assisted
the availability of a greater-than-ever *range* of choice, and in
many ways reduced the real power of fashion. Whereas in the
past each age had a circumscribed area of the popular and
well-regarded, ours has an array of patches, often overlapping,
but certainly not always linked in the same or even similar
combinations. Dr Johnson's 'Common Reader' lasted well into
this century. There was a strong possibility, at least until the
First World War, of educated people sharing the same tastes
and judgements. Whether you look at architecture, clothing,
furniture, books, pictures, or music, fashion was in fact *more*
dominant in the past. In today's plural society taste has
fragmented.

The technological revolution has combined with the taste
revolution to provide a vast interlocking range of possible
options. The reader of this book may be listening in his home
to authentic baroque, medieval plain-chant, or a full romantic
symphony orchestra, primitive tribal ritual music, swing, jazz,
pop, or electronic music. As the reader looks up to his or her
wall, he may see a Etruscan wall painting, a fresco from
Florence, Picasso, Van Gogh, an abstract, a Russian icon, or a
poster. The technical facility that makes this eclecticism possible is in fact less remarkable than the human facility that has
come with it. We are capable of responding to this staggering
range of aesthetics[1] to an extent never before known in British
taste. The Victorian country house, the Edwardian villa, the
Georgian terrace, the Queen Anne mansion, the Elizabethan
farmhouse are all *available* to our admiration. This is a staggering human and social feat which is possible only in the age of
eclecticism. The thirteen-year-old will, of course, not be aware
of all this, but as a child of his age, he will, too, be an eclectic
within his own scope. Every pupil who enters the secondary

[1] Although commentators such as Edgar Wind in his 1960 Reith
lectures have doubted whether the appreciation of such diverse stimuli is
in fact as deep as in less eclectic ages: 'Diffusion brings with it a loss of
density. We are much given to art, but it touches us lightly, and that is why
we can take so much of it, and so much *of so many different kinds*.' (My
italics) *Art and Anarchy* (Faber and Faber, 1963), p. 9.

school is at heart an eclectic – and it is a hard fact for schools to digest. The curriculum has already shifted as our notion of 'the educated man' has splintered, and as we have opened up the options for all. No longer, for instance, do the less able in most schools have a significantly smaller range of choice than the most able – whenever they can, pupils opt for options. Pastorally, though, the eclectic experience of the pupils has been less easy to accommodate. The comparison of the super-market is often used by time-tablers to describe their arrange-ments for fourth- and fifth-formers. But, to take one instance only, how does the pastoral system adjust to school-uniform attitudes for a generation brought up on a choice of a range of brilliant shirt colours at cheap prices in Marks and Spencer?

It is an accepted commonplace to describe our world as one of rapid change. Many teachers would feel that this is all the more reason for school's placing additional emphasis on sta-bility and continuity, while others would see it as justification for flexible adaptation. The changes are coming in all aspects of our lives at an ever-increasing pace, and spreading with great speed across the entire community. Many commentators have noted this, as Alvin Toffler does in his book *Future Shock :*[1]

> We invent more machines than ever before – and, what is more import-ant, we rush to apply them faster. (A whole management technology is devoted to the acceleration of innovation.) The first English patent on a typewriting machine was issued in 1714. It took a century and a half before the first typewriters became commercially available. Today we scarcely wait a decade and a half before moving from patent to market-place. Whether we look at antibiotics, integrated circuits, transistor radios, tape cassette players, or a thousand other technical items we find the rate of diffusion rising. In turn, this accelerating diffusion affects our lives in myriad ways, forcing small, almost un-noticed 'micro-adjustments' along with the more evident ones. It makes some jobs obsolete and demands that we crash-train for new ones. It alters the way we spend our time, the way we communicate, the way we react to the culture around us.[2]

This process has been going on throughout the lives of our pupils, and is almost fully assimilated into their systems. How-ever, the situation is less understood by teachers and schools. This is partly because not only is change coming faster, it is affecting society in a different *order :*

> Contemporary change is diffused rapidly by the mass media with little chance to pass slowly through the mediating sieve of a powerful and

[1] Toffler, Alvin, *Future Shock* (Bodley Head, 1970; Pan, 1972).
[2] This quotation is Toffler's own summary for *The Observer* of 31 December, 1972. For a full account see Chapter 2 of *Future Shock*.

more or less educated leadership group. In fact – because high education and high intelligence diminish suggestibility – many of the
intelligentsia of today are much less deeply affected than are young
people and the general run of citizens. The cultural, emotional and
intellectual distance between, for example, a working class adolescent
and his grammar school teacher may amount to a century of change, as
indeed may that between a primary school child, his parents and his
teacher.[1]

This whole process is dependent on organizational and technological means certainly, but it also seems to reflect a change
in the spirit of the age. The process is encouraged by more
movement of families around the country, or at least from
home to home. An indication of how little geared to this schools
are can be found in the usually inadequate admission arrangements that most schools have. The presumption is that 'our'
children will stay – and this affects the mechanical organization
and the atmosphere of the school. In actual fact the 1971 census
showed an unprecedented movement around the country. I
have mentioned this as contributing to change of social patterns. Toffler, whom I quoted earlier, sees it also as contributing
to a new kind of 'temporary' human relationships:

> Turnover . . . is rising in our relationships with place. Once we were
> all linked for a lifetime to a particular bit of geography or real estate;
> now our lives are short term. We, in America, were the first to smash
> this pattern and create a new nomadism. But the British are not so far
> behind. Thus, according to *New Society*, 'The English are a more
> mobile race than perhaps they thought. . . . No less than 11 per cent
> of all the people in England and Wales in 1961 had lived in their
> present usual residence less than a year. . . . In certain parts of England,
> in fact, it appears that the migratory movements are nothing less than
> frenetic. In Kensington over 25 per cent had lived in their homes less
> than a year, in Hampstead 20 per cent, in Chelsea 19 per cent.' And
> Anne Lapping, in the same journal, states that 'new houseowners
> expect to move house many more times than their parents. The average
> life of a mortgage is eight to nine years.' It may surprise some Britons
> to know that this is only slightly longer than in the US.

Such developing trends mirror those in the US and other countries
and they amount to an extremely important shift toward the ephe-
meralization of human and organizational ties. It means that, certainly
not for all Britons but for significant groups, the ties with place, with
job, with company, with ideas, with values, and, above all, with other
human beings are growing more and more temporary. When I was a
boy growing up in New York, a best friend was someone who stayed
in your life from the time you were seven or eight on through adolescence. Today more and more American youngsters have sequential
'best friends', none of whom last more than a year or two, because their

[1] Wall, W. D., *Adolescents in School and Society* (NFER, 1968), p. 6.

fathers are being transferred from one place to another. I doubt that
this process is anywhere near as advanced on this side of the Atlantic;
but I suspect it is beginning. The more change in society, and the more
mobility, the more temporary the human ties.[1]

With such forces at work it is not surprising that the standards of society are uncertain, and there is rarely a consensus
of expectation of behaviour. The spirit of the age of eclectism
can be seen as much in the sphere of morals and personal
relationships as in aesthetics. Organized religion has faded, the
cementing belief in the after-life has gone, and only a tiny
minority of our pupils have a set of standards taken at first
hand from the parental teaching of a religious faith – but the
school community, again, displays the vestigial remains of an
age of a single religious faith.

Associated with this is the attitudes to leaders and public
figures of all kinds. The Second World War, social mobility,
and a host of other forces have removed the public leader from
the pedestal. After two generations of increasing frankness in
the Press, so that everyone was used to seeing public figures
warts and all, television found that the close-up was the most
compelling device in its repertoire. Its exploitation brought
many fascinating insights to the homes of the entire nation. It
also brought with it the exposure of slips, failure, temper, and
personal traits – the leader was finally fully humanized, and
frequently satirized with a force unknown since the eighteenth
century

It is no wonder that Professor Frank Musgrove charac-
terizes the present age as seeing 'the decline of deference'.
Previous generations have limited the questioning of the established rules to a minority; ours has seen it as the habit of many,
possibly even the majority. In his well-known 1962 Reith
Lectures, Professor G. M. Carstairs, then Professor of Psychological Medicine at the University of Edinburgh and now
Vice-Chancellor of York University, could already see this
rejection as well established: 'During this century we have
learned to reject authority, or at any rate to challenge those
who claim authority to produce evidence to validate their
claims.'[2] Since then, we have experienced a further 'decline in
deference' to the extent that very rarely can a teacher *rely* on
acceptance and obedience: the right to lead has to be earned.

[1] Again this is Toffler's own summary, of Chapters 5 and 6 of *Future
Shock* in *The Observer*, December 31, 1972.
[2] Carstairs, G. M., *This Island Now* (The Hogarth Press, 1963), p. 91.

As Musgrove points out: 'we have to learn how to run schools without deference.'[1] And nowhere is the difficulty greater than in the pastoral work of a school at a time when 'People fear less and want more'.[2]

Such an opening up of the possibilities of choice in beliefs, morals, and standards, and such a sour scrutiny of public figures and leaders of all sorts has had its gains, certainly. Chief among these has been a reduction in hypocrisy. (That is not to say that there is not sometimes a more subtle form of hypocrisy, which hides behind a simulated or even believed-in frankness.) Within a school it is associated with difficult changes of attitude. These range from those of the teacher who is quite unable to 'impose' demands in which he does not fully 'believe', to those of the pupil who is unwilling to follow instructions of which he 'doesn't see the point'. These refusals to act in a way which feels hypocritical is quite alien to the public pattern of schools of the past, in which there were clear understandings of what could be openly accepted, and what was done, known about, but mutually ignored. The traditional back ways in over walls for Oxbridge undergraduates stand for the old order: an accepted but suppressed arrangement that is quite out of the spirit of today.

The reduction of hypocrisy is most evident in the sphere of sexuality. Enough has been written about this for it to be unnecessary to labour the point. The eleven-year-olds who came to secondary schools for the academic year in which I have been writing this book were born in the year in which the Director of Public Prosecutions failed in the case against Penguin Books for the publication of the complete edition of *Lady Chatterley's Lover* (October 1961). That case is interesting for a number of legal and literary points,[3] but there is no doubt that that trial, whether as cause or effect is less certain, marked the changing point. Since then, children have been brought up with the regular, frequent, frank, and vivid experience of sexual description of all sorts. The changes in what is acceptable have accelerated, and have been given strength by the technical developments that have given sexual frankness such visual strength. This includes television and, less often remarked, the greater skill of photographic reproduction, including the vivid

---

[1] Musgrove, op. cit., p. 2.

[2] Shanks, Michael, 'Personal View', Radio 3 (27 January, 1973).

[3] An edited transcript is available, and is lively and historically relevant reading, in Rolph, C. H., *The Trial of Lady Chatterley* (Penguin, 1961).

use of colour. Has this change been properly digested by the adult world in general and the school in particular? The teenage magazines have certainly digested the changes, and, indeed, contribute to them. The pastoral staff of a school might well subscribe to *Petticoat, Honey, Nineteen* (so titled, but read at fourteen) and the rest as a basic piece of in-service training. The acceptance of sex and the sensual there, and its blatant exploitation on poster and magazine stall, is largely suppressed or ignored in the school.

This trend is too easily associated in people's minds with a supposed decline in family relationships. It is true that the nature of the family has changed in a number of ways – one of which I shall refer to later. However, a notable feature of society today is precisely the opposite. The family is in fact the 'success story' of the mid-century. Teachers too often forget this. Ronald Fletcher analysed it in his survey *Family and Marriage* in 1962, and in his revised edition eleven years later was even more emphatic: 'Marriage and the family in our society continue to enjoy a tremendous popularity; benefiting from the culmination of reforms set firmly afoot during the nineteen thirties.'[1] Glibly quoted divorce figures should not be looked at as contradicting this. As Fletcher points out: 'May it not be that high standards and expectations of marriage and family life actually *entail* a high rate of resort to divorce? . . . A high rate of divorce might well be indicative of a higher conception, a healthier condition, of marriage in society, rather than a worsening of it.'[2]

Following his researches, Frank Musgrove describes the place of the family today thus:

> The modern family is our most successful social institution. Geographical migration and the social services have given it a new importance and have promoted its unity; social mobility (children rising above the social level of their parents) has not been shown to weaken the cohesion of the family or seriously to impair the bonds between parents and their prospering children; young people were seldom so deeply embedded in their families, particularly in the middle class; and as education becomes ever more protracted for more people, the prolonged dependence of the young into adult years is likely to become a marked feature of life at all social levels.[3]

[1] Fletcher, Ronald, *The Family and Marriage in Britain* (Penguin, 1973), p. 15.
[2] Ibid., pp. 16–17.
[3] Musgrove, Frank, *The Family, Education and Society* (Routledge and Kegan Paul, 1966), p. 31.

In Chapters 8 and 9 this book explores some of the practical
implications for what has come to be known in a rather limiting
phrase as 'home-school relations'. There is, though, a more
general point: the school stands in a tradition, as I have said, of
being apart from society in general and the family in particular.
The incidence of stubbornly difficult problem families and the
strictly limited teacher-time available for helping them has
overshadowed this central truth: the family has never been so
strong, and has developed as a caring and loving group as
never before. As Musgrove goes on: 'The modern family
specializes in affection. It can do this job precisely because it
need do little else.'[1] In other words, the pressures on the family
have been sufficiently reduced for it to flourish primarily as a
companionship group.

There is ample evidence for this view of the family, despite
the excruciating problems of the inadequate or broken families. Among the most detailed is that in the final comparative
chapter, 'Then and Now', of the Newsoms' first research report
on child-rearing practices today:

> Many mothers emphasized that, beyond the mere relaxation of disci-
> pline, there is a new warmth and companionship in the present-day
> relationship between parents and children; and it is possible that this
> trend, too, is the result of a more general change in the social back-
> ground which makes it possible for families today to enjoy much more
> real leisure together. The advent of the forty-hour week and the ten-
> dency to finish the week's work on a Friday night mean either that the
> breadwinner can enjoy two clear days of domestic relaxation with his
> family at the weekend, or that he is making considerable overtime
> money, some of which will probably be spent on acquiring new labour-
> saving devices in the home.[2]

However, one fairly widespread effect of the new styles of
family life, that is perhaps not so desirable, has resulted from the
break-up of the extended family and the increased warmth and
closeness of the nuclear family. It is the decline in the number
of what sociologists call 'moderated' relationships. Parents are
in most cases fully devoted to the growing adolescent, and thus
tensions are inevitable. In the mobile, nucleated urban and
suburban pattern there is not such a network of other adults
who are able and willing to enter into a suitable relationship
with the young person as there is in many a small town or

---

[1] op. cit., p. 37.
[2] Newsom, John and Elizabeth, *Patterns of Infant Care* (Penguin, 1965),
p. 243. See also Gorer, Geoffrey, *Sex and Marriage in England Today*
(Nelson, 1970).

village. Such 'moderated' relationships ideally shade off from the continuous concern of close relatives to the nodding acquaintance of the farmer down the village. Such a range provides a 'moderated' sequence of relationships for the young person between his parents and the world. The classic pattern of Gran taking the child's side or permitting slightly more lax behaviour is an example. Lacking such 'moderated' relationships, and relying too much on the totally demanding parental relationship, many of the young, especially of course from caring homes, are driven to a spurious rebellion against their parents. Conversely, the possibility of moderated relationships is one of the major strengths that the pastoral system of a school has to offer. Pupils are, almost without exception, grateful for such relationships.

One way in which pressure has been relieved in the family itself is by the generally rising standards of affluence. It is still true that the poor are horribly far behind, and that many sections of the population are having serious difficulties in coping financially, but the general level of family finance, and the comparative financial well-being of business life, has built up an expectation of life that is not always met within school. Life is expected to be reasonably comfortable, whereas the school tradition is squarely against lushness – almost as if comfort and colour were immoral. Television can be associated with this expectation. Amongst its least commented-on influences has been its immense emphasis on effective presentation. The credit titles might be taken as an example: they are ingenious, lively, gripping, and highly skilled. The graphic designer is one of today's most influential people. This generation expects competent presentation at the turn of a knob. Schools, with their muddles, mess, and mundane presentation show up badly in this comparison with the intense and vivid presentation of television both at home and, even more closely to hand for comparison, in school programmes.

I have described aspects of our time that I see to be especially significant for the pastoral work of a school: the eclectic attitudes to life-styles; the increasing speed of change, and the way in which change is hitting society unselectively; the pluralistic standards; the decline in the acceptance of authority; the rejection of hypocrisy; the increase in the consciousness of sexuality; the increased importance of the family; the increase in wealth; and, lastly, the general expectation of high virtuosity in presentation. In describing these features, I have already

described some of their direct effects on the young people
who have been brought up in this period. Now I shall concentrate more closely on a few of the particular characteristics
of the young people of today – the clients of our pastoral
organization – from the point of view of that organization.
Are there any special features of youth today on which we
should focus if we are scrutinizing the pastoral systems of our
schools?

The earlier maturity of the young today is the characteristic
that is most frequently commented on, and this is supported
by reference to the hard fact that the mean age of the first
menstruation of girls has dropped.[1] It is undoubtedly true that
for physical reasons of diet, housing, and physical education the
onset of puberty is now lower. The paradox that this has
happened at a time when larger numbers have been encouraged,
and now compelled, to remain at school has been often pointed
out. The adolescent school experience is now for all. As W. D.
Wall puts it:

> In so far as the phenomena of adolescence are provoked by the environ-
> ment and particularly by the prolongation of the period of dependence
> between childhood and full acceptance into adult society, the last half-
> century has been a steady extension through the social groups of cir-
> cumstances originally confined to one or two. Adolescence has become
> democratized.[2]

The pastoral pattern devised for *either* the pre-pubescent *or*
the tiny basically middle-class socially motivated pupil needs
re-considering for those new young adults. I should put the
emphasis, however, less on physical maturity than emotional
and attitudinal. Some regret it as meaning that children can
never be 'children' today. Few teachers, it seems to me, have
really faced this issue. As a result of the change in family feeling
and patterns of child-rearing, the eleven-year-old of many
families is used to expressing views, to joining in conversations
with adults, above all to sensing adult situations and their interactions and feelings. Television has been a major influence here.
The mid-teenager is not an extensive television-viewer, but by
then he has a lifetime of viewing of the adult world behind
him. This television experience has included the extremities of
violence (20,000 fictitious homicides by sixteen, for instance, for

[1] 'Age at menarch has been getting earlier by some 4 months per decade
in Western Europe over the period 1830–1960 . . . There is little evidence
that the trend has stopped.' Tanner, J. M., *Growth of Adolescence* (Blackwell,
second edition, 1962), p. 154.
[2] Wall, W. D., *Adolescents in School and Society* (NFER, 1968), pp. 3–4.

American youth), but even more significant are the many
episodes of plays, serials, and current-affairs programmes which
show adult interchange of various sorts. As Marshall McLuhan
put it in the US context: 'By the age of three, the North American child has ... seen more adult life than Methuselah.' Any
English teacher could illustrate this point by the range of
reactions from pupils to the situations in literature. I remember,
for instance, listening to the BBC Radio 4 production of a play
by David Campton, called *Boo*, with a third-year group. The
play told of the violent behaviour of a group of young children
who had been despised and teased by an adult man. It was that
part of the theme which I had thought would impinge on the
group. What I had not fully expected was the shrewd and involved analysis of the marriage of the man which we were soon
embarked upon. It was not merely that the group could argue
whether it was a happy marriage or not; they went on to show
in what specific ways it was failing: the husband thought
that he could cheer up his wife by superficial pleasantries.
The legacy of those years of television viewing was an adult
awareness that has not been present in previous generations
of school children, and which demands a suitable pastoral
context.

With this maturity has come a relatively high level of personal spending money, which in its turn has given a feeling of
independence. The drive towards the adult world shows itself
in a variety of ways. The Saturday job, for instance, which
schools used to think of as the sad necessity of the poorer
family, is now part of the teenage life-pattern and is concerned with independence rather than helping the family
finances. It seems to me both that this kind of drive towards
independent work and earning is admirable, and that schools
are only reluctantly willing to concede that such jobs should be
undertaken.

The 'democratization' of adolescence has worked in other
directions also. Early heterosexual experience in previous
generations was probably more extensive among the working
class than among the middle class. This correlation has faded,
and sexual experience is spread more evenly across the classes,
at any rate from fifteen upwards. The overall totals may still
not be as high as snide attacks on 'modern youth' make out.
Schofield's 1968 survey (based on earlier data)[1] suggests that a

[1] Schofield, M., *The Sexual Behaviour of Young People* (revised edition,
Penguin, 1968).

quarter of boys have had intercourse by 17 and a third by 18.[1] His detailed analysis is worth studying. More recent figures would undoubtedly show higher figures for lower ages. The important point is, as Schofield puts it:

> Our results have made it clear that premarital sexual relations are a long way from being universal among teenagers as over two-thirds of the boys and three-quarters of the girls in our sample have not engaged in sexual intercourse. On the other hand it is equally apparent that teenage premarital intercourse is not a minority problem confined to a few deviates. It is an activity common enough to be seen as one manifestation of teenage conformity.[2]

The establishing of a sexual role, to which I referred on page 9 as a central pastoral need, is one of the potential sources of tension and conflict between the generations. As one psychiatrist described the situation that comes when young people are achieving sexuality at a time when their parents are ageing and 'losing the creative significance of sexuality':

> Unless parents have sublimated their own sexuality, have displaced it to some appreciable degree on to other things, they may strongly resent their children achieving an adult sexual role. Envy of the young often lies behind the criticisms of them. Destructive envy like this can poison the relationship between parents and their children.[3]

It is difficult not to feel that similar envies occur in teachers.

Such points, and other instances of general unease, have led many people to talk of 'the generation gap'. It is very important to the running of a secondary school to determine what, if anything, this phrase means. Another of the journalistic theories is that there is a yawning and unbridgeable chasm between the generations. This belief has led to adults, with the best possible motives, sinking money into clubs and centres designed for 'the adolescent', and doing all they can to create a virtually self-contained adolescent environment, a world which only a few 'licensed' adults can visit – and then only if they go through the statutory motions.

There is, though, strong evidence that the gap is largely a myth – and that the drive to adulthood is stronger and more frequent than is believed. Attitudes are not all that different during adolescence from those of adulthood. The attack on the whole concept of adolescence as a separate state, an attack which is highly relevant to a school's planning of its social

[1] ibid., p. 49.
[2] ibid., p. 224.
[3] Crowcroft, Andrew, *The Psychotic* (Penguin, 1967), p. 175.

system and pastoral care, was led in 1964 by Frank Musgrove in his important book *Youth and the Social Order*:

> The adolescent was invented at the same time as the steam-engine. The principal architect of the latter was Watt in 1765, of the former Rousseau in 1762. Having invented the adolescent, society has been faced with two major problems: how and where to accommodate him in the social structure, and how to make his behaviour accord with the specifications.[1]

His own research into history convinced him that the adolescent was not always regarded as he is today, and his sociological research showed that the inter-generation attitudes were not as popularly supposed. He found that 'Young adolescents showed themselves better disposed towards adults than adults were disposed towards them'.[2] The vast majority of the adolescents were identifying with adult values, and approving of the adults they knew. In a later book he did further research into the attitudes of young people to their homes:

> There were no indications in this inquiry that there is, in general, a great gulf between teenage children and their parents; that they are unable to communicate; that children throughout their teens do not place high value on their parents' support and approval. All the evidence is to the contrary.[3]

Similar results have been found by researchers in other parts of the world. A Montreal research report puts it clearly:

> The adolescent, by the age of 14 and 15, have already internalized the ideals and values of the surrounding adult society. The adolescent appreciate the keen interest of the parents in their activities and feel that their parents are working on their behalf; they are in close agreement with their parents on general career and marriage goals and the manner in which these goals are to be achieved ... they do not reject adult values or participate in an anti-adult 'youth culture' ...[4]

Similarly, Peter Wilmott, studying boys in Bethnal Green, was forced to modify the generally accepted picture:

> There is little sign either of what has been called 'the war of the generations', or of any widespread feeling of resentment against adult society. When the boys in the sample were asked if they thought they had 'as much chance to enjoy life as you should have', over four-fifths said they had. Asked whether they thought they had 'as much chance to get on

[1] Musgrove, Frank, *Youth and the Social Order* (Routledge and Kegan Paul, 1964), p. 33.
[2] ibid., p. 104.
[3] Musgrove, Frank, *Family, Education, and Society* (Routledge and Kegan Paul, 1966), p. 129.
[4] Westley, Williams A., and Elkin, Frederic, *The Protective Environment and Adolescent Socialisation* quoted in Musgrove, ibid., p. 131.

in life' as they ought to, nearly nine out of ten said 'Yes'. Even allowing
for a tendency to make the best of things, the consensus is impressive.

These findings are broadly in line with other studies in, for instance,
Sheffield, a north Midlands town, Stepney and Poplar. Such research
as has been carried out does not support the more gloomy or dramatic
accounts of working-class adolescent rebellion.[1]

Looking more specifically at sexual roles, Schofield had similarly found: '. . . it is obvious that this teenage subculture has
been created by the adult world, not by the young people
themselves.'[2] The evidence from all sides supports my feeling
as a teacher and parent that the extent and nature of the 'gap'
have been exaggerated, and the adult view is forcing adolescents, who would otherwise wish to identify more fully with
adult society, into a non-world. The evidence is that the classic
adolescent turmoil has some, but only some, basis in physiology.
Even if we cannot go as far as maintaining with Musgrove that
it has been 'invented', we can see how the contemporary world
has made it a more difficult period than any other time has done.
Anyone who has read the anthropologists such as Ruth Bene-
dick[3] and Margaret Mead[4] must have pondered on this
question. Professor Carstairs has posed it like this: 'Are the dis-
turbances which vex our adolescents due to the nature of
adolescence itself or to the civilization? Under different
conditions does adolescence present a different picture?'[5] He
goes on to give Margaret Mead's answer:

She discovered that in Samoa adolescent stress and turmoil was as
exceptional as it is usual in Western Society, and she attributed this
ease of transition to certain characteristics of Samoan society – Its pre-
vailing casualness, the absence of deep interpersonal relationships
either within the family or between friends; and, as in most simple,
homogeneous cultures, the absence of choice in matters of belief and
conduct.[6]

Such an approach makes us look more critically at how we
arrange matters, especially in school and especially in our
pastoral organizations. Could it be that difficulties are there
as a result of the approaches of adults, conditioned as they are
by post-Rousseau theory? A Canadian psychologist analyses
adolescent stress as largely society-created:

[1] Willmott, Peter, *Adolescent Boys in East London* (Routledge and Kegan
Paul, 1966; revised edition, Penguin 1969), p. 179.
[2] Schofield, op. cit., p. 235.
[3] *Patterns of Culture* (Routledge and Kegan Paul, 1935).
[4] *Coming of Age in Samoa*, and *Growing up in New Guinea*.
[5] Carstairs, G. M., *This Island Now* (The Hogarth Press, 1962), p. 46.
[6] ibid., p. 46.

Our consumer-orientated society demands a person be able to perform a job, consume goods, and pay taxes. If he cannot, he must be taken care of by friends, family, or the state. In our society the teen-age years are spent in a nebulous limbo during which most individuals are not capable of maintaining a job, starting a family, engaging in sanctioned sexual behaviour, or contributing to the general well-being of the dominant society. The adolescent has virtually no alternative other than a dependency status which strongly contradicts his growing sense of autonomy and independence. The only real function adolescents have in our society today is to attend school. It is a preparatory age during which the individual is groomed for adult roles and skills, serving no other functional purpose to the larger society. Adolescents do not contribute to the ESSENTIAL work of society; they provide neither brain power nor physical energy for the construction activities of society; they have almost no voice in the legal machinery which regulates society. From the point of view of most adults, adolescence is simply a zone through which all children must phase before they are entitled to early adulthood. It is recognized as troublesome; a period of disruption and anguish, hostility and rebellion; a period of sensuality and bizarre carryings-on. Thus, we see that alienation of youth is not only an experience but part of our contemporary cultural design.[1]

This 'nebulous limbo', then, is without status-recognized function. We tend to make this worse by creating situations – clubs, sixth-form suites, community centres, etc. – in which we hope to replace significance by a status based on separateness. In reporting on a very important action research study, John Bazalgette sensed that:

> Given that young people by the age of 16 or 17 have met many adults in different roles, the accumulated effect of this experience causes them to view with suspicion the institutions set up ostensibly to help them by herding them together out of touch with adult society.[2]

Indeed, even the school as a whole could be seen as part of this 'herding them together'. As Musgrove tartly puts it:

> It was formerly supposed that the child could learn nothing from other children except vice; it is now assumed that he can learn little of value from anybody else. It is one of the oddities of our day that contact between the young and the mature, except certified neuters such as priests, teachers, youth leaders and kinsmen, is regarded as dangerous and even immoral.[3]

Bazalgette's researches made it clear to him that:

> Structures intended to help young people, need to provide them with opportunities of interacting with adults who understand their own roles

[1] Mitchell, John, J., *Adolescence, Some Critical Issues* (Holt, Rinehart and Winston of Canada, 1971), pp. 50, 51.

[2] Bazalgette, John, *Freedom, Authority, and the Young Adult* (Pitman, 1971), p. 97.

[3] Musgrove, Frank, *Family, Education and Society* (Routledge and Kegan Paul, 1966), p. 143.

in society and are able to maintain this understanding in their dealings with young people.[1]

And he concludes:

> In the end the problem which has emerged as central has been to create ways in which young people can take a place in adult society, not creating special young people's areas in which adults can find a place, but finding ways of helping them to be alongside adults and to take a full part in an adult situation.[2]

I have spent some time on the question of the essentially adult motivation and learning of the late adolescent because it runs counter to much current theory and practice. The fact is that the last decade has seen maturity start earlier, and adult wishes and ideas spread wider for most of the young population than in the nineteenth and early twentieth centuries. Our clients would rather identify with the adult world than the teenage area we delimit for them. We have invented and perpetuated adolescence, and are hoist with our own petard.

This partial maturity manifests itself in the teenage anti-authority attitude. No doubt much of this has been taken over from the general trends in society which I described on pages 25–33. These, though, are mediated to the young by the child-rearing pattern, which itself adds further elements. The pupils in schools in the 'sixties were the generation whose formative early years came *after* post-war austerity. There had been a reaction against the war; fathers with memories of service authoritarianism looked differently at their children. Both parents had high hopes for their children's future, and had been influenced, at however remote a level, by the psychological and even artistic theories that were making people look differently at the childhood experience – the large-circulation papers were efficient and vivid popularizers of the 'advanced' theories. Dr Spock himself may have been read only by the professional classes, but ideas based on his book reached through to all but the least privileged. The relative practical comforts and increased prosperity itself affected child-rearing ways. As the Newsoms commented:

> It is widely recognized, for instance, that today children of every age enjoy a great deal more personal freedom in all sorts of ways than did their parents. Some of these mothers thought, however, that this was at least partly due to very practical considerations bound up with

[1] ibid., p. 105.
[2] ibid., p. 120.

higher standards of living. Nowadays, parents literally can afford to
let their children do more as they please. If a child has several changes
of clothing upstairs, it matters so much less if, on occasion, he gets
thoroughly dirty; and, when this happens, it is no longer necessary to
put him to bed while his clothes are washed and dried again. Similarly
the cost of replacing clothes is no longer quite such a nightmare to most
mothers, so that they are able to worry less about the damage and
wear caused by crawling, climbing, and enjoying an occasional rough
and tumble on the ground. When it is not quite so necessary to save
shoes to pass on from one child to the next, scuffed toecaps are no
longer a major calamity. Perhaps an additional factor in this freedom
is that the general standard of children's clothing is so high that the
difference between 'ordinary' and 'best' clothes is not now so great; nor
should we forget that today's frilly petticoat is something to be worn
every day, rinsed through and dripped dry over the sink at night,
whereas twenty years ago it might represent half an hour's solid work
in washing and ironing.[1]

The interrelationship between the practical aspects of life and
influences on the bringing up of the young is a fascinating
study, on which there is very little evidence for our society
(much more for primitive societies, ironically!). The Newsoms'
two reports are the fullest evidence readily available, and the
verbatim quotations illustrate clearly that the pastoral situation in schools has been changed drastically. These remarks
from a scaffolder's wife and a garage-owner's wife illustrate the
points:

> 'I'm bringing them up better. They used to stick to routine too much.
> They weren't allowed to have their freedom. You know, play and do
> things. I wasn't allowed to do things like playing with soil and things
> like that, like Lynn does – I wasn't allowed to ever get dirty. I was never
> allowed to make a mess.'[2]

> 'We're a bit more free and easy; I mean, Sundays, when we were young,
> meant best clothes and no toys and sit still, but my children wear jeans
> on Sunday and we go up to the allotment and get really messy. They
> did go to Sunday School for a bit, but Brenda said "It's nothing but
> standing up and sitting down, we'd rather come to the allotment
> with you".'[3]

I personally also wonder about the effects of modern medical
care, particularly the ready availability of drugs such as peni-
cillin. Before the mid-'fifties the careful mother had to worry
constantly about children's health. As the polio figures rose

[1] Newsom, John and Elizabeth, *Patterns of Infant Care* (Penguin, 1965)
pp. 239–240.
[2] ibid., p. 240.
[3] ibid., p. 241.

every summer, and when a cold could become pneumonia, hand-washing, clothes-changing, and general fretting were a necessary strand of childhood life, creating expectation of discipline. The generation born in the late 'fifties never knew this. We feel the difference in the secondary school. The primary schools have adjusted, and pedagogical theories of the time fitted the necessary adjustments well. The primary experience reinforced the home experience, and the combination has produced a secondary pupil whose expectations of authority are quite different from those of the pupils for whom the secondary school was devised.

These family patterns, together with the general tendencies of society, have stressed the individual and his or her personal assessment of whether an experience is meaningful as a criterion of its suitability. This has meant not only a growing dislike of organized groups and, for instance, an increase in interest in individual and informal sports (golf, canoeing, riding, badminton) in place of team games, but also, and more fundamentally, a demand for personal dignity as a right. This is held fiercely even by eleven-year-olds, who will no longer, for instance, accept arbitrary cuffing and other trappings of the past, however jocular the administration of them may be.

The 'demand for a meaningful personal identity as a right'[1] has obvious pastoral implications. At its extreme the children of our age when they come to their late teens have 'an exultation of subjective experience . . . looking towards a millenium of effortless bliss.' The words are those of Professor Carstairs in a series of talks in 1972 on the changes he has observed since his famous Reith lectures a decade earlier. He commented on the reluctance of many young people to regard the postponement of gratification as desirable. They are moving, as he puts it, 'away from doing towards feeling'. This is the so-called 'counter-culture'[2] which, while its full expression may not, and may never, have been felt in its full force in most schools, is nevertheless a potent influence. Musgrove sees the move as an essential by-product of the present computerized technological revolution and the growth of a 'personal service society'. Good taste, he argues, which once meant restraint, is now inclusive. Careers, which were once linear, are now in-

[1] Musgrove, Frank, 'The Decline of Deference', op. cit., p. 5.
[2] See, for instance, Theodore Rozak's book: *The Making of a Counter Culture* (Faber, 1970).

creasingly episodic. The younger generation, he goes as far as to say, are Dionysiac rather than Apollonian. His references to Nietzsche's *Birth of Tragedy* neatly label the two polarities.[1] The Apollonian atmosphere and relationships of our school patterns are shuddering at the moment under the onslaught of the hordes of Dionysiacs or semi-Dionysiacs. The pastoral system is the only possible way of reconciliation.

In childhood and early teens another formative influence was again at work outside the school, one which both reflected and at the same time intensified social trends and increased Dionysiac man: the pop music culture, which can be dated to Bill Haley in 1957, or more powerfully to the Beatles in 1963. A sociological and psychological analysis of pop music would have a great deal to teach schools. Pop groups of all sorts are virtually classless in a way that no previous popular entertainment has been. Clothing, style, accent (hence the importance of mid-Atlantic), and the whole manner of presentation owe no allegiance to class – in the way that, for instance, George Formby and Billy Cotton on the one hand, or Ambrose and Henry Hall, on the other, clearly did. There is a virtually complete rejection of class and any associated privileges by the young. This manifests itself in their choice of clothes, accents, and cultural experience. It also exercises itself in a continuous erosion of any situation of privilege that are built into schools organization.

A further feature of the pop-music scene is the apparent availability of an easy success. There is no doubt that the effect of this is devastatingly powerful on the young adolescent. This is partly a technical point: the electric guitar produces a seductively rapturous sound at first pluck. There is little compared with the problem of embouchure of a wind instrument or the even more taxing tone difficulties of string instruments. But one of the virtues of much group pop music, it seems to me, is that it depends on inventiveness and group creation, and does

[1] Nietzsche's formulation of the 'Apollonian–Dionysiac duality' is described in the first section of his essay on the arts, *The Birth of Tragedy*. Musgrove uses the terms to describe cultural changes in these words: 'The Apollonian values are these: a concern for order, discipline, codification; foresight; rationality; ability to defer gratification; methodical and systematic effort; chastity; frugality; reliability and predictability; propriety; caution and circumspection. . . . The opposite of Apollonian virtues, in Nietszche's typology are Dionysiac. Dionysiac characteristics are intuitive, non-rational, spontaneous, extravagant, incautious, prodigal, virile, tactile – even ecstatic, frenzied and boundary-bursting.' (Musgrove, *The Decline of Deference*, op. cit., pp. 3–4).

not require the virtuoso playing of an instrument after years of devoted practice. On the other hand a repeated five-note pattern on a bass electric guitar can be powerfully fascinating. That fact, plus the apparent casualness of presentation, and the immense publicity and wealth of the successful groups, produces fantasies in boys' minds, and erases the idea that devotion to a long training and development of skills will be worthwhile. To a considerable extent the publicity blurbs encourage this. A radio life-story of the Beatles, for instance, had one of the group telling how they were given a commission to produce a new number. It was to be an important step in their careers. 'So we went off to play Monopoly for a fortnight!' said one. Now it does not really matter how true that remark was. It illustrates the fact that many young performers seem to the thirteen-year-old to have achieved an easy success.

*   *   *   *   *

I have selected some features of the pupils in their times that seem to need consideration before we can look at practical procedures. I have omitted reference to the special problems of immigrants, and to the extra problems of inner-city areas. The immigrant-family problem is certainly different, but requires a whole study.[1] The inner-city problem adds a layer of instability to the situation, and pre-selects, because of the effects of urban depopulation, an extra high proportion of pupils from parents faced with acute difficulties.

I have described a mature young person pushing for personal meaning and adult status, and with a fairly strong, if variable, identification with adult values. He is in a mobile, changing, family-oriented, world of eclecticism, in which choice is the theme, and mobility and the media have put a wide range of life-styles, occupations, clothes, moral standards, and modes of behaviour apparently on offer. There is a great variety of adult roles available, and with that come the stresses and decision difficulties which such choice inevitably brings. No wonder that the maturity is shot through with anxiety about expectation, role and the future. Stability may limit, but it comforts. Choice may extend, but it bewilders. W. D. Wall, whom I quoted earlier, in no way underestimates the disadvantages of the past,

[1] See, for instance, Bowker, Gordon, *The Teaching of Immigrants* (Longman, 1970).

but to understand the pastoral needs of today it is worth studying his analysis of the differences between our own age and the Victorian era:

> Whatever he may have lacked in material and intellectual terms, the child from the village or even the slum of a century ago enjoyed certain psychological advantages. He was part of a small, coherent and comprehensible community within which he was known. His environment was peopled with figures with recognizable functions and provided for him experiences of danger and adventure. Not infrequently he was part of a large family group providing a gradation of emotional relationships and many substitutes for or variants to his emotional links with his parents.[1]

> However, the well fed, well housed, physically well cared for modern child may lack a number of psychological essentials. The environment of the town or suburb – the home of considerably more than half our children – has been rendered unsafe for play by the motor car and rarely provides a natural challenge to physical adventure. Adult work takes place behind walls and away from the dwelling place. Hence the environment is not peopled by adults ready to intervene, if necessary to punish or protect. Nor does the child see before his eyes the nature of work. The suburb does not present a coherent, comprehensible and completely articulated community. In about half the cases, his family is geographically or socially mobile or both. He will be uprooted a number of times and the tissue of relationships outside his immediate family may be broken or never in fact developed – he is too uniquely dependent upon a small immediate family.[2]

That pattern suggests the special function of a pastoral system to offer stability and relationships – even an emotional component. The other powerful need is help in the preparation for choice:

> Even half a century ago, vocational choice, political views, religious belief and many other important aspects of life were by and large restricted if not uniquely determined by the station (and the place in life) to which it had pleased the good God to call one. The choice was conformity or revolt – and revolt, as Jude the Obscure found, was tragically difficult and almost certainly unsuccessful. Theoretically at least today, any job is open to the lad or lass o'pairts; and what is more, the actual range of types of job is vastly greater. Similarly, political and social philosophies abound; there is a wide gamut of beliefs and non-beliefs cutting across social class; in manners, morals and behaviour there are many modes and the old associations between them and social groups are no longer intact. Pressed on by rising expectations, beset by the notion that you have only one life to live (and that may be shortened by the cataclysm), provoked to anxiety by ignorance of the demands and possibilities of the apparently limitless alternatives, it

[1] Wall, W. D., op. cit., p. 1.
[2] ibid., p. 2.

is not surprising that contemporary adolescents react with anxiety, bewilderment or even outright rejection of choice.[1]

A school must be able to offer guidance without dictation, advice without domination, and a firm framework for growth. Above all it must know its pupils closely enough to be able to relate to them.

[1] ibid., pp. 7–8.

4 Groups and Groupings

How can we meet the needs for care, guidance, and counselling which I have described, for the young people of our age whom I have pictured?

In many ways education has over-stated the possibilities which schools can achieve; our ambitions have underestimated the intractable personal and social barriers to the work of a school. Yet, it does also seem true that some schools have barely explored the organizational factors which are available to them for deployment. It may be that there is more strength in a school organization than has been realized. Each organizational element needs consideration separately in the first instance. It seems that too often a school faced with reorganization asks the larger questions first, such as: what overall organizational pattern shall we have? The inner details – many of them fundamental – are considered only later. My suggestion is the reverse. It is that each detailed variable should be focused on in turn as an element considered separately. From provisional decisions made on each factor it is possible to build up an overall total care system. The logic of this is simple: pastoral care involves the adult and the young person face to face. The purpose of any larger school structure is to help this situation work best. It is therefore reasonable to start from the detailed and work outwards.

The elements of a care system which I shall describe are not each self-contained, nor are they of equal importance. Some of them, indeed, are of broader significance, such as the delegation structure of the school. However, the full organizational potential of school planning is seen only if each is firstly considered separately. In this way it is possible to see the alternatives more clearly, with their advantages and disadvantages. It is also possible to see the implication for other elements of the system of each one in turn.

The start is obviously the group which receives the pupils in the first place, and the next aspect to consider is the way these groups are linked together.

(a) The Base-Unit

For the pupil, the reality of pastoral care is that embodied in the most frequent meeting, which is usually of the registration unit. I shall call this the 'base-unit' (except in descriptions of particular schools, when I use their own nomenclature). It is the combination of this group, its frequency of meeting, its function, and the way it is run which are the most important aspects of pastoral care. This is why I am considering the base-unit first, and why, indeed, there is a whole book in the series devoted to the role of its leader.[1]

The original purpose of having any group in a school other than a teaching group was to fulfil the legal requirements of registration. In the wholly class-taught school, such as the majority of infant schools, the registration function can be absorbed into the teaching function. It is important to realize this. The infant, or even junior, pupil starts his working day as he enters the room; the formal registration can be subordinated to significant activities, and done after work has started. In the more complex secondary school in which 'teaching' has split off from 'registration', and split further into subjects, possibly involving the changing of pupil groupings, there are many possibilities for the organization of this base-group. It can be argued that this separation of the base-group from teaching groups is the cause of many of the difficulties in the secondary school – and later I shall consider some of the possible strategies for avoiding this, especially with younger groups. If, though, there is to be a separation, this is surely to be exploited. Something can be made of it so that it becomes a virtue, not merely a makeshift. If the base-unit is not controlled by teaching requirements, its composition can be considered for purely pastoral requirements. Too many comprehensive schools have developed sophisticated pupil-grouping techniques for their teaching, but retained a base-unit which has not been freshly thought out from the point of view of the quality of care offered.

The first question is whether there need be a group for the base-unit at all. Could pupils be cared for individually at the first level? This no doubt seems a ludicrous question, and probably even if any system of purely individual tutoring were worked out the tutor would feel the need to gather his pupils together from time to time to give out information common to all, and probably some form of regular grouping would re-emerge. However, it is worth pondering whether we are well advised to spend so much time in groups. One could, for instance, envisage a sixth-form system in which pupils are 'on the books' of one particular tutor among those working with the sixth form. In this kind of situation the grouping of pupils would be in some form of semi-open social area by their own

[1] *The Tutor*, by Keith Blackburn (Heinemann, 1974).

friendship patterns. The tutor would have a desk, work area, or office, and the students would visit the tutor when there was a reason for doing so. 'Registration' would be some form of 'signing in'. Solihull High School for Girls is an example of a number of schools that go some way in this direction by basing sixth-form tutorial relationships on friendship groups. Towards the end of the fifth year girls are asked to give in the names, preferably in pairs or threes, to indicate who would like to be together. These self-chosen groups are then put into six tutor groups, each one having approximately twelve in the Lower Sixth and twelve in the Upper Sixth (thus, incidentally, keeping the same tutorial relationship for the two years).

Such a system would remove the weakest part of all conventional pastoral systems: that the teacher working with the base-unit (whom I shall call the tutor) has to spend a disproportionate time achieving order, running the group, and so on. With younger pupils it is difficult to envisage very much breaking up of the base group. With sixth forms it seems that a great deal would be gained: essentially pastoral work would be individual. And wouldn't there be advantages for the 15- and 16-year-olds also? So much of the tutor's energy is devoted to group management that individual work has very little time. Many of the individual consultations inevitably take place in a crowded 'form-room', where twenty-nine others are champing at the bit. It is not surprising, then, that his patience is tried, and that the individual relationships are weaker than they need to be. Indeed it is amazing that so much is achieved. Of course, his presence 'running the group' is one of his important sources of strength in dealing with the individuals; for it is one of the ways the tutor gets the feel of his pupils. However, I suspect we are going to work towards a greater individualization and a reduced emphasis on the group. Nevertheless, the group will no doubt always be with us for a proportion of the time. How, then, should it be formed?

Size
The first question is one of size. The standard size of 30, sometimes 31 or 32, is too readily accepted as the norm. How have we come to accept this? Because of the historic growth of the basic pastoral unit out of the normal teaching group, we have thought of 30 as inevitable. The 'form-entry' is taken as the standard definition of the intake size of a school, and this is taken as X times 30. In many schools the accommodation is

based on the number of 'form bases' required, and this is deduced by dividing the year group by thirty. Only the more unsuitable specialist rooms, such as a pottery room or chemistry laboratory, are available above this minimum. However, typical staffing ratios in all-through secondary schools run between 1:14 and 1:20. In some there are rooms unused for basic pastoral units, and in many there are devices for using less suitable rooms, or even open spaces. These points offer possibilities. In one area an eight-form-entry comprehensive school was working with basic groups of only twenty-four pupils while a neighbouring school still struggled with the standard thirty plus. Woodroffe School, Dorset, is able to reduce the size of groups to seventeen, by asking every teacher on the staff, other than the Head and Deputy, to take groups. (The extreme example of this is possible only in a sixth-form college. In Itchen College, Southampton, for instance, base-units are as low as eleven or twelve. Obviously this is possible only with the luxurious staff ratio permitted by the present points system to a school all of whose pupils are over sixteen.)

Clearly there are arguments against using such a high proportion of the teaching staff as this requires in a tutorial capacity: it means that major heads of department, even intermediate pastoral heads, career teachers, and so on, all have their burden of routine tutoring. Arguably, their time is better used helping their teams of teachers, or coping with individual pupils who have serious troubles temporary or permanent. On the other hand, it is very noticeable that the nature of what happens between adult and young person in the much smaller group is radically different from that which takes place in the considerably larger group. I should say that this difference is so valuable as to be well worth working for: it can alter the whole nature of relationships in the school community.[1] Such a decision would probably force a school away from using teaching groups as the basic pastoral unit. It also opens up questions of the grouping of the base-units (discussed on pages 62–7). Some overall patterns (e.g. streamed pastoral groups or even mixed-ability single-age house groups) make it harder to vary the size of the basic units than others. Thus, houses with ten vertical groups can easily spread to twelve if circumstances permit, but houses with two groups *per year* cannot.

[1] cf. 'It was mentioned in the schools visited that the size of the tutor groups (=30 pupils) during the first four years was generally too large.' Moore, B. M., *Guidance in Comprehensive Schools* (NFER, 1970), p. 76.

Composition

Whatever the size, what shall the composition of the groups be? The first question concerns ages: should the pupils in one group be all of the same chronological year-group?

Our schools are firmly based on age divisions for most purposes, certainly for the bulk of secondary-school teaching. Many find the idea of mixed ages for pastoral care curious – though it is the normally expected pattern for extra-curricular activities: entrance to the first eleven or a part in the school play is gained by skill and suitable physical maturity. There are grounds for challenging the rigidity of our age-layering, although I must largely take it for granted as a definite part of at least the purely teaching aspects of a school.

The most trenchant critic of the system is Frank Musgrove, Professor of Education at the University of Manchester, whose views on the adolescent identification with the adult world I have already quoted. He declares: 'Our schools breed an exaggerated respect for the often irrelevant criteria of age. Increasingly they have been organized and stratified according to the precise distinctions of age.'[1] While the continental system of 'keeping pupils down' if they fail to achieve a certain grade can have undesirable social effects, it also has powerful effects on raising the average performance levels of pupils (though possibly depressing the levels of the most able).[2] For the purposes of this book the points at issue concern the way young people are treated by the teachers and the interaction between the young people themselves.

As Musgrove says:

> Age may be a most misleading index of abilities. . . . As the size of the scatter in individual growth patterns increases in adolescence, it is even less a reliable index of physical, social, mental, or emotional maturity. Age becomes even more an irrelevant criterion of fitness to undertake a wide range of tasks and responsibilities.'[3]

And, one might add, even more irrelevant as the basis for relationships – as simple observation of the workings of a family, or the pattern of sixth-form boys with fourth-form girl-friends makes clear. The well-documented findings of Tanner

[1] Musgrove, Frank, *Youth and the Social Order* (Routledge and Kegan Paul, 1964), p. 158.
[2] For a discussion of this see Pidgeon, Douglas, A., *Expectation and Pupil Performance* (NFER, 1970), and Yates, A., *Organising Schooling* (Routledge and Kegan Paul, 1971).
[3] Musgrove, Frank, op. cit.

about adolescent growth confirm this, but seem to have barely affected our thinking in schools.[1]

Once the stable homogeneous 'form' as a teaching unit has been eroded (as it has in most modern fourth- and fifth-year patterns), the administrative convenience of the pastoral unit based on age has possibly gone also. If, then, one looks at the criteria for a successful social pastoral group one might well ask whether there are more subtle methods than the rigid date-of-birth classification. We might *choose* which pupils to put into which group by their personal characteristics and teacher compatibility, perhaps by what Tanner calls their 'skeletal age' or 'general physiological status'. The nearest we have got to this flexibility is in those schools where the basic-unit has pupils who span all or some of the years of a school on a strict quota basis. This latter method is often called 'vertical' grouping or 'family' grouping (because its span of ages is in some ways similar to that of a large family, and some people feel that it has some of the virtues also). It is important to realize that the choice is wider than merely that between single-age or fully vertical. The second has a number of variations: the ages spanned can be less than the full 11–18 range. One school, for instance, started with years 1–6 in the same groups, but found that the sixth form had to come out; a year after that the fifth form were taken out also, leaving groups spanning years 1–4 only. The school described on pages 184–8 (with no sixth form) had groups spanning years 2–5, with the first year as a reception and induction year. It is conceivable, though not very likely, that a vertical grouping could be combined with ability grouping: but it is not a very attractive thought to consider the possibility of the 'less-able school' within the school that this could create, and which would be more marked than in even a streamed age-grouped school.

A final variation should be noted before we look at the pros and cons of the different systems: a school does not have to have the same pattern over the whole of the age-range. For instance, a number of schools have their sixth form in combined base-units, with upper and lower grouped together. This is a modest form of vertical grouping which is often combined with conventional age-grouping for the rest of the school. Schools with strong horizontal breaks at the end of the third year might very well adopt a two-year mixing over the unified fourth and fifth years, while maintaining single-year grouping

[1] Tanner, J. M., *Growth at Adolescence* (Blackwell, second edition, 1962).

in the lower school. Split-site schools, wishing to make a virtue of separation by considering the needs of the pupils on each site as single-mindedly as possible, often decide to have single-age groupings for one building, perhaps the younger years, and vertical groupings in the building for the older pupils. The reverse seems to be very rare, although a school with only years one and two in a separate building might well integrate them, to fit a system of teaching nearer to that of a junior school, while keeping years three and upwards separate. It is important, then, to realize there is no invariable need for a stereotyped pattern in all seven years.

Now it is necessary to look at the advantages and disadvantages of the two main age-grouping methods in outline:

FROM THE TUTOR'S POINT OF VIEW

Vertical	*Single-Age*
Easier for the tutor to think of the pupils as individuals and to relate to them on a one-to-one basis;	Easier to create group loyalties;
Harder to find a group activity to occupy the whole group;	Easier for the tutor to find a suitable subject for group discussion, and a suitable voice with which to address the group;
Less heavy burden of work for tutor at any one time of the year, as not more than a section of his group is involved in, e.g. option choices, examination entries;	Easier to brief tutors on such age-dominated procedures as option-choices, examination entries, induction to school, etc., as fewer tutors involved in any one such exercise;
Easier to keep order as not so many, e.g., lively first-years or large aggressive fourth-years congregated together;	Group management more difficult;

FROM THE PUPIL'S POINT OF VIEW

Vertical	*Single-Age*
Older pupils can sometimes give help and advice, and offer patterns of behaviour to emulate;	Pupils of the same age give a wide range for possible close friendships;
Somewhat greater possibility of continuity and stability, as there is always a coherent group (especially if it crosses four or more years) from which only a few join each year;	Can be harder to establish yourself in at first;

Vertical	*Single-Age*
Tutor likely to be insufficiently informed about the important procedures and advice relevant to own age.	Too many others of same age jostling for tutor's attention at peak times.

Obviously there is no simple answer: each school will have its own features, and a factor like great staff stability may make the advantages of the 'vertical' less compelling in one school than in another with a more mobile staff. Equally obviously, the decision cannot be made after considering only the base-unit, for whereas either grouping method can be accommodated in the so-called 'house' system (see pages 64–5), 'vertical' grouping within base-units will not fit the year-grouping of the base-units (usually called 'horizontal' – see pages 62–7).[1] Similarly, vertical grouping cannot easily be combined with homogeneous or banded ability – for an all-age less-able group would be an extreme kind of 'streaming' which I cannot imagine anyone justifying: it would create a special school within a school (but compare the points on pages 59–60). Over all, I suspect the crux of the single-age versus mixed-age controversy (especially if the mixture of ages covers a wider range than two years) centres on the decision about what could be called group counselling versus individual counselling:

The single-age group tends towards handling pupils as a group, and individual work is important but secondary;

The mixed-age group tends towards handling pupils singly or in pairs, and group approaches are important but secondary.

Abilities

The majority of the preliminary and first-phase comprehensive schools settled for single-age base-units, though the exceptions were notable ones. (I have avoided saying 'chose', because I suspect the other possibilities in composing base-units were barely explored.) There are, though, various factors that can be brought into the selection of pupils for the base-units: the most important of these is whether the pupils are grouped by ability in the basic pastoral unit, or balanced, with a mixture of measured abilities.

The established pattern, of course, which the comprehensive school inherited was the streamed pastoral unit (the 'form'),

[1] Except that base groups combining pupils of only, say, two age-groups could be related to a similar age-based horizontal organization.

which coincided with the streamed teaching unit. It is not within the scope of this book to discuss the question of pupil grouping for teaching and learning purposes except to the very real extent that the pastoral situation *is* a teaching/learning situation itself.

Most of the streamed schools used the inherited streamed pastoral unit, and this was particularly so of those which used the 'year' as the larger grouping (see pages 184–202). However, from the first a number of schools adopting house organizations grouped pupils into pastoral units based on these houses, and drawing from the full ability range of pupils within the house. (Such mixed-ability pastoral base-units are, of course, also compatible with year-based larger groupings.) Again, the choice is not merely between 'streamed' or 'mixed-ability' pastoral units. It is possible, but rare, to 'band' a large intake into broadly homogeneous groups of about ninety, and create semi-mixed-ability pastoral base-units within each band. It is worth noting, in this context as elsewhere, that grouping techniques have a different effect according to the *size* of the intake: thus in the large (say, ten-form-entry) school the so-called 'broad-banding' with mixed-ability groups within the band produces a grouping which is just as homogeneous as 'streaming' in a small (say, three-form-entry) selective school.

Rather more common than equal banding is the 'tailing' of an intake by having a number of parallel mixed-ability pastoral base-units covering the majority of the intake, but with one or more 'remedial' units as well. Thus one eight-form-entry boys' school covering 80 per cent of the ability range (described in the case study on pages 184–8) has six parallel groups, one 'semi-remedial' and one 'fully remedial'. Another school (mixed) of similar size has remedial groups derived from two of the four houses each. Yet another school has house groups as the fourth- and fifth-year pastoral base, but each of the two house groups in each year is drawn from rather different combinations of options: thus there is an 'Academic' group and a 'Commercial/Technical group' in the fourth year of each house. This is rather like the traditional grouping of sixth form pupils into pastoral units based on their science- or arts-based courses – although it implies an ability grouping also. The sixth-form decision would seem to me simpler these days as the science/arts division has been made less distinct. Few schools, I fancy, would want to build in such divisions for the future.

It is possible to tabulate the pros and cons of these aspects of

pastoral grouping, though, as in all such listing, the polarities
are somewhat artificial:

PASTORAL BASE-UNITS

Homogeneous	*Mixed Ability*
Likely to reinforce any labelling arising from sets or streams in teachers;	Likely to encourage pupil mixing, and to discourage premature typing of pupils;
Easier to find suitable mode of address and atmosphere for group;	Can be harder to run group discussion and to explain matters;
Mechanical administration, announcements, checking, briefing, etc., made easier;	Transfer between teaching groups easier, as base unit not changed and thus friendship patterns not broken;
In a streamed school close control of pupils made easier;	Possible to make the group nearer to a cross-section of the school as social unit;
Easier to create links with subject teaching in a basically streamed school;	Easier to link with subject teaching in a basically non-streamed school;
Tendency towards group leadership.	Tendency towards individual counselling.

There is very little research on the effects of either of the two
forms. A small survey by the sociologist Barry Sugarman (now
of the Farmington Trust)[1] showed that in a streamed school
there were significant friendships within mixed-ability groups
cutting across streams, but this was a limited pattern. Ford's
study of comprehensive, selective, and non-selective schools[2]
showed what little effect a mere comprehensive organization
has in a fully streamed school. The NFER research also looks
at this.[3] However, the sum total of this guidance gives schools
very few firm conclusions. My overall impression is that when a
mixed-ability pastoral unit supports a streamed teaching pattern, the friendships are influenced largely by the dominating
teaching pattern, but that nevertheless the mixed-ability pastoral unit considerably softens the harsh effects of streaming on
the less able especially.

The familiar low-stream behaviour and attitude problems

---

[1] TS, privately circulated, 1963.

[2] Ford, Julienne, *Social Class and the Comprehensive School* (Routledge and Kegan Paul, 1969).

[3] J. M. Ross, *et al.*, *A Critical Appraisal of Comprehensive Education* (NFER, 1972), Chapters 4 and 11 especially.

have been shown as substantially the results of streaming, and not merely the inevitable differences resulting from a range of abilities and social backgrounds. David H. Hargreaves has documented this in his study of a secondary-modern school, which has especial relevance to a consideration of pastoral care: *Social Relations in a Secondary School*.[1] He maintains of that school: 'We have found that subcultural development is generated by a number of mutually reinforcing factors, of which the organization of pupils into streams is the basic structural component.'[2] The evidence of that study supports the pragmatic findings of many comprehensive schools that the mixing in the pastoral unit goes some way to blur the sub-culture antipathies. As Hargreaves puts it: 'If these mutually hostile subcultures are to be eliminated – either in a comprehensive or a Secondary Modern School – the school must provide greater opportunities for members of different streams to interact, preferably in a co-operative enterprise'.[3]

There are also more limitedly administrative differences between the effects of the two forms of pastoral units. The more homogeneous the pastoral base-unit is, the tidier the effect is: discipline is likely to be more rigid but less personal a thing. The nearer to mixed a unit is, the less tidy, but possibly the more personal it will be. The first helps to keep a school 'in control', but the second can help to create a community of contact. It can be seen that in most respects my analysis inevitably leads me towards preferring the mixed unit, but especial thought is worth giving to the difficult pupil who needs support. The concept of the 'remedial' *teaching* group, giving smaller group teaching and supposedly special subject tuition to pupils who are however based in mixed-ability pastoral/registration units, is open to considerable scrutiny. It rests on the assumption that some mixing is desirable if the less able, the backward, or the disturbed pupil is to benefit from the school, and not be merely confirmed in his or her present condition. This is an assumption that very few, if any, would challenge – though there may well be debate about the range of pupils within which the mixing is profitable for the backward, and possibly even more debate about the range within which such mixing is *mutually* profitable. The scrutiny, it increasingly seems to me, should focus on the kind of activity in which the mixing takes

---

[1] Routledge and Kegan Paul, 1967.
[2] op. cit., p. 192.
[3] op. cit., p. 187.

place. The 'learning' activity takes the longest time, and it is that in which, inevitably, and in any kind of school, the greatest status is invested. In one sense, and from one point of view, the pastoral work of a school is a 'support' activity, designed, to put it crudely, to ensure that the pupil is fit to benefit from his learning activities, and, at a slightly higher level of ambition, to help the pupil to integrate this learning with his personality and growing independent self. (In this sense the whole process is a 'vicious circle'.)

There are separate arguments for the establishment of at least a substantial minority of teaching time, if not the majority, in mixed-ability groups. My present concern is to ask whether it is not sometimes valuable for some part of the pastoral care to be analagous to the 'remedial' teaching for which staffing and accommodation resources are willingly found. Certain pupils need not so much special 'teaching' as special 'caring'. The 'clever' disturbed child might well be best helped by a special very small pastoral unit, feeding the ordinary teaching groups. The 'slow learner' might be better in the normal mixed-ability pastoral units feeding special teaching groups. This kind of paradox is hidden by the crude effects of normal streaming when the disturbed and the slow gravitate to produce not only unteachable teaching groups, but also unmanageable pastoral groups.

A 'remedial pastoral group' would be especially suitable for pupils who could profit by being in mixed-ability teaching groups, but need additional close care with their personal organization. Special 'nurture groups'[1] of as few as five or six might be established, say within each house, or from a group of tutor groups. The special tutor would concentrate on preparing the pupils for the day's timetable, and, acting as a kind of 'super Mum', would ensure that each pupil left for the right place with the right equipment.

A scheme along similar lines has been set up at Garforth Comprehensive School near Leeds. This school has a daily 'Form Tutor' period of half an hour. Ten or twelve of the teachers without full group tutorial responsibilities take two or three children each for three out of the five weekly tutorial sessions. Their objectives are: '(i) Extra help with reading, arithmetic, or any academic problems, and (ii) To form special relationships, for many of these children are maladjusted and/or

---

[1] This is a phrase coined by London infant and junior schools for the special teaching groups within schools set up for disturbed children.

come from deprived homes.' As one senior member of staff commented, 'In many cases only (ii) is attempted, and is in fact deemed sufficient'. My observation of occasions when *ad hoc* arrangements have been forced on a school to cope with an individual pupil who has been totally unable to function without daily help suggests that regular arrangements for discriminatory pastoral care may be necessary in some schools for at least part of the year.

The grouping of pupils by ability in any case depends on the availability of some form of 'measured' grades. Many authorities administer verbal reasoning tests as part of the junior-school transfer procedure. Those few authorities that are either dropping such tests, or simplifying them into a smaller, and thus coarser, number of points on a scale, are obviously making the creation of both streamed and mixed-ability groups harder, for you cannot mix abilities if you do not know them. In a medium or small school, certainly, a purely random selection might well produce very unbalanced groups: the standard size of pastoral units (around thirty) is too small to be sure that chance will not produce certain groups with an unequally large weighting of markedly more able pupils. The results of this are felt for years as one group not only has a high centre of academic gravity, but also produces an unusually high number of contributors to the extra-curricular and cultural life of the school.

Area Divisions
Mention must be made of ways of grouping pupils into pastoral base-units other than those relating to general ability. Family relationships, for instance, are usually noted so that members of one family, however many years apart, would have the same house affiliations. Certain interests or aspects of background can be usefully exploited to a minor degree. For instance, at Pimlico, a large London comprehensive school which has special provision for musically able children, those with special musical interests are placed in related groups. More unusual still, perhaps, but successful, and in its way very practical, was the procedure in a three-form-entry girls' selective school when the headmistress grouped first-year pupils by 'maturity' and seeming sophistication. Thus one of the three groups had what she called her 'Alice in Wonderland' little girls.

The most important of such factors is that of intake areas and contributory schools. Some schools, especially those with house systems, arrange mixed-ability groups to coincide with intake patterns. In this way pupils from certain contributory junior schools are kept together. In a rural school, this has important geographical relevance, for pupils from nearby villages are kept together.

The advantages of such grouping are powerful:

(i) Junior/secondary liaison is easier than it would otherwise be, certainly in a house system, as each head of house has only a limited number of schools with which he has to make close contact. Thus the transfer can be smoothed, and, for instance, heads of houses can visit their contributory schools to meet the pupils each year.

(ii) Certain practical problems like coach journeys delivering pupils back after special events can be managed more easily.

(iii) The identity of the pastoral units is reinforced by the external factors.

However, there are two serious disadvantages, and once again only the individual school can assess whether they are major factors in the particular case or not.

(i) Different contributory areas can have different characters and very different ability profiles. Thus in a large urban school that has adopted this system, it has been found that the houses within the school develop in awkwardly different ways, one house becoming the 'rough' one because of the placing of its contributory schools. A large urban comprehensive in Leeds analysed the geographical distribution of its remedial and maladjusted pupils. The map showed quite clearly that they clustered largely in one small section of the estate. An area pastoral division would have been disastrous. An interesting example which highlights this unplanned effect, and which well reveals the dilemma, is the house affiliation of the boarding lodge for 120 pupils which is part of Crown Woods School, a thirteen-form-entry mixed comprehensive school in south-east London. For the important reasons of ease of communication, the boarding house was originally associated with one house only, and fed all the mixed-ability tutor groups of that house. A boarding establishment, especially one provided primarily to help the children of service families overseas, does not tend to attract the parents of the least able. Further, being on site all the time, pupils from the boarding lodge had a stronger motivation towards extra-curricular activities. It was soon found that these two factors subtly but powerfully altered the balance of

the six houses, and the one fed by the boarding lodge, although
its members were only about a quarter of the house, became
prominent in many ways, and its 'mixed-ability' groups were
different in character to the others. It will be found that
similar, though perhaps less striking, variations will occur
in certain areas if groups recruit according to contributory
schools.

(ii) Secondly, the advantages of mixing are lost, and pupils
are retained within the friendship group of their earlier years.
Some heads argue that the wider mix is essential.

The advantages of togetherness and good communication
are great: the decision is difficult.

Choice
All the criteria discussed so far have, of course, been ones leading to directive action by the school to the pupils. There is a
basic flaw in all such methods: the school is virtually directing
a teacher (the tutor) to create 'a good relationship' with a
pupil. Is this the only way of doing it? It is possible to argue
that for some age-levels at least tutor and pupil should choose
each other. This is difficult in the arbitrary or house-based
system of groupings, but fairly easy in an age-based system. I
know a school that does this with mixed fourth- and fifth-year
groups, and another that allows such choice within a sixth-form
tutor-group pattern. The chosen relationship with a general
practitioner is considered desirable. Might it not also be so with
older pupils and their general guides?

(b) The Linking of Base-Groups

In the small school of, say, three-form-entry, the fifteen base-
groups in the first five years of a traditional pattern can be
regarded as a single community. In any larger school this is
really not possible. Each of us needs someone to whom to go for
briefing, advice, and support; each person needs a recognizable
leader who will guide, commend, and if necessarily criticize.
Even in the three-form-entry school it is arguable that the
pastoral system suffers from the failure that lies within the
presumption that the head can lead all his tutors (probably
called form teachers) direct. It is the old romantic fallacy of the
small school to believe that in this 'single-order system' (see
page 93) there is naturally good leadership. Usually the

form teacher in such a school lacks precisely that support and encouragement that is supposedly one of the virtues of the small school. My evidence is that the 'tutor subordinate' role of the right-hand column on page 75 is often carried to extremes in small schools: I have spoken to many such 'form teachers' who maintain that 'the head keeps everything to himself'. There is probably an approximate optimum number for a team of colleagues: the pastoral staff of all but the smallest schools is almost certainly too numerous for single leadership.

Some people would not accept that argument, but would see the pastoral staff of the large school as needing sub-division. It is this bringing together of tutors into workable teams that I should see as the first function of any linking of base-groups. It is more normal, I know, to see the function of larger groupings as primarily providing *pupil* communities. I'm not at all sure that this is their prime function, though (as I shall describe later), it is, of course, very important. But I should start with the tutors.

If you accept that the tutor is the key figure, but that he cannot work in isolation, needing to be part of a supportive team, and to have a leader (whom I shall call the 'intermediate pastoral head'), the next question is how to group tutors, and thus base-units of pupils also. Is there a way of relating base-units so that they have something in common? Obviously this depends on the method of grouping into those base-units. A few theoretical possibilities are immediately apparent:

Method of composing base-group	*Possible ways of linking base-groups*
streamed (and therefore single-age):	(i) by ability (e.g. top two streams for each year); *or* (ii) by age (e.g. all streams from one year);
'vertical' (i.e. mixed-age and mixed-ability) derived from contributory schools:	(iii) contributory schools;
the same selected randomly:	(iv) arbitrary;
mixed-ability but single-age:	(v) age (i.e. all groups of one year); *or* (vi) arbitrary

At first glance method (i) may seem ludicrous, but it is the way multi-lateral schools, or multi-lateral schools disguised as

comprehensive schools, work. However, I do not offer it as a
hopeful scheme. It will be seen that there are really *three* ways
of linking the base-units: two of them have recognizable criteria: age or source (i.e. contributory school). This second
(which suffers from the advantages and disadvantages described
on pages 60–2) is less common and in many cases is not practical. The third possibility I call 'arbitrary', that is, a workable
number of groups are linked together and thus given an arbitrary unity arising in the first place merely out of the teaming
of tutors. With a base-group pattern which is 'vertical' this
may result in a working system which is exactly the same as that
resulting from linking by 'source' of pupils (i.e. contributory
schools).

Thus the main choice is between 'arbitrary' or 'age-based'
links (although, once again, there may be variations at different
points in the school). The first of these we usually call a 'house',
but this word contains a beguilingly misleading metaphor.
These two major systems are often called 'vertical' (i.e. arbitrary) or 'horizontal' (i.e. age-based). Obviously the age-based
does not have to comprise a single year, for pairs of years will
also work (e.g. fourth and fifth). Both the arbitrary (house)
and the age-based linkages also have something of an effect of
creating smaller pupil communities within the school, and thus
affecting pupil relationships. Apart from teaching (which is
discussed later), these two methods of creating the smaller
communities do work in different ways. As a pupil walks
around the school, he probably always has a strong feeling of
his year affiliation, for teaching is almost invariably year-
based. The question is, to what extent does the overlaying of the
arbitrary or house linkage modify this *year* consciousness?
Assemblies in houses symbolize the vertical grouping, as do any
visual representations by tie, badge, or colour. The weekly
games may utilize the house affiliation to help with teams,
though the greater range of options, and the greater emphasis
on individual physical athletics in older years, is certainly
reducing the community effect of the house in games. Over all,
though, I should say that the individual pupil does not feel his
house or year affiliation primarily in these ways. His moment
of feeling the affiliation is when a teacher in some context of
work or play, when needing to criticize or praise, asks the
crucial question 'What house are you in?' It is the repeated
putting and answering of the question which speaks 'house' to
the pupil – together, of course, with the fact that he is sent for,

or goes to see, a house head when in trouble or in need of advice.

I am arguing, then, that the essence of linking base-units, even when that arbitrary linking is called 'a house', is not a *geographical* aspect of the school (though the placing of tutor rooms in year or house complexes may emphasize the linkage very strongly indeed); I do not even consider that the essence of the linkage is pupil-to-pupil loyalty, shocking as that disclaimer may seem, especially to advocates of the house system. Rather I see the essence of the linkage as a *chain of responsibility*. It is the knowledge that a certain 'intermediate pastoral head' cares, and will make a fuss if necessary, that imprints 'house' or 'year' in a pupil's understanding. What is the reader's visual image of a house? Is it of pupils playing team games? Or is it of pupils socializing together over board games and snacks? Mine is neither in the first instance: it is simply of a young person talking individually to an adult with whom he has a continuous relationship. Its prime architectural articulation is the interview-room, not the dining-room; and its symbol a small table and two chairs, not an open space.

Attempts have been made to discuss the pros and cons of the age-based and the arbitrary methods of linking, but usually such discussions have been by headteachers who have naturally had to choose for their schools, and their accounts are naturally biased by their decisions.[1] These accounts tend to rationalize whichever system was felt to be right for the particular school with which the writer was familiar. Moore, more objectively, says of the two possibilities: 'To know their true level of effectiveness would require intensive study.'[2] This is by no means as easy an argument as staffroom platitudes would suggest it to be. When architecture sways the decision, it is certainly easy, but otherwise the balance of advantages and disadvantages of either pattern is subtle. The consideration is made the more difficult by the fact that if you look at the linkage, as I have done, primarily as a teaming of tutors under an intermediate pastoral head, then many of the conventional arguments, for instance about the relative merits of the competitive spirit, are less important. Once again we can, however crudely, tabulate the points:

[1] e.g. Margaret Miles in section 5 of her *Comprehensive Schooling* (Longman, 1968), or Albert Rowe on page 102 of *The School as a Guidance Community* (Pearson Press, 1971).
[2] Moore, B. M., *Guidance in Comprehensive Schools* (NFER, 1970).

Arbitrary (vertical)	*Age-based* (horizontal)
Difficult to find mode of address and treatment which is equally applicable over full age-range;	More homogeneous and therefore easier to give feeling of coherence (e.g. in assembly);
	Easier to create appropriate atmosphere for various ages;
Exposure to older and more senior pupils helps to mature;	Danger of exaggeration of age differences;
	Intermediate pastoral head can specialize in needs of different age-groups;
	Easier to relate pastoral to the curricular;
Inter-house competition can be developed;	Competitive element almost certainly impossible between years;
Houses can develop their own characters and atmospheres;	Easier to get similar treatment in age-groups and thus avoid unfair variable treatment;
Tutors and pastoral heads able to assess pupils' problems in the context of whole age-range;	
Pupils more likely to feel a loyalty to a house than a year;	Pupils can more easily identify with pupils of their own age;
Continuity of care easier;	Difficult to provide strong continuity;
Knowledge of families easier to link;	
	Especially suits split-site schools;
	Less likely to be hierarchical; and mixing therefore more easy;
Induction of new pupils to base-unit more pleasant;	Induction of new pupils more effective as whole year geared to this as a prime function;
Easier to diffuse specialist advice (e.g. vocational guidance) naturally and gradually into the normal sequence of day-to-day pastoral care.	Easier to beam specialist advice (e.g. vocational guidance) at the appropriate age-range;

In each case I have tried to list both sides as fairly as possible, and it will be seen how difficult it is to assess the relative merits of the two columns. There seem to me to be two major aspects that need especial thought: continuity and curriculum.

Continuity

In the traditional three-form-entry grammar school, a pupil's form teacher often changes each year. Serious attempts are now made to provide continuity in comprehensive schools by leaving a tutor with a group for a number of years. Although continuity of tutor is important, it is also important that there should be the organizational continuity of the sort that goes beyond the individual tutor, the kind of stability that rests in a *school's* continuity and knowledge of the individual. In our context this has to be invested in the linking of pastoral units and in the person of the intermediate pastoral head. The arbitrary and the age-based links need careful testing against this criterion. Under an age-based system, heads of year sometimes stay put, exploiting their special expertise as (for example) head of first year. This means that the pastoral head's knowledge can be passed on only on paper. If the tutors go on, then the head of year also wastes the relationship he has built with them; if they stay put, on the other hand, then no knowledge goes forward. There is thus a potential loss of experience of the pupils which the tutors and the intermediate pastoral head have built up over the year. If, on the other hand, the whole team moves forward, something of the specialism which is the strength of the system is lost. Many horizontally organized schools compromise by keeping perhaps the first and the fifth year heads stable, and rotating the others. It must be pointed out, though, that in an area of many large families any ingenious variation of the horizontal system still suffers from the lack of continuity for the *family*. It takes time to get to know a pupil, and even more to get to know his family; this is an investment of the intermediate pastoral head's time and energy. In a house system, it is a valuable investment, but less so in a horizontal system. (An interesting variation is operated in one London age-based school: the Heads of Year move up with their year until the Fifth. They then have a fallow year during which they are expected to pick up the Junior School liaison for their incoming first year twelve-months later.)

Curriculum

Many of the first generation of comprehensive schools set up a pastoral system as something separate from the teaching system, and many thus unwittingly created an academic/pastoral split. This was not designed, but resulted from the admirable intentions of trying to create an additional perspective to the school organization: one that would, as it were, give strength to a teaching system that was felt to be fairly static and acceptable as it stood. In considering the linking of pastoral groups, the relationship of the pastoral work to the teaching work should be closely studied. They are complementary, not separate, activities, and the school organization must help this relationship, not make it more awkward.

In a largely streamed teaching pattern there is no doubt that it is easier to relate the pastoral and curricular aspects of base-. groups that are linked on an age-base pattern: each year has a slightly differentiated curriculum, and the head of year can express an opinion on the needs of his year. He can oversee the distribution of the timetable. The pastoral tutors will be responsible to him, and the year group will have a marked unity. It is very difficult for an arbitrary or house-based pastoral system to have a close relationship with streamed groups, for obvious reasons. In these schools there certainly does seem to be a separation, and very often the pastoral heads are widely divorced from the academic life.

There is ample evidence of the difficulties which this split can produce. Equally clear are the opportunities that are thus missed. For instance, slow learners are taught by a 'department' which has only tenuous or tangled relations with the 'house' which knows the pupils. The DES did a nationwide survey of *Slow Learners in Secondary Schools*. The writers reported:

> Schools were asked to indicate what they considered to be the primary function of a house unit; 39 considered this to be to provide for informal social activities, 30 for registration, and only 14 for providing educational guidance. Most schools saw the primary purpose of a house as a vehicle for the organisation of various sporting activities. Rarely were the houses used as a basis of teaching groups (109 no; 19 yes), and when they were it was usually for art, drama, physical or religious education. A few heads, however, made more imaginative use of their house system. In one school, for example:
>
>> The first year boys had their form master as house tutor; thus some lessons were taken in house groups. The aim was to prevent the boys, who came from 22 contributory schools, from being immediately separated from their known companions.

In reply to a question whether the house organisation influenced the curricular needs of the slow learners, the answer was generally 'No'. In general, the significance of house/tutor groupings in this aspect of the education of the slow learners seemed slight.[1]

Obviously, the introduction of non-streamed work, which can be based on a house mixed-ability group, changes this problem. Where a school has created the mixed-ability teaching group, the pastoral/academic link can be as easily created through a house system. One truism is certain: the planning of the curriculum and that of the pastoral system must be integrated.

I must add a warning: the debate between an age-based and an arbitrary method of linking pastoral units is not one that will produce a clear answer in any school. There is, though, always a need for some element of the discarded system to be retained. For instance, any school, it seems, that devises a strongly vertical system will need a horizontal component of some sort. This was recognized in Moore's NFER survey, for example: 'The structure is essentially vertical although the head has found it necessary to introduce certain horizontal elements.'[2] These were 'course co-ordinators' and 'year tutors'. This is most noticeable in the sixth form, for some degree of separate organization is almost always found necessary here, partly to cope with the need of the sixth form to feel more adult, and partly to provide the kind of specialized educational guidance which sixth-form timetables require. Similarly, though, strong co-ordination and leadership is likely to be required to help the tutors in, for example, the third year in guiding pupils into their middle school options. Conversely, a heavily layered age-based system is led by pastoral heads whose vision is rightly focused on to the needs of a year. This can mean that longitudinal care is less developed than when the intermediate pastoral head has pupils of all ages in his care. He can easily, for instance, see his task as 'getting safely through the year', rather than having a vision of the pupil's growing needs. Some schools meet this by building up the careers guidance within a strong department that gives, as it were, vertical continuity. Similarly, the role of Director of Studies can be built up to give a stronger all-through basis to educational guidance.

Finally, of course, the composition of the base-groups and of

[1] Department of Education and Science, *Slow Learners in Secondary Schools*, being *Education Survey 15* (HMSO, 1971).
[2] Moore, op. cit., p. 21.

the linked groups cannot be considered without asking about the roles and responsibilities of the teachers who lead both, and indeed of all senior roles in the school. It is therefore the question of teacher roles and responsibilities which the next chapter explores.

5 Roles and Responsibilities

It is one of the frequent organizational failures of schools not to provide newcomers with a clear job-description. This is partly because of the burden of work and the shortage of time and clerical help, but it is also because it is often presumed that all roles are clear and self-defining. This is very far from true, and, indeed, roles are becoming less clear or easy to pick up as they are coming to vary more from school to school. Similarly, it is important that the situation into which these roles fit should be logically devised and clearly articulated. The lack of definition masks but does not solve inconsistencies and difficulties in the work of the school. At a time of change in institutions, role definition is vital.

The more clearly the structure of a school is understood, the more likely it is that young teachers will have encouraging conditions in which to work, and the greater the possibility of their voices being really taken into account. Paradoxically, in even a medium-sized organization it is the apparently very informal set-up that is the most frustrating for the individual. For teachers to work effectively, lines of communication must be well defined, and roles and responsibilities must be clearly but flexibly laid down.

It is helpful to think of a large school as having an overall leader, the head, and under him three responsibility layers. These are not as hierarchical as they may sound; but they do reflect responsibility patterns.

Firstly there are the senior staff such as deputy head, second deputy, senior assistant, etc. These are people who, at any rate in a well-shaped school, have defined responsibilities for decisions that are essentially those of the head of an organization. These roles thus embody aspects of the work of the head of a small school, especially in that the responsibilities are across the school. (I discuss these roles in some detail on page 91.)

Then, secondly, there are those whom industry would call 'middle management'. The phrase 'middle management' sounds awkward in school conversation, but it is useful in indicating a fairly clear stage in the functional hierarchy. Heads of departments and intermediate pastoral heads (heads of year or heads of houses) are the most common titles. These people are '*middle*' in that they have considerable autonomy, but it is largely for implementing overall policy. Certainly their voices are important for the formulating of policy,[1] but on their own

[1] cf. Chapter 10 of my *Head of Department* in this series.

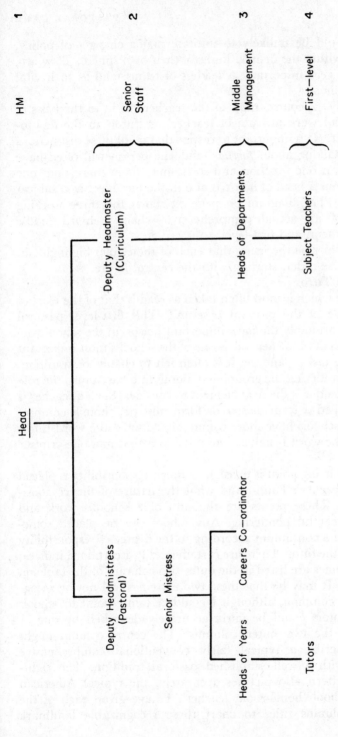

A typical (but not necessarily ideal) modern school structure, to show responsibility layers

1   HM

2   Senior Staff

3   Middle Management

4   First-level

Head

Deputy Headmaster (Curriculum)

Heads of Departments

Subject Teachers

Deputy Headmistress (Pastoral)

Senior Mistress

Careers Co-ordinator

Heads of Years

Tutors

they would be unlikely to inititate major changes of policy,
except within the defined limits of their own sphere. They are,
though, very important as leaders of teams, and as such vital
to the school.

Finally, of course, most of the teachers fit in to the basis of
the school work as 'subject teacher' or 'tutor' in the day-to-
day layer. (It is important to realize that in all these distinctions
we are talking about *function*, and one person will often have
more than one function and so he may fit in more than one
place; thus a head of house is also in the first layer as a subject
teacher.) The diagram on page 73 shows the three working
layers of an actual comprehensive school: senior, middle
management, and first-level.
I shall describe the issues that each of these roles highlights in
the reverse order, starting with the central figure.

(a) The Tutor

The role which is most often taken as read is that of the teacher
in charge of the pastoral base-unit. This first-level pastoral
figure is arguably the most important person in the school: the
definition of his or her role is one of the school's most important
planning tasks – and yet it is often left to chance or tradition.
After considering the grouping of pupils into base-units, the role
of their leader is the next element to consider. Such a teacher is
often called a form master or form mistress, though comprehensive schools have more commonly adopted the word tutor.
This is the word I shall use, for it is a somethat more descriptive
word.

The starting point is to ask how much responsibility is placed
in this teacher's hands, and what the nature of this responsibility is. These points are the nub of a school's work and
deserve careful pondering. Any school can be placed somewhere on a continuum according to the degree of responsibility
given to the tutor. There are certain readily ascertained indices:
the extremes are listed in the outer two columns of the table on
page 75. It may be that these two extremes will not be recognized as common, although I could certainly point to schools
whose tutors could be fairly accurately described by one or
other of the two outer columns. The centre column might
well describe a typical fairly conventional comprehensive
school with a well-established pastoral tradition. The right-
hand pattern also pictures accurately, the typical American
High School 'home-room teacher'. I have given each of the
three columns titles to chart three recognizable landmark

patterns as a basis for analysis and planning. It is these details which show you a school's pastoral focus:

	Tutor Ascendant	Tutor Neutral	Tutor Subordinate
A	Tutor is obliged to have full access to all information on pupils;	Information mostly available on request;	Tutor not given confidential information on pupils;
B	Tutor vital part of reception and induction process;	Tutor fully informed in advance that new pupil will arrive;	New pupils sent to join group without prior notification;
C	Subject teachers contact tutor in the first instance when worried;	Subject teachers sometimes keep tutor in touch, but not regularly;	Subject teachers always go direct to pastoral head in serious cases;
D	Letters home written by tutor on his own initiative;	Tutor can suggest letter required;	Tutor not normally shown pastoral head's correspondence;
E	Tutor basically responsible for attendance, calling for help when he feels the need;	Pastoral head follows up absence queries initiated by tutor;	Tutor merely marks absences in register, and takes no further action;
F	Tutor plays major advisory part in vocational and educational decisions;	Tutor's assessment noted in writing;	All vocational and educational advice centralized;
G	Tutor present at all major interviews with parents, careers advisory officers, etc.;	Tutor told what took place at interview;	Tutor not informed such interviews are to happen;
H	Tutor's views usually solicited by senior staff before pupil seen by them;	Tutor informed reasonably fully of any action by senior staff	Summary action taken by senior staff without notification to tutor;
I	Tutor feels primary responsibility;	Tutor feels significant assistant in care process;	Tutor feels basically a register checker.

It is usual that a school placed towards the right of the continuum on one of the factors near the top of the list will be towards the right throughout. Further, it is likely that there will be a correlation between a school's position on this continuum and other factors, particularly those concerned with staff participation, but probably also attitudes to the academic grouping of pupils. There seems to be a clear correlation with attitudes to discipline: schools on the right experience a demand from teachers for 'tougher measures' at the top. This is because the teachers in day-to-day contact observe difficulties, but lack the motivation or scope to act. It therefore appears that those 'at the top' could and should take firmer action 'to support' them. Schools to the left involve the entire staff in responsibility, and it appears that this leads staff away from authoritarian discipline, certainly away from physical discipline, towards a personalized control based on relationships. A tutor in a school of the 'tutor ascendant' pattern, for instance, would not relish handing over one of 'his' pupils for a caning.

Of course, it is easy to see the motives for schools to move to (or remain in, as this is in fact nearer to the typical grammar-school pattern) the 'subordinate' mould. It will be argued that the school possesses insufficient reliable, conscientious, tactful tutors ('imagine old Fred trying to write home! He can't even spell, and he'd put his foot in it anyway'); their time is too full as normal subject teachers; the pastoral heads are *paid* to do it all; there will be serious variations of procedure if tutors have too much freedom; above all, no one will know what's happening – or not happening.

My observation is that although there is truth in all these fears, and although one sympathizes with the school overwhelmed with them, in practice the opposite is even more true: a school *creates* good tutors by the degree they are taken into its confidence, and the degree of responsibility they are given. It is these two factors that lead to concern, and from concern comes ability. I have observed tutors performing markedly better and relishing their roles more when they have been put more into the picture and given more responsibility. I have also been struck by current American attempts to extend the role of the 'home-room teacher' in this direction.

A school far to the 'subordinate' side seems unable to monitor a pupil's progress, and when a pattern of difficulties and failure is at last perceived it is impotent to help, for it has no power to influence at close quarters. In a school with tutor roles defined in this way (or allowed to become thus accepted by the very lack of definition) it is usual for a tutor to know so little of a young person directly, and to hear so little from subject-teacher colleagues, that only the strikingly successful or strikingly unsuccessful pupil is noticed. In one such school it was discovered only from an end-of-term report survey that one particular second-year base-unit had nine pupils with serious patterns of failure, and this figure was half the total in the (small) school judged to be serious problems. This caused great surprise but not apparently any criticism of the tutor – although I would see the late discovery of this as a drastic failure on his part. One new careers master complained of the difficulty of getting to know about pupils as a result of a similar failing: 'If I want to find out something about a pupil, I have to go to the form teacher. He normally doesn't know much, and so I am forced back on the house heads – but they are all tied up with current problems.'

The tutor can spot the vulnerable pupil only if he has the power to do so – and yet only he *can* have the power to do so; he can help the pupil in difficulty only if he has the information at as early a stage as possible. Chapter 6 on page 105 shows how involved a tutor can be, and I hope it also shows how valuable such involvement is. Being able to talk with subject teachers easily enough, often enough, and above all soon enough is most important. And then the school as a whole and the tutor himself must make ready communication from the pupils possible. In one school that prided itself on a good pastoral system a conscientious tutor nevertheless was the last person to find out when two of his fourth-year not very academically successful pupils had used their initiative and dangerously climbed down a drainpipe to discover why an elderly lady they visited could not answer that door. They sadly discovered her dead, and informed the police. The tutor first heard of this when a colleague showed him a cutting from the local paper! The habit of talking had not been established. The ordinary day-to-day events of pupils' lives, such as their participation in extra-curricular activities, should be fed into the tutor's work, both by formal school machinery and by informal tutor-group procedures. The first should include regular slips from extra-curricular teachers to tutors, and the second might include a version of the 'News' sessions so beloved of primary schools, and regular 'review' sessions.

Should the tutor teach his group if possible? The old form teacher was primarily a subject teacher with some marginal pastoral responsibilities. Because (in most cases at least) he or she taught the group for a small part of the week knowledge was accumulated. It has always seemed to me, though, that there were dangers arising out of this apparent source of knowledge, and I shall submit that many three-form-entry schools with form-teacher systems reveal to the outsider by their glaring lack of knowledge of the pupils just what these dangers are: because the fact of teaching the group makes it look as if form teachers have a sufficient source of knowledge, no other need is expressed and no other source of knowledge built into the system.

Obviously in a streamed school with a mixed-ability pastoral unit, the tutor cannot teach his group; equally with any fourth- and fifth-year pattern that offers a multi-option choice, the base-unit cannot often be a teaching unit. In these kinds of situations the tutor does not have the supposed advantage for getting to know the group of teaching them a subject. He often finds, though, that what he is forced back onto is in fact superior: getting to know the pupils by talk, informal activities, proper documentation, and real guidance tasks (such as playing a part in careers advice). It can be argued that the very lack of a subject-teaching relationship can be an advantage. The relationship is almost purely 'personal' and not didactic. As Moore points out: 'He is in a good position to get to know the individuals in his group without the direct intrusion of any classroom overtones.'[1] This seems especially true in the older years.

However, there are those who would look at it the other way, and say that pastoral teams should have prime responsibility for teaching programmes, thus creating what some recent commentators call a 'mini-school'. Certainly I think that any school with some mixed-ability teaching groups in the early years would try to make the tutors teach their groups when possible. With careful planning, many of the teachers can work with groups of their own house. The tutor thus becomes something of a team leader for those teachers, especially if his subject is a central one, or if there is a measure of integrated team-teaching for part of the week. The head of house naturally can take a close interest in the actual work, and the tutor thus becomes his special representative across the curriculum.

A nice question of priorities comes when the new year's staffing is being worked out and there is, as often happens, a conflict between keeping the tutor with the same group of pupils for continuity, and retaining a teacher/tutor link. I should myself put continuity first.

Knowledge and the mutual respect of having shared some experience together are the core of a tutor's work with a pupil. From this core will come the influence that a tutor has, and on this influence, I strongly submit, depends the influence of the school. No remote figure has the power to influence pupils' interest, attendance, work, and behaviour in the way that a really close tutor can. A pupil is less likely to stay away from school if he knows that his tutor can make a pretty shrewd guess if it is a genuine absence or not (note or no note): he is

[1] Moore, op. cit., page 76.

less likely to be anti-social around the school if he knows he will have to justify his behaviour to his tutor. There remains one point about the role of the tutor which needs mention. On pages 50–1 I spoke of the possible variation in the size of groups. One way of producing somewhat similar results to those of a small group when room availability does not allow actual group reduction is to put more than one tutor to a group. Co-tutors considerably alter the role of the tutor.[1] By working as partners (not, it must be emphasized, doing one day on and one day off!), it is possible to give pupils a closer and more detailed degree of care. The 'clients' within the group are divided between the two co-tutors – either *could* cope, but for normal counselling and care each pupil has an attachment. The whole group atmosphere is liable to change, and authoritarian direction is likely to tend towards more relaxed and individual approaches: you can't shout so often when your colleague may be there!

In defining the role of a tutor, a school needs to consider:

   (i)   whether or not he should teach the group:
   (ii) the provision of information;
  (iii) the processes of communication;
  (iv) the advisability or otherwise of his including some vocational and educational guidance in his role (cf. pages 214–221);
   (v) to whom he is responsible, and in what ways;
  (vi) the channels of authority and responsibility;
 (vii) his actions over attendance problems;
(viii) his disciplinary power;
  (ix) the amount of autonomy granted to him.

It is quite clear from talking to pupils how much the real tutor is valued by the pupils, and what a yawning gap there is in the pastoral life if the role is not well filled. The Introduction and Chapter 3 have defined, I hope, some of the pastoral needs of pupils of this age-range. My observation, experience, and study of the research into schools convince me that it is the tutor who must meet the main demand.

All the evidence is that this indeed is the central role, that teachers respond well to its development, that pupils do well in a guidance system that is tutor-orientated, and, finally, that

[1] cf. *Two in a Classroom*, a valuable discussion of shared teaching roles, by Nancy Martin and others, University of London *Bulletin* Number 7 (Autumn 1968).

pupils themselves recognize their needs. As a survey of sixth-form provision[1] made abundantly clear yet again: 'What was wanted of the form teacher was to be a sympathetic and tolerant adviser with a personal interest in each of his students.' The actual phrases used by the sixth-formers are revealing – and encouraging: 'There were references to what was variously described as a "father-figure", "a big brother", "a confidant-cum-tutor-cum-parent", "a confessor/counsellor who should be able to listen sympathetically to one's troubles", "a friend rather than a teacher, a Marjorie Proops in some ways".' As the researcher commented, and this could stand over this section: 'The recipe is obviously difficult to follow, requiring a fine blend of tact, restrained guidance, personal but unfussy interest, and tolerance.'[2]

Only if he has a close responsibility for the oversight of the studies of his pupils is the tutor likely to have the necessary grist to his mill. The weakness of the tutoring concept is the difficulty of relating to another person with no shared activity on which to base that relating. The oversight of studies is the easiest to manage, and the most flexible. Any shared enterprises, from camping to theatre visits, from decorating the room to helping a younger class, are necessary second ingredients. Group talks, discussions, careers sessions, and the like can be arranged. But there remains the vital need for regular 'review sessions' in which the tutor works methodically through his group in private interview, say, twice a year. A check-list interview *pro forma* is a valuable basis, but these sessions permit the otherwise submerged difficulties to surface.

Finally, the role in the particular school must be actually defined and described: the new tutor should be able to read a 'tutor's handbook' as readily as he can a subject syllabus.

I shall not attempt to define 'the ideal recipe' here – for my thesis is essentially that there is no such stereotype. The personal 'diary' of a tutor included as Chapter 6 should assist as evidence, and I hope that by considering this together with the issues raised in this section a reader with a particular school in mind will be able to initiate discussion on the tutor's role, and arrive at a provisional job-specification that suits his school.

[1] Edwards, Tony and Webb, David, 'Freedom and Responsibility in the Sixth Form', *Educational Research*, Volume 14, No. 1 (NFER, November 1971), page 47.
[2] op. cit., p. 47.

(b) The Intermediate Pastoral Head

I have argued elsewhere that: 'The understanding, skill and energy of what might be called "the middle management" are vital to a reasonable level of success. But where is the help for which applicants for and holders of such posts must look, the guidance which it can only too often be seen they need?'[1] The more I see, the more convinced I am of the truth of this. Defining the role of the intermediate pastoral head is one of the central planning decisions, for it is a pivotal role without which the tutor will not know his job and the senior staff will be both impotent and cut off. As in all the other roles described in this book there are serious problems if the posts are not well defined. 'Well defined' does not mean finally or rigidly defined, but the focus of the job should be clear, and its relationships to other posts worked out. Possibly the relationship to more specifically 'curricular' posts are the ones which give greatest difficulty. Outsiders can often see the cause of stresses and dissatisfaction as lying clearly in this failure to define. One researcher, who looked at larger comprehensive schools in seven different LEAs, commented:

> In some schools the roles of housemaster and year tutor were clearly understood, normally because they had become established by practice, but in some the position of housemaster bristled with conflict. In this survey the housemaster role rather than that of the year tutor was more prone to misunderstanding. The latter appeared much the same from school to school, whereas there were marked variations of responsibility in housemaster posts.[2]

A starting point in considering the definition of the intermediate pastoral head's role is to scrutinize the conventional range of activities and responsibilities which are sometimes regarded as his duties of:

Discipline
Attendance
Welfare
Counselling
Educational Guidance
Vocational Guidance
Records

[1] *Head of Department* (Heinemann, 1970), p. 3.
[2] Nash, Barry, 'Large Comprehensive Schools', in *Comprehensive Education*, No. 21 (Summer 1972).

Relationships with parents
Testimonials and applications (UCCA, etc.) for pupils

These are activities that can be closely defined in relation to the pupils in the units for which the pastoral heads are directly responsible. In addition they may also have broader 'school' responsibilities, such as the supervision of prefects or of staff duties, which do not refer solely or mainly to their pupils.

There are three main ways of considering their roles. One is to look at the extent to which their prime responsibility is for pupils direct, and the extent to which they they lead teams of teachers. The second is to look at the disciplinary function of their jobs: are they expected to impose a recognized school discipline, or are they nearer to non-directive counsellors – who question and listen but do not judge or direct? The third plane of consideration is the extent to which they have total pupil responsibilities, and the extent to which some of these are separated off to specialists. It is possible to find examples of schools where almost every one of the duties mentioned above has been given to someone *other* than the intermediate pastoral head.

Here, then, are the three continua:

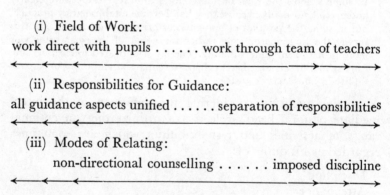

  (i) Field of Work:
work direct with pupils . . . . . . work through team of teachers
←——←——←——————————————————→——→——→

  (ii) Responsibilities for Guidance:
all guidance aspects unified . . . . . . separation of responsibilities
←——←——←——————————————————→——→——→

  (iii) Modes of Relating:
          non-directional counselling . . . . . . imposed discipline
←——←——←——————————————————→——→——→

In this section I am not attempting to describe how they can work, still less to give personal advice: rather I am concerned with the organizational framework into which they fit. I shall look at each of the three aspects of role definition first; I shall then consider what part the pastoral head can play outside his or her own pupils' groups, and finally add a brief note on 'The Person for the Job'.

(i) Field of Work

The pastoral tradition as we know it has been strongly influenced by the boarding-house tradition of the public boarding schools in certain respects. In particular the *direct* responsibility which was possible in that model has left its mark, even on teachers who have never visited a public boarding school. In the classic 'house' there were certain elements that made direct knowledge and influence possible. The first of these was the intensive and extensive time-scale: pupils during term-time were in 'the house' whenever they were not actually being taught. Secondly, the numbers were comparatively small: Winchester has houses of 50; Christ's Hospital of 50; Merchant Taylors of 88. These numbers make the task of the House far more like what I called the 'Tutor Ascendant' pattern (page 75), for the house is really the *base-unit*. As a result of their traditions, staffing pattern, and residential emphasis these schools are able to build up the base-unit to be the most significant unit in the school, and its leader, the housemaster, to be a very powerful (some would say too powerful) figure.

This does not transfer to the typical state day-school pattern, and it is the role of the housemaster that is one of the main changes. Yet this notion of almost always working *directly* with pupils still lingers. It might be possible to create a some-what similar pattern if houses were kept very small indeed. Some schools add a deputy to the pastoral head, and this has the effect of reducing the pupil case-load. Can the case-load ever be reduced sufficiently for the direct influence of the house-master to be paramount?[1] I doubt it, and I suspect that schools that hanker for this are hoping for the impossible. In doing so they may well be missing the opportunities for structuring a pattern based on the day-to-day work of the tutor.

The alternative is for the pastoral head to see himself pri-marily as leader of a team of teachers. He will still need to 'know' all his pupils, but he will regard his tutors as the main means of knowing them, and keep himself as primarily a team leader. Indeed I should use virtually the same words as I did of the work of a head of department: 'He is the catalyst and co-ordinator of a team of people; he is the link between that team and other groups; his aims are to create atmosphere,

---

[1] A DES study in 1967–1969 found the mean size of the 'main pastoral unit' (what I have called the linked basic groups) to be 260 – far above boarding-school house sizes! (My own calculations are based on figures in COSMOS paper 2/70.)

encourage thought, and devise procedures. He must continu-
ously pick up and give back, so that there is a mutually stimu-
lating, and mutually supporting team.'[1]

For this to work he will carefully consider the placing of his
tutors, he will be substantially responsible for their briefing,
he will above all convene and lead fairly frequent discussions
between the tutors in which they can put their difficulties and
their ideas. The age-based links of a 'horizontal' system probably work better with this team arrangement than the arbitrary or house system, for the focus of concern in the first is closer.

The head of house will no doubt be the channel for referral
to outside agencies, but the extent of this, and whether referral
to other school-based advice and help (e.g. from a careers
teacher) should be from the intermediate pastoral head level
or direct from the tutor is obviously open to careful scrutiny.

Is all this to say that he does not work directly with pupils
at all? Obviously not. Indeed my impression is that, paradoxically, the pastoral head who sees himself as primarily working
through his team of teachers has more opportunity for rich
relationships and significant work with the pupils by the very
fact that he has divested himself of the over-powering burden
of the entire population of his group of units, and of routine
matters. He will need to establish clear procedures about when
he does want to see the pupil and he will want to establish
'sampling' visits as well. His main work, though, will be to
give second opinions when called for, to see each pupil at key
times, to see pupils in difficulties, or those who merely 'want a
word'. (However his role is defined, it is essential to try to remove the usual impression that only 'difficulties', 'crises', or
'being in trouble' are reasons for seeing the intermediate
pastoral head. I know of no school where success in this is
complete: it does seem possible with separate counsellors, and
in my view is one of the main arguments in their favour.)

(ii) Responsibilities for Guidance

It has become accepted as convenient to look at three aspects
of guidance: educational, vocational, and personal.[2] To these
may be added other normally accepted aspects of 'care' such
as those listed earlier on page 81. It is easy to see how various
aspects of these can be separated off. In the very small secondary school the headmaster often used to, and still indeed

[1] Marland, M., op. cit., p. 99.
[2] cf. Moore, B. M., *Guidance in Comprehensive Schools* (NFER, 1970).

does, regard some tasks as especially his. These can include, for instance, checking on attendance, or careers guidance. In one of my case-study samples (see page 193) the reader will find that attendance-checking is looked after by a senior member of staff rather than by heads of houses. In another, one of the crucial areas of educational guidance, the choice of fourth-year options, was almost entirely removed from the pastoral organization. The presence in, or alongside, an organization of a specially trained counsellor might well be seen as another form of separation. Some 'careers teachers' see their work as expanding to a wide range of aspects of guidance, and would set up a 'Guidance Department', with career teachers handling many sides of personal guidance.[1]

Once again this is the kind of question that is rarely debated in schools, or if it is, it is not debated in detail. It is, though, a fundamental question for the organization of pastoral care and for the creation of the context in which the pastoral head works. Put simply, the question is whether the pastoral head is responsible for 'the whole man' or not.

On the side of some degree of separation are the arguments about the need for specialist expertise: educational guidance in a complex option system must be centralized with the academic expert; careers guidance today requires such a mass of information that only the devoted specialist can cope with it; personal guidance requires a professional who is not only apart from the disciplinary sanctions of the school, but also has had the relevant training, as described by C. James Gill on pages 121–31. It is even logical to argue, in a way which is complementary to this last point, that in schools without separate counsellors it is reasonable to separate off the major disciplinary sanctions, so that the pastoral heads can establish relationships unsullied by the need to impose sanctions. Such separatism is certainly found: the American High School, where, typically, there is a 'Guidance and Counselling Department' and a Vice Principal for 'discipline'.

Many readers would take the point of separating one or the other of these, but would firmly insist that all the others should remain integrated. The arguments are seen at their strongest over the question of vocational guidance. Can an all-rounder

---

[1] cf. MacIntyre, V. A., 'The Careers and Guidance Department', in Heppell, Raymond, *A Practical Handbook of Careers Education and Guidance.* I find this a muddled concept, applicable only to a small school with no properly developed pastoral organization.

hope to offer the kind of knowledge required? Moore's conclusions were unexpectedly firm and clear:

> Definitions submitted by heads and guidance staff indicated that
> vocational guidance could, if need be, function more or less as a
> separate entity. But, clearly, its greatest value was to be realized through
> being integrated with educational guidance.[1]

*If you integrate vocational guidance you risk losing expertise; if you
separate it the risk is that you merely make available facts on demand to
virtually unknown clients.* There is no doubt in my mind that the
very existence of a well-established careers teacher, with recognized status in the school, tends to draw a great deal of vocational work away from the pastoral staff unless there is a
definite policy to the contrary. This may be equally so if there
is a separate but nevertheless weak careers function in the
school. The 1965 DES report found a number of such schools:

> Still in far too many schools the work of the careers teacher is regarded
> as no more than of marginal importance, an out-of-school activity for
> which no training or preparation is necessary. In too many schools the
> careers teacher is expected to do no more than make arrangements for
> the Youth Employment Officer to give a school talk, to interview the
> leavers, and to distribute leaflets which are given to schools by enter-
> prising firms.[2]

In such a situation, again, it is unlikely that the pastoral heads
will feel they have much responsibility for vocational guidance.

There is, I think, a compromise solution that avoids the two
polarities, and is in line with other similar organizational shifts
in modern secondary schools. I have described in my chapter
on 'The Complementary Team' in *Head of Department* how
'advisers' are needed within certain large departments to build
up expertise within the team. Similarly it seems to me that the
Remedial 'Department' is a confusing misnomer. What is
required is a Remedial *Adviser* who would not be precisely
analogous to the head of, for example, Geography, but would
have wider responsibilities, leading not only his own departmental team of teachers, but more generally the whole staff.
In a not too different way a school should probably have not a
separate 'Careers Department', but a person whom I should
dub 'Careers Adviser'. This person would maintain the relevant
expertise within the school, would advise the curriculum co-
ordinator of the timetabling requirements of education for
work, the librarian of the resources requirements, and the
pastoral heads and their team of tutors.

[1] Moore, B. M., op. cit., p. 66.
[2] DES, *Careers Guidance in Schools* (HMSO, 1965), p. 77.

Such a solution, which I elaborate from the careers point of view in Chapter 12, would leave an essentially integrated role for the head of house, who would be somewhat like a GP, able to call on specialist advice when required. His central focus would be the whole pupil, and the careers adviser would be one of the many specialists on whom he could call when it seemed wise. A counsellor is probably best seen in this way also – as an adjunct to the main pastoral head, not a competitor. Moore sees this when he continues from the point I quoted on page 86 about integrated vocational and educational guidance:

> Personal guidance, though qualitatively different from the others, and in this sense perhaps separable, fulfils an important *integrating* function. This was possibly because its concern and focus include a good deal of the overall educational and social development of the pupil, and by virtue of a closer relationship at a personal level between teacher and pupil and fairly frequent meetings between them other aspects of guidance are inevitably incorporated.[1]

I see, then, the need for an all-embracing definition of the pastoral head's role, with specialist help, but no hint of the filtering off of any aspects. Such a role requires time (a maximum of a three-fifths teaching timetable I should say), good accommodation, and adequate secretarial facilities. Here, as a sample, is a job description of a southern comprehensive school's head of middle school.

> It is the school policy to allow the maximum autonomy to the Heads of Schools and to devolve a great deal of responsibility to them. In view of this the Head of Middle School will be responsible for the day to day care of his pupils, for administering the Report and Record Card system, meeting parents individually and holding parents' evenings, attending meetings of the Parent–Teachers' Association, for liaising with outside specialist agencies and welfare services as well as the Heads of Lower and Upper Schools, and the Director of Counselling and Careers, supervising the homework programme for the Middle School, conducting Middle School staff meetings, initiating, organising and supervising extra-curricular activities where these relate to the Middle School, supervising the Middle School Council and attending meetings of the School Council; discipline and appearance of the Middle School pupils, conducting Assemblies, attending meetings of the senior staff and such other duties as may be agreed. The Head of Middle School will be expected to teach his or her subject about one-third of the time. Subject speciality or the possession or non-possession of a Degree is not important.

(iii) Modes of Relating

A school must be clear what it expects of its pastoral heads, and, indeed, a pastoral head applying for a new post needs to know

[1] Moore, B. M., op. cit., p. 63.

what will be expected of him. It is also essential that there is not too fundamental a divergence between the various pastoral heads within one school. It is not sufficient to leave each to establish his own pattern, nor is it fair for unwritten and undiscussed assumptions of role to mould the individual pastoral head without his having a chance to contribute to an ongoing debate.

There are schools in which the pastoral heads, whatever their individual humanity and care, tend towards the role of dominant disciplinarians, and there are others in which, whatever their involvement in the executive running in the school, they tend towards the 'non-judgemental' or 'non-directive' as described in the purely counselling situation described by C. James Gill on page 121.

The position chosen on the continuum will obviously depend on a range of factors outside the individual, including the philosophies of the senior staff, the traditions of the school, the pupil intake, and so on. It is harder to draw up a balance sheet of the advantages and disadvantages of the two extreme positions, let alone the more likely compromise positions. Carried too far the authoritarian role denies the pupil both intimacy and true choice. The opposite, in a pastoral head, can make the school disorderly. It is probably true that most schools in the next decade are likely to need to temper authoritarianism in their pastoral heads, rather than the reverse. An over-authoritarian interpretation of the role seems to lead towards the alienation of the older pupils especially, and arguably to the over-rapid persuasion of all pupils into personal, educational, or even vocational choices which are later seen as wrong. The art of remaining authoritative without automatically exercising directive authority on every occasion is the art of the pastoral head. The frequent jibe in America that 'Guidance and Counselling Departments' are really 'Pushing and Shoving Departments' has a wider cautionary truth.

(iv) Other Duties

I mentioned earlier that intermediate pastoral heads sometimes attract school-wide responsibilities that do not relate intrinsically to the care of their own pupils. Such a process is natural: as a school changes in various ways over the years, responding to a variety of probably unexpected pressures, the need for a certain task to be done is suddenly felt. The need may be urgent, but the job at first may not seem too time-consuming. It is felt that a 'senior member of staff' ought to take on this new task. This is perhaps because it is traditional that senior people do school-wide administrative tasks, even though in many cases younger and newer teachers could do them just as well. It is felt, maybe rightly, that other teachers are less likely to query, at least openly, the possibly arbitrary decisions that will need to be made. 'Seniority' seems necessary – whether it is for allocating coat-pegs or supervising examination entries. In the second place there may be a pastoral head who from one point of view looks as if he has grown out of his job: 'His' year or house seems to be well run: he's got it all buttoned up; he's just ready to take on something else. And, thirdly, despite the pressure of work on middle management, there is more flexibility in the use of their time as their basic timetable class-contact time is usually considerably less than the norm for the school.

For these reasons, intermediate pastoral heads in some schools sport a variety of such tasks. There are both advantages and disadvantages in allowing this to happen. Often there is no choice at the time because the process happens gradually and virtually unnoticed: only after a number of years have gone by is it realized that the basic responsibility pattern has been overlaid by a criss-crossing network of other responsibilities. When it has been realized, though, or preferably before it happens, the situation needs reviewing to see where the balance of advantage lies.

It may be argued that it is good to 'get these people off their patches' – to allow them to have wider perspectives. It could be felt that the linking of some non-house activity to a house responsibility gives added strength; that to take on some sphere that involves pupils of another age gives balance to a year responsibility. There is almost certainly the argument that the rest of the staff are used to taking direction from such people. Probably, though unconsciously, there is also the fact that by far the easiest way of coping with a new demand is to tack it on the back of an old responsibility; this avoids re-arranging responsibilities in a more complex way, and very likely avoids drawing on the school's pool of allowance points.

Yet there is a price to be paid for such 'ad-hoc-ery'. It can imply a difficulty in the overall planning of the school, perhaps inevitable when situations change and the old staff and responsibility patterns change. If the duties don't relate to each other coherently, it is doubtful if they ought to be linked. Diversity can pull apart: it is very difficult, for instance, for a house-master

to maintain a fully personal and active leadership of his team
of teachers and his pupils if he has a further responsibility
which is quite other, such as a sixth-form General Studies
programme. Smaller schools often have to economize with
such pairings – some intermediate pastoral heads even carry the
headship of major departments as well. My observation leads
me to suggest that only in the exceptional situation should the
exceptional person be asked to do this. The structure of the
school should be shaped so that there aren't isolated tasks to
be doled out round the pastoral heads. Either these tasks
should be absorbed by their 'natural' post, or a new post
should be created to take them on. In general the focus of an
intermediate pastoral head should be on his or her team of
teachers and pupils; he or she will frequently, of course, look
up, but then it should be to advise on any or all of the broader
aspects of the school with the advantage of the experience
gained. If he looks up only to plunge straight into some other
detailed task his unit will lose his full force and the school will
lose his full wisdom.

(v) The Person for the Job

We are only just starting to see the difficulties of the career
structure, and the problems of selection. Which kind of people
are attracted to these posts, and how do they perceive the posts
in career terms? There is certainly an obvious and unhappy
arts/science split. One observer analyses it thus: 'Scientists feel
that they have more to lose by moving into the pastoral area,
whereas arts teachers, in moving in that direction, feel that they
are extending interests and skills that have always been important to them in their teaching function.'[1]

There is certainly need for thought about the kinds of people
who should be appointed to these positions. In some schools and
even certain areas the intermediate-pastoral-head roles are seen
as the special niche for the non-graduate getting on in years who
is known to be 'strong' in his own classroom. In this kind of
ambience phrases like 'He looks good on the pastoral side'
tend to be used as politer ways of suggesting that he's not much
good in any thinking or leadership role. There are serious disadvantages in allowing a situation in which a certain type of
person, and only that type, is regarded as 'just right' for these
posts. In the first place, thought *is* needed for any leadership
post, and surely none the less because the leadership is respon-

[1] Richardson, Elizabeth, *The Teacher, The School, and the Task of
Management* (Heinemann, 1973), p. 106.

sible for all aspects of a young person's life, not merely one segment of learning. Also a certain breadth of vision is required: it is impossible to lead discussion within a team of teachers if the leader lacks the perspectives gained from wider knowledge, the ability to analyse, and some 'cultural breadth'. Equally important, a school with a band of too similar people as intermediate pastoral heads is going to lack the variety of outlook necessary for medium-term and long-term planning. The whole structure of the teaching profession, certainly in the secondary field, is changing. Large schools have forced the pace, but it is not essentially a matter of size. The main point is that the greater demands placed on education, and the necessarily great rate of change, require thoughtful and responsive leadership at all levels. There is no way in which the clock can be put back so that teaching can become a matter merely of the imparting of skills and knowledge to pupils who are served up in a ready disciplined state! The ferment of school change that has centred round the curriculum in the 'sixties, far from abating, will spread to other aspects of the school. We are going to evaluate our success in even such seemingly spontaneous aspects as extra-curricular activities.[1] When research produces hard confirmation of our worst fears, as it so often does, we are going to be forced to think, to research further, to develop. This book itself is a modest part of the process. In this kind of era the intermediate pastoral head will have intellectual and organizational problems, as well as those of staff management and leadership, which are of a new order of complexity. The posts are far from suitable as a reward for long service or stability, or classroom confidence – important as all these qualities still are. These are posts for outstanding professional people, *with the expert training that is necessary for such a post.*

(c) Senior Staff

There is little or no work that has been done on the various possible roles of senior staff in the secondary school. (Thus, for instance, when in 1971 the very important Burnham decision to permit a Second Deputy in schools of Group 11 and above and to pay the Senior Assistants on the same salary scale was announced, its significance as a major factor in planning schools was barely discussed in print.) There is a tiny handful of books by headmasters on how to be headmasters: there is a

[1] cf. Reid, M., 'Comprehensive Integration Outside the Classroom, Educational Research, Volume 14, No. 2 (February 1972).

fascinating study of staff-room relationships by Hargreaves,[1] and a pungent and contentious chapter by Frank Musgrove on 'The Good Headteacher',[2] in which he declares:

> His power is distinctly dull, its exercise felt to be a tedious burden. The source of power for headmasters is their bureaucratic office rather than their personal charisma. The problems of recruiting able men to boring positions of power in schools as in other organisations may in future be a serious one.[3]

There is one book-length study of roles of senior staff[4] and a brief research article by Barry Nash,[5] to which I have already referred (page 81), and a very useful article by Denys John.[6] There is, though, nothing much else to guide the school planning of these roles.

I should advance the initial thesis that only in a few schools have they really been planned. In most they have merely grown. Heycock's hilarious attempts to find out the roles of the senior mistresses in his study schools are proof enough of that: he finds an odd assortment of tasks, and usually what he calls 'role conflict' or 'lack of role definition'.

Barry Nash finds an equally appalling picture of 'the lack of definition in many cases in the role of lady deputy head-teachers and senior mistresses'.

Secondly I should advance the thesis that many of the problems of schools arise from this. Confusion has been institutionalized at the core of the school. If a school has been planned outwards from the basic group, as I described in Chapter 4, and the roles of the staff have been defined upwards from that of the tutor, it will be found that the co-ordinating and leadership roles of the senior staff come clear fairly easily. However, if they are not made clear, and if they do not have a logical relationship with each other and with all the other elements in the structure of the school, the pastoral system is unlikely to work well, however much effort is invested in it.

[1] Hargreaves, David H., *Staff Relations* (Routledge and Kegan Paul, 1972).
[2] Musgrove, Frank, *Patterns of Power and Authority in English Education* (Methuen, 1971).
[3] ibid., p. 109.
[4] Clayton Heycock's *Internal Organisations and Management* (Sceptre, 1970).
[5] in *Comprehensive Schooling*, No. 21 (Summer 1972).
[6] John, Denys, *The Roles of Senior Staff*, in *Trends in Education*, No. 30, April 1973. I am also very indebted to a number of points which he made in a talk on 'Planning and Decision Making' in January 1972.

When the early comprehensive schools were planned, they were forced to borrow from the patterns of other schools. This is nowhere more noticeable than in the definition of senior roles. In the 'traditional' single-sex three-form-entry secondary school the hierarchy was clear, as in this one:

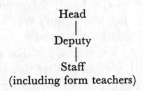

Head
|
Deputy
|
Staff
(including form teachers)

School A: three-form-entry boys' secondary modern

Theoretically the headteacher knew all. He was responsible for all the pupils – and thus correspondence normally went to and from him alone. The deputy was in many ways not so much a 'deputy', in the sense that his primary job was deputizing, but a mundane extension of the head, seeing to the trivia and the daily routine of detail. The point about this pattern is that, theoretically at least, the day-to-day pastoral figure, the form teacher, knew who his leader was: it was the headmaster, or his extension, the deputy. If a subject teacher wanted to inquire about a pupil or was concerned over some aspect of his welfare, he could fairly easily turn to the pupil's form teacher. (Although, as I have insisted in my Introduction, this happened far less than it is reputed to have done.) If he needed support, advice, or stronger action, the form teacher could turn direct to the head or deputy. Such a school can usefully be termed a 'single-order' school: there is a single triangle of control and communication:

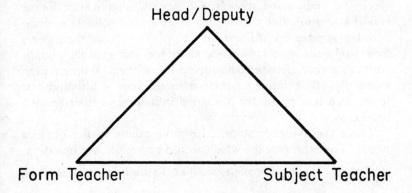

Head/Deputy

Form Teacher   Subject Teacher

However, a mixed-sex version immediately introduced a complication, one which has left an unhappy legacy in the comprehensive school. It was usually felt that the deputy should be of the opposite sex from the head. If the deputy had ever been thought of as more truly a 'deputy' rather than the 'mundane extension' of the head, this would presumably not have been necessary. But the deputy was felt to be the means by which the head could still handle the old village-school day-by-day control. As it was also felt that men dealt best with boys and women with girls, a further day-to-day person of the opposite sex to the deputy was then required. There had traditionally been a 'senior assistant' paid extra to be the 'gaffer', interpreting the unhappiness of the staff to the head/deputy, and mediating the whims and directives of that combination to the staff. What better than to use this figure as the sexual complement to the deputy?

It is dubious, to say the least, whether the disciplinary/ pastoral relationship is best carried out on a sexual basis. The fullest analysis of this has been done by R. R. Dale in a series of papers, culminating in a major book.[1] His concern, though, was to analyse as far as possible the differences between types of schools, not between the sexes within mixed schools. Further, when he looks at the pupils' recollections of mixed schools he is, naturally for his purposes, mainly examining the recollection of the *total* school experience by his subjects. On discipline, a sample of ex-pupils (though hardly representative, as they were drawn from College of Education students) clearly found a 'greater satisfaction' with the discipline of mixed schools than with single-sex schools; but the satisfaction recorded by women was far greater than that recorded by men, for whom there was only a slight difference in 'satisfaction' levels between single-sex and mixed schools. Of especial significance for us was the finding that the women from mixed schools remembered a greater friendliness and helpfulness than their peers from single-sex schools, whereas there was not a similar significant difference between the memories of men. Women were especially appreciative of their men teachers – although far fewer men had praise for 'the good influence' of their women teachers.

There the evidence stops. Musgrove points to the obvious need: 'The relationships which would repay further investiga-

[1] Dale, R. R., *Mixed or Single-Sex School* (Routledge and Kegan Paul, 1969).

tion are those between male teachers and female pupils on the one hand and their male pupils on the other.'[1] His own conclusions on such evidence as there is led him to conclude: 'All the indications are that girls in secondary schools moderate the power or drive of their male teachers; boys in secondary schools have no such effect on their male or female teachers.'[2] This is hardly strong support for the insistence on a deputy-equivalent of opposite sex in mixed-sex schools to look after the 'welfare and discipline' of pupils of that sex. Very little psychological work has been done on the relationships between pupils and teachers, but it seems fairly clear that there are various sexual tensions. Musgrove's thesis of the 'moderating' force of the female pupil on the male teacher does not go as far as to make clear whether the effect is beneficial or harmful. It certainly gives us little knowledge about the complementary question: What effects do female pupils have on *female* teachers? There can certainly be jealousy-tinged tensions between the adolescent girl beginning to be aware of her womanhood and the woman teacher. These tensions seem to me to be at best negative, and at worst to be eroding humanity and driving towards a carping and destructive relationship. Similarly men can often be thoughtless to the older adolescent boy, resenting his 'freedom', his difference from them (which is an implicit challenge to their standards and tastes), and his very maleness. Contrary to popular ideas, male teachers, it seems to me, are often more sympathetic to the younger secondary boy than they are to the late adolescent boy.

Of course, these are no more than subjective hunches, but they cannot be denied by firm evidence, and only that would justify the sexual division of senior roles in a mixed-sex school into 'boys' discipline' and 'girls' discipline'. It is, of course, very valuable that mixed (and, indeed, I should say even single-sex) schools have both men and women making up the team of senior colleagues leading the school and contributing to its shaping and decisions. Also, and equally obviously, there are occasions when an intimate personal matter will require advice from an adult of the same sex. But this last reason has never prevented us having mixed basic groups of pupils and a single tutor of either sex, and should in my submission not force us to divide the pastoral responsibility at senior levels between a man and a woman.

[1] Musgrove, Frank, op. cit., p. 54.
[2] ibid., p. 9.

The mixed-sex version of the single-order school pattern, which I described on page 93, thus looks like this diagram of an actual school, typical of very many:

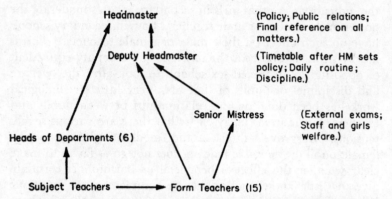

SCHOOL B, three–form–entry secondary school, 420 mixed, 1971–2

My contention is that this division does not in fact work very well even in a small single-order school. This is not only because the sexual division is pointless and possibly harmful in the more specifically pastoral tasks, but also because it is confusing in a bureaucratic analysis. To whom does the day-to-day teacher look for guidance? How does the senior mistress relate to the channels of communication and decision-making?

School C shows very clearly the fallacy of the senior mistress in the complex school, and how the borrowing of old patterns and role assumptions from smaller schools is dangerous:

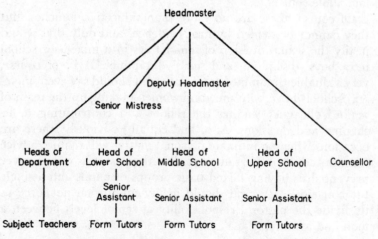

SCHOOL C, urban comprehensive, eight–form–entry, mixed

ROLES AND RESPONSIBILITIES

Whatever the snags may be in the single-order school, the borrowing of this pattern in complex larger schools is little short of disastrous. This is because the introduction of an an intermediate layer of responsibility (head of year or head of house) between the day-to-day teacher and the deputy and senior mistress makes the 'discipline and welfare' roles of those two obscure, and it often forces the senior mistress out on to a limb, having literally no 'place' in the hierarchical pattern. This school (age-grouped, with years further grouped into 'schools') has introduced intermediate pastoral heads with the expected responsibilities for discipline, attendance, welfare, and guidance. The deputy headmaster is seen as their point of reference. What, then, is the senior mistress's role in terms of the heads of school? The deputy headmaster 'does the time-table', although heads of departments refer directly to the headmster for policy decisions. What, then, is her role in relation to them? Finally, a counsellor is employed, standing deliberately to one side of the structure, for those needs which are ultra-personal, and seeing the headmaster as his or her point of reference. It is not surprising, therefore, that in this school, and very many like it, the senior mistress feels, and indeed actually is, out of the main stream. (No wonder, also, that the job often attracts such miscellaneous tasks as looking after stationery and receiving visitors!) Barry Nash has a section headed 'Are Girls Welfare Posts Really Needed?'[1] He describes the 'nebulous responsibility, sometimes tenaciously held', and gives one case typical of many:

> One example of conflict arising from the expectation of a role was that of a particular senior mistress who by judgement and past experience assumed on appointment that she would have a voice in the policy decisions of the school, a considerable amount of contact with older pupils, some careers and education guidance and responsibility in a general way over female pupils and staff. But as her duties became clear, the principal aspects of her work were the allocation of first-year entrants to forms and an overall supervision of the lower school.

That last, of course, is actually more than many senior mistresses have. Nash's conclusion, published some time after I had collected my case-studies, strongly confirms my conclusions. He declares:

[1] op cit., p. 9. See also Richardson, Elizabeth, op. cit., pp. 218ff.

There appears no logical explanation for the senior lady teachers to
have such vague responsibilities, unless it be that this is the natural
development of the role of the senior mistress in the small school, and
that little thought has been given to re-assessing the role in the large
school. . . . There is no sound case for a senior mistress.

It is not necessary here to explore all the implications of these
points for school management, but it will be seen that there are
serious results for pastoral organization. In schools A and B the
senior pastoral figure, whether deputy head or senior mistress,
is likely to know the pupils fairly well, for the schools are small
(although 450 is really too large a population for detailed
knowledge). It is therefore possible for them to take on the
support roles for the tutors. However, in school C, and others
like it, the total population is over 1,000 and no single person,
or pair of people, can know the range of pupils even moderately
well. Thus the roles of 'boys' discipline' or 'girls' discipline' are
ineffective because the senior figures are too remote from the
pupils for whom the 'discipline' is necessary. It is impossible to
take major action, indeed any action except a strictly temporary
holding action in emergency, without knowledge. In a 'complex' pattern the knowledge lies with the intermediate pastoral
head. The ordinary teachers, therefore, need to refer pupils to
these people, not to 'the top'. There is nothing more depressing
in the large school than the disciplinary figure, male or female,
stalking the corridors to reap up the wrongdoers, or sitting in
a study to receive those dispatched for admonishment from on
high. This is wrong because it demands summary action without knowledge, and because it cuts out the intermediate and
knowledgeable figure.

It is interesting to note that the large school has anyway
seriously changed the position of the old, senior assistant in a
further respect. In the single-order school, he or she had, as I
have indicated earlier, an interpretative and mediating role
between 'the staff room' and the head. For the staff were less
differentiated and there was relatively little hierarchical responsibility among them. The greater complexity of the larger
school, and especially the immensely increased authority of
middle management, has meant that the head and his deputy
have more frequent and more structured relationships with the
staff. The growth of definite elements of staff participation,
and above all the regular and properly run heads of department
meetings, has meant that the old interpretative (or 'gaffer') role
of the senior assistant has withered away, or, perhaps more

accurately, been dispersed among the members of middle management. When held by one person the role involved immense power, for both 'sides' were dependent on this 'go-between' for news and for his or her goodwill. It is paradoxical that in some respects the newer head of the larger school has more direct contact with staff than his predecessor in the smaller school. Certainly, though, the *raison d'etre* of the senior assistant has vanished.

What, then, is the logical and useful role for senior staff? It follows through from the definitions of the roles of tutors and intermediate pastoral heads. Just as the tutors need briefing, encouraging, and if necessary criticizing by the intermediate pastoral heads, so they in their turn require similar leadership from above. Just as the tutor will feed significant information and requests for help to his team leader, so intermediate pastoral heads will want to ask their leader for a second opinion, for advice, for support in mobilizing other agencies and resources. There will be occasions when they will want to refer a case upwards: then it will be with full documentation and only after their attempts to cope have appeared insufficient. If, as I have strongly argued, the old models of the smaller schools are inappropriate for the comprehensive school, what is a possible grouping of senior staff that is able to offer purposeful leadership? This question inevitably broadens into larger questions of school management that are beyond the scope of the book (although my case-studies in Chapter 11 explore them a little). There is a basic principle: everyone should have a task which coheres, is satisfying, is easily recognizable, and which does not have too much overlap with others. I should further contend that these roles should be differentiated by *sphere of responsibility*, not by hierarchy. In the larger school the vertical linear seniority should be replaced by a horizontal relationship based on tasks.

This starts with defining the role of the deputy. In many schools it has been poorly defined, and in the larger school this lack of definition is painful to watch. The essential point was made by the Headmistress of Mayfield, Margaret Miles, in her book on comprehensive schools:

It had always been my intention that the Deputy Head should be more in the nature of a partner, or a second or alternative Head, than an assistant to the Head in the way that a Senior Mistress or a Deputy Head in a small school often is. . . . This means that instead of the less important things being discussed by the Deputy and the more important

by the Head, the division must be in other ways; there must be
specific matters of equal importance, some of which are done by the
Deputy and some by the Head.[1]

She is, in fact, rejecting the role of 'mundane extension' and
pleading for the deputy to have a *job*. Actually deputizing is, of
course, one important job, but the difficulties spring from the
failure to realize that this is not a full-time job: some other
definite area of responsibility is required also.

Compiling the timetable has been one of the traditional tasks
of the deputy. Without going into the major question of academic policy-making, I shall merely state baldly that it is
desirable for curriculum planning to be the responsibility of the
timetable manipulator – the two are integrally linked. Also, if
the deputy takes timetable manipulating and everything else,
he or she will have insufficient time for real planning and
thought, and conservatism will be built into the timetable. I
should extend Margaret Miles' point by saying that a school
should define a number of leadership roles. (The head teacher
can take one of these if it really seems practical, but he or she
will probably need to remain as co-ordinator and overall
leader.) Each role should cohere, in that as far as possible the
elements should have a family relationship to each other. For
example, oversight of student teachers probably goes better
with academic leadership than with a purely pastoral role, but
because timetabling has had more status than caring for students, the student-training role has often been passed down to
a senior assistant. The executive chores should as far as possible
go with the responsibility for researching and leading *thought*.
Intermediate staff should be clear about whom they should
relate to. And, finally, care should be taken to avoid a complete
teaching/caring dichotomy – the yawning academic/pastoral
chasm of many comprehensive schools.

Many of the examples in this book were noted before the
Burnham agreement of 1971 altered the scale of senior responsibility posts. The result of that salary award, though, is to
make it far easier for schools to plan roles in the way which I
recommend. Put simply, the new awards pay the Senior
Assistant on the same scale as a deputy head – thus giving
financial recognition to the broad equality that I have been
recommending. Further, and of great significance for my thesis,
the award allowed LEAs to give schools of Group 10 and above

[1] Miles, Margaret, *Comprehensive Schooling* (Longman, 1968), p. 33.

a second deputy on the same salary scale. These large schools can then look for *three* complementary areas of responsibility for each of these people. One of the three can then, additionally, have the responsibility of actually deputizing – but 'the' deputy must have, and must be seen to have, a clear area of responsibility as well. This is difficult for some schools, too many of whom are merely using the money to pay another senior figure without a clearly defined role:

School D:
(1,900 boys and girls) large 6th form (Headmaster). Group 11 but likely to be Group 12 from April 1973. Required Sept. Second Deputy Head (man); this newly created post calls for a teacher of high calibre to work closely with Head and Deputy on day to day organisation, making school policy, maintaining high standard of work and broadening the range of school activities. Particular responsibilities will probably include boys' discipline, organisation of school camps and journeys, and general oversight of school's visual aids programme. Should possess initiative, enthusiasm and sympathetic understanding of adolescent problems.

Clearly school D has not had an *organizational* need for another person, nor has it re-defined spheres of responsibility. This second deputy has no real job, and it is unlikely that he will 'broaden the range of school activities' from the base of such a poorly defined role. It is no surprise to find 'visual aids' flung in as a make-weight to convince LEA and Governors that this really is a weighty role. Barry Nash quotes a similar case of one headmaster who 'described the role of deputy as "the usual duties of a deputy"'!

On page 102 is a diagram showing the organization of a Midlands urban mixed comprehensive school that used its old triple hierarchy (before the possibility of second deputy) sensibly. Although it appeared that the senior mistress was clearly less senior than the deputy headmaster, in their basic functions they were broadly equal. The senior mistress was, in fact, the pastoral head, and co-ordinated the pastoral work of the intermediate pastoral heads.

School F, of similar size and intake, established a fourfold hierarchy before the Burnham award by creating a senior mistress at the old Grade E, the highest responsibility payment under that of the 'senior assistant', and this is shown on page 102. It is interesting to note that soon after this was made there was a change of staff, and the Burnham award allowed the senior mistress post to be dropped, in favour of a second deputy.

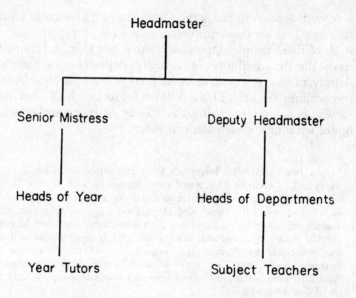

SCHOOL E, eight—form—entry urban mixed comprehensive

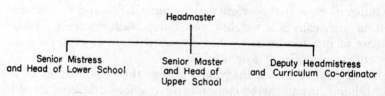

SCHOOL F, eight—form—entry urban mixed comprehensive

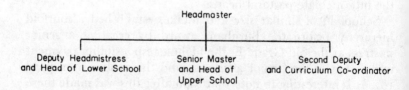

SCHOOL F, after Burnham 1971 award

The deputy-linked roles were then changed as shown in the second diagram.

The 'deputy headmistress' still had the functions of (*a*) deputizing (and was thus recognized as the senior of the three colleagues on any occasion when seniority counted), and (*b*) daily routine, but these two functions had shifted from the person whose *central* task was curricular (and thus responsible for the work of the heads of departments) to the person whose *central* role was the pastoral responsibility for the first three years. Here is a closer breakdown of school F's responsibilities:

Deputy Headmistress
and Head of Lower School
    Oversight of all aspects of Years 1–3, including attendance, welfare, discipline, academic standards;
    Co-ordination of the houses in matters affecting those years;
    Liaison with junior schools;
    Daily routine;
    Staff welfare;
    Deputizing for headmaster.

Senior Master
and Head of Upper School
    Oversight of all aspects of Years 4–7, including attendance, welfare, discipline, academic standards;
    Co-ordination of the houses in matters affecting these years;
    Oversight of careers guidance programme;
    Co-ordination of extra-curricular activities;
    General co-ordination of houses where whole school affected.

Second Deputy
and Curriculum Co-ordinator
    Curricular development;
    The work of the heads of departments;
    External and internal examinations;
    The librarian and the media resources officer;
    Student teachers;
    Staff duties (done in departmental teams).

One of the interesting general points is that heads of horizontal or age-based units can have, and should have, academic as well as pastoral responsibilities – that is, they should have views growing out of their close experience of dealing with the pupils that will lead towards teaching policy. In School F, therefore, the curriculum co-ordinator must consult the heads of upper and lower schools in his curriculum thinking, and in devising his timetable.

Such a scheme potentially suffers from a split in the pastoral responsibility. There is not one overall 'pastoral head'. This can make co-ordination between houses more difficult, and co-ordination is one of the main tasks of senior staff. Such a split would be in no way difficult in an age-based school, for the two pastoral heads would have different sectors and thus be responsible for different teams of intermediate pastoral heads. Either way such a division is defensible in that it splits the case-load, but objectionable in that it breaks continuity and dislocates rather than co-ordinates. The many schools granted a group of four senior staff (head plus three) are obviously faced with a dilemma. One left a single pastoral head, but gave the third member the following list of duties:

> community relations
> recreation and extra-curricular activities
> student teachers
> staff tutoring.

It will be seen that this role barely coheres, but in a community school does have strength and interest. As this person also took a third share of staff coverage and daily routine the overall pastoral head had sufficient time to specialize, and to linger over pupils when advisable. A number of schools are devising the second deputy's role very clearly round community functions.

Schools cannot continue to organize themselves as sloppily as some of them have in the past. The role of each person, spheres of responsibility, and the links between them need careful planning *as a total system* if the individual pupil is to have the care he or she needs, and if the school is to be a well-ordered community.

6 A Tutorial Sample

by Bob Grove

The reality of pastoral care, I have argued, lies at the day-to-day level. It is the frequent, continuous contact of the everyday teacher that is the starting point. The most effective, skilful, experienced, and humane senior teacher is powerless to help more than a few pupils personally, and is powerless to help them if he or she meets the problems too late, or after an unsuitable preparation. The purpose of the entire organization is to put the first-level tutor in the most effective position for his or her job.

Here is a sample of that job. It is a description by a young teacher of the task of a tutor, written from his own point of view, and highlighting the difficulties and rewards of the task as he sees them. The school is a large suburban mixed comprehensive one. The tensions are similar to those found in many schools. This school, by the writer's own description, is well organized on many counts, and yet he feels the job is not as successful as it should be.

Are the tensions and difficulties he describes serious, or does he exaggerate? Is there an inevitable conflict between the school's need for order and the individual pupil's personal need for sympathy? If the conflicts are real, can they be avoided? By fuller training? By different procedures? In particular, can a school's pastoral care be organized to improve on this?

It is the first day of term. This is your first teaching appointment and you are nervous. At college you were taught a good deal of theory, and on teaching practice tried out some ideas for lessons. But even then you were working with an experienced teacher who had initially set up the situation in which you worked with the children. It is not until you see the crowd of totally unfamiliar faces in the playground that you realize how much you looked at the children through the other teacher's eyes. The next teaching situation will have to be set up by you, and you wonder how on earth the person you feel yourself to have been until now will ever achieve any kind of *rapport* with the self-absorbed young people that you see before you. They do not appear to be nervous or lonely, but rather the reverse; at ease, and pleased to see one another. You have been told that in addition to your teaching you will have one form for whom you will have special responsibility. You are told in the staff handbook that in addition to administrative tasks you are expected to look after the general welfare of the child: 'A tutor must know well each individual in his group – the home background, leisure activities, attitude, work and behaviour in school.' Looking at the faces of the children in the playground, this seems a very tall order: and what exactly does one do with such information? The handbook merely goes on to describe the allocation of monitorial jobs and routine procedures.

At five minutes past nine you meet your tutor group. The house head informs them that this is Mr Grove who will be taking them over from Miss Wood. He knows that they will miss their previous tutor but he is sure that they will get on well with Mr Grove. As a parting shot he says somewhat ambiguously: 'If you have any difficulties just come and see me.'

You turn round to face thirty-three children who clearly know each other well but you not at all. With as much confidence as you can muster you sail straight into the administrative work, and after a while perhaps introduce a sly joke as a means of establishing your humanity. The children do not respond.

After a week, timetables have been given out, you have met your new classes and the tide of duplicated sheets is beginning to ebb. Despite rigorous attention to the various procedures for checking pupils' progress, then the appointment of room stewards, blackboard monitors, etc., you don't seem to have made much progress in getting to know the group. You have read something of their past histories on the school files, but you can't very well start off a conversation on Peter's record or Janet's last report. Perhaps you could adopt the headmaster's suggestion that tutor groups should discuss 'important' issues like uniform. ('What's the point – they never do anything about it') or assemblies (ditto).

At this moment you are heading for the first of many bouts of discouragement which always hit new (and not-so-new) teachers. With luck you will find a sympathetic colleague who will admit that he has felt much the same many times and that the first rule is patience. Meanwhile you must hold the fort and begin to introduce periods of tutorial time devoted to less formal and non-compulsory activities. Almost any activity that keeps them busy or happy will do: chess, draughts, reading (bring in some paperbacks and magazines and start a library), table tennis if you have the space, or just talking about last night's activities. Don't be afraid of noise and movement within reason, or of disapproving faces peering through the window.

Gradually faces and personalities become more distinct and as trust increases you begin to learn something of how each pupil relates to teachers and other pupils. Jimmy doesn't like his maths teacher; Peter's French teacher doesn't like him;

Carol and Pauline are deadly enemies; Fred is bullied in class. In isolation such information may not seem relevant, but it helps to build up a pattern of knowledge about a child. Not only is it the tutor's job to get to know his children but in the first instance to refrain from moral judgements. When a child divulges some information about other pupils or teachers, it is very easy to slip into one of two dangerous stances at first. One is rejection – the attitude that the child should not criticize those in authority or not pass his judgements on. The other is that of tacit sympathy – the acceptance of what the child says at face value either because you don't like the look of the person concerned, or because you want to be friendly towards the child. In the first case you may be branded irretrievably as a part of the system, and in the second as gullible.

I shall now leave the story of the first few weeks and look back over the three years in which I have known my tutor-group. During those years both they and I have changed so much in our relationship to the school and to each other that I find it hard to analyse the developments as a sequence. I cannot generalize about my group nor can I pretend that I am neutral towards them individually. Some of them are now approaching their last year at school and are thinking about careers. Others are still on the long road to university. Just recently the situation as regards the two most difficult problems has changed radically. But I shall return to them later.

First let it be said that the majority of the group are not problems. They are reasonably well adjusted to school and if not always well-motivated academically are able to get by without too much trouble. But for each member of the group there have been instances where in a greater or lesser degree it has been necessary for me to intervene with advice or help. One aspect of this is the liaison between home and school. This is continuous via the pupil's 'Daybook',[1] in which a parent or teacher can write at any time. Inevitably the system is under-used, but valuable none the less. At report time the tutor's function is more vital than perhaps one realizes. Colin was very pressing that I should write him a good report last year, since his 'old lady' was debating whether or not to buy him a 'sheep-skin' for his birthday. I pointed out that as I didn't teach him the matter of his coat was out of my hands. I could only summarize the other teachers' comments. 'Well, that's it,' he replied, 'She doesn't read the rest properly. If you say I'm

[1] cf. Sample format on page 163.

doing OK, that's all she wants to know.' Fortunately he got his good report. On another occasion John came to see me after I had really slated him in his report for lack of effort. When his Dad saw that, he'd keep him in for a fortnight, he pointed out. My response was frosty. Did he expect me to write less than the truth to improve his social life? Oh no, he agreed with what I'd written, but the least I could do after a slating like that was to give him his report after the weekend so that he could go to his mate's birthday. His report stayed in my desk until the Monday.

Possibly the most critical stage of a pupil's career at our school is at the end of the third year when he chooses his middle-school course. Inevitably the subjects chosen then will determine to some extent the directions he will take when he leaves school, so it is important that the school and parent assess the child's potential and interests as accurately as possible. The consultations and meetings are arduous but very necessary. Even with the best reporting system, some parents still grossly overestimate or underestimate their child's potential. Most difficult of all are parents who frankly admit that they have lost all contact with their child. Chris lives with his grandparents, his parents having split up, and they came to school for the parents' evening obviously quite lost. Chris never told them anything; they only knew about the meeting from another boy's parents. Was he doing well? Did he ever say anything to me? I was very surprised at this since Chris seemed to me a hard-working, happy, well-adjusted boy and I assumed he got a great deal of support from his grandparents. I lived fairly close, and as Chris was away when the choice forms were given out I made the excuse to visit them and to go over the forms with the boy and the grandparents. It was quite obvious that Chris was the one who was going to make the decisions, and he seemed politely surprised when I tried to draw his grandparents into the conversation. Since then I have asked after his grandparents and although he has been prepared to answer quite cheerfully Chris is obviously very self-sufficient and lives his own life.

Other major and minor crises which have affected their school lives have occurred at different times to most of the group. The death of a parent, or a parent's re-marriage, are times of stress at which the most one can do is be as tactful and normal as possible and to advise close school friends on how they can help ease the situation when the child returns to school.

Less serious, though vital to the child concerned, are matters such as bullying. Great tact is required here as mishandling can make matters worse, and the child will not confide again if the first attempt to deal with matters fails. Jenny in my group once feigned illness for two weeks to avoid a particular girl who had threatened her. In fact I knew that the threat would not be carried out and that the real trouble came from Jenny's own 'friends' whose gossip had built up the situation out of proportion. I visited her home and explained what was happening as I saw it to her parents, and then contacted the other girl's tutor to try and find a way to ensure that Jenny's imagination was not fed with any more fears. The tutor saw the girl and was very frank, saying that Jenny was very worried and that although she knew that she had no intention of harming her, Jenny didn't. So to avoid misunderstanding and wrongful accusations she must stay clear of Jenny.

I could cite numerous small matters from daily school life which one has to deal with – small thefts, classroom disputes, etc. One of the more unusual was when Michael, a very over-mothered boy, came to me one day and asked if our house head could tell his mother that his friends were allowed to stay out till 10.30 at week-ends and that having to go in at 9.00 was very humiliating for him. This was arranged, and I gathered that that problem was then solved.

Apart from this, for most of the rest of the time I am a listener to stories of achievement, and complaints, and a gateway to pupils' involvement in social and school activities. In addition to the perennial house sports, a few are willing to run charity discotheques, some enjoy helping in the school bookshop that I run and at drama productions; and a number of others can be coerced into joining in. It is most rewarding to build upon relationships by showing practical interest in their schemes, and by drawing the more reticent or self-conscious into group activities. Even the most scornful boys find it hard to resist coming to a charity disco which the girls have organized, and after a little arguing with me, to show the world that they are not really interested and are only doing me a personal favour by coming, they will even pay the entrance fee. There is a point however, at which coercion must stop, and the right of the child to opt out acknowledged. The hearty individual who tries to bluster everyone into joining in his own schemes at a party is never invited again.

For a few children, however, such activities are peripheral to their problems, problems which probably originate outside school but which of necessity they bring with them to school. I shall devote the rest of this article to three children at risk. I say they are at risk because what happens to them in school is more important than what happens to those children who adapt well and enjoy school. Disturbed children are acutely sensitive to the attitudes of adults towards them and may continually test a teacher, to provoke him into rejecting them, as other adults, possibly parents, have done in the past. If it is important to avoid over-hasty judgements about any child, it is crucial with the disturbed child. It is almost impossible for a class teacher to be aware of and sensitive to the potential needs of all the children he teaches all the time. Therefore it falls upon the individual tutor or ultimately the head of house to provide the disturbed child with the consistency and security he needs. Before continuing, I should like to say that the school to which I refer is in general a humane institution with a justly good reputation for dealing with difficult children. But it is only through rigorous self-analysis by schools who take their duties seriously that individual failures and institutional shortcomings can be avoided.

As the first example I shall give demonstrates, it is very hard to sort out failure and success. There may be in an apparent total breakdown of relationships, a kind of success that will become apparent only afterwards.

Mary[1]

Mary is in the care of the local authority, along with most of her brothers and sisters. Her parents are separated and have established other relationships which exclude the children. Mary has obviously accepted the house-mother of her cottage as a mother-substitute, but her relationship with her father is unresolved. There is a good deal of mutual affection between father and daughter which, coupled with his guilt at abandoning her, makes him unable to refuse her anything. Mary wants to go and live with her father and has in fact been promised that she can when she is 15. At one stage Mary tried to force the situation by behaving so badly at the home that her father would be obliged to take her away. This for many reasons was impractical at the time, but Mary would not accept the situation.

[1] The names of the children have been changed but I feel it is important to stay as close to the facts as possible.

As she had truanted from school one day I went down to the home, as I had done several times previously, to find out what was going on. The next morning, instead of announcing my visit to 'her aunty' or 'her house' to the rest of the group with a certain amount of pleasure, as usual, she accused me of interfering and 'making so that she couldn't live with her Dad'. I was surprised, and told her that although I agreed with the decision I had nothing to do with making it. She continued to condemn me loudly, however, and I became irritable. I said that I had told her the truth and she could believe it or not as she liked. There followed a period of hostile silence during which I regretted my irritation, and tried to analyse her (and my own) behaviour. Mary's relationship with me is in any case erratic, alternating between confiding affection and wilful defiance, which has as its objective making me angry: in which, incidentally, she succeeds more than any child I know. In this particular case it would seem that she had found it convenient to blame me rather than her father or the faceless local authority for her disappointment. Having worked out her anger, peaceful relationships were resumed as though nothing had happened. Obviously the confrontation had been necessary to her and it was equally necessary that I should be visibly perturbed by her accusation. The important thing was that such crises should not be unnecessarily prolonged by my continuing the silence. I had to make the first move towards re-establishing communication. My own reaction is worth a comment because I am sure it is not unusual. I was hurt at the apparent unreasoning hostility of someone whom I had been concerned to help. The temptation to surrender to one's own feeling that the child is 'ungrateful' and to build up tension which will hurt the child is quite strong. Of course a child will not show it is hurt, but will just put up a barrier and feel confirmed in its belief that adults are fundamentally untrustworthy. The temptation to sulk, ironically, is most strong with teachers who care deeply about the children in their charge, teachers who perhaps rarely show anger or loss of control. Anger in itself in fact can serve the healthy function of defining a positive relationship. The desire to hurt, however well disguised, can only destroy a relationship.

In general Mary's relationship with teachers is good. She is pretty and can be very appealing. However her basic insecurity is reflected in relationships with other children. Her friendships with other girls tend to be highly traumatic. She herself once told me that she is 'easily led'. Part of her wants to identify with the 'tough' girls who had rejected their home and the adult world, and the other part is desperate for affection and reassurance from her friends, which makes her sometimes impossibly demanding.

Two examples will illustrate this, and also how easy it is for a school unwittingly to reinforce the negative side of a child's personality. Last term we had a new girl in the group who had been sent to us because her previous school could not cope with her. To Mary she epitomized the tough, lawless, worldly figure that she wanted to become. She truanted with this girl and was involved in a house-breaking incident. Her first thought was that she had successfully embraced the identity of a delinquent. Her defiant silence was studiously modelled on that of the other girl, and she responded to all questioning with raised eyebrows and the often repeated words 'Don't care'. Shortly after this the other girl left and Mary was without support. She came to me then to test her delinquent identity, to see if she really was 'beyond the pale'. She described her crime in great detail, and the likely actions of the police and court. When this failed to impress she tried a more direct approach. Did I think she would be 'given the push'? I said there was no likelihood of that. Would I then tell 'them' that she should be sat outside the house head's room – the recognized parking point for school delinquents? Clearly Mary had not grasped that the school was not of necessity a part of the institutions which had identified her as a delinquent.

The school's capacity for type-casting on the basis of such encounters with the law, however, was brought home dramatically some weeks later when Mary was involved in a fight with one of her 'friends'. The argument stemmed from a piece of 'bitching' concerning both their parents, and was unusual only in that the violence was physical rather than verbal. Mary in her anger won the fight and frightened her opponent. Possibly in order to salvage self-respect and gain some protection, the other girl complained to various members of staff not only that Mary had threatened her, but that she was the leader of a gang of female thugs from the home who would join in. To anyone who knew Mary this would have been, firstly, comic, but owing to her previous brush with the law the idea of her as a potential female Al Capone gained currency. She was not only sat outside the house head's room, but threatened with removal from her class. This sudden reaction of the school caught her by surprise. She felt that she had been unjustly treated, and to be cast in an anti-social role in such circumstances aggrieved her. Her behaviour became sullen and very reminiscent of that which she had tried unsuccessfully to maintain after the house-breaking. Fortunately I was able to protest on her behalf on a fairly informed basis, and the humanity of those in authority instantly asserted itself to right the situation. Such a happy outcome is not always the case, however. The other two children I shall mention are for separate reasons labelled as trouble-makers, and far from inspiring the affection which Mary can easily command in her more charming moments, seem to be felt as a threat to the authority of the school.

Jimmy

I shall not go into the details of Jimmy's background, but it is fairly horrific. He is in the care of the local authority and lives at an excellent hostel which, so far at any rate, seems to have proved wrong the prophecies of serious delinquency which have dogged the boy from an early age. The situation is still precarious, however, and there are several factors which work against Jimmy as far as appearances are concerned. Firstly he is coloured, and therefore easily identified in a school with few coloured children. Secondly he is very slow-witted and basically mistrustful of adults (with good reason, incidentally). Thus when questioned or told off, he appears not to respond at all. Thirdly he is very strong, and though never violent unless provoked he has the reputation of a fighter. He has some talent as a boxer but his disturbance shows through in his alternation between unwillingness to compete and, when in the ring, going berserk.

There are other sides to him however. He is very popular with the other children, and not merely the delinquent element. He has a charming smile when relaxed, and a very dry sense of humour which takes the listener by surprise because of the deadpan delivery. Significantly the weaker members of his form and the group are not afraid of him, something unusual for a boy of his reputation. The basic stability however which enables most children to take the periodic hostility of the adult world in their stride is not there with Jimmy. Despite appearances he is very sensitive to the intentions of adults and can easily be thrown into periods of black depression in which his violence comes very near the surface.

Jimmy's school career has, by comparison with that of some of our children, been relatively calm. He likes the school, and undoubtedly, together with the hostel, school provides an element of security vital to Jimmy's sanity. To be forced out of the school would be the second worst thing that could happen to him. Yet, because of the factors I have mentioned earlier, the two major conflicts he has had with the school have nearly resulted in his expulsion.

The first concerned a fight with a boy both bigger and older than himself in which Jimmy went berserk and bruised the boy badly. This was fairly untypical behaviour in that although fascinated by violence Jimmy usually prefers to watch. It *is* typical however that having become involved he would go to any lengths to win. What happened exactly we will never know. The point is that the assumptions which were made were all against Jimmy. The other boy's head of house called in the police without consulting anyone, and tried to get the parents to bring a charge of assault. The parents, although upset, did not want to become involved in what was essentially just a playground fight. In view of Jimmy's previous good record one would have thought that the matter would have been left there. However, again without consultation with those responsible for Jimmy within the school, moves were made to get the headmaster to expel him. On this occasion I went directly to the headmaster to put the facts into the context of Jimmy's background, and Jimmy was only given a warning. The unsettling effect of all this undoubtedly played a part in the second and for Jimmy more serious incident. This involved taking drugs, and understandably the police were called in to track down sources. The interpretation which the school put on the evidence that the police found, however, is hard to understand, except in relation to Jimmy's reputation as a trouble-maker. As far as the police were able to find out, Jimmy had been taking barbiturates, initially possibly for kicks, but later to escape situations in school and outside which increased his tension. Without them he was depressed and anxious and therefore needed a continual supply. The cycle is familiar, and almost without anyone suspecting anything, Jimmy became psychologically dependent on them. The source was in fact traced to a girl who had got them from her mother, and it was suspected that some had been obtained at a local youth club. At one stage Jimmy also asked a boy in his class if he could get him some pills, and on this was based the theory that Jimmy was about to start a drug ring and was a menace to the school. The fact that the pills were supplied to him quite willingly by other children who were already in contact with sources of supply, that no threats were used, and that Jimmy never passed any on but used them solely to satisfy his own increasing dependence, did not seem to count with the school. Interestingly there was no suggestion that those who *supplied* the pills should be expelled.

Once again the warden of Jimmy's hostel and I sorted out the facts and tried to put them into some kind of perspective. This time a psychiatrist's report had to be produced to convince the school that it was necessary for Jimmy to stay on.

At the moment of writing, Jimmy has in fact broken his dependence on the drugs and seems much more cheerful. The problems are still with us, however, and with every minor scrape he gets into, the reasoning of the previous occasions is forgotten and the credibility of those who spoke for him, including myself, is undermined. Each over-reaction builds into a self-fulfilling prophecy, and confirms the belief not only of the school but of the boy himself in his own badness. One can only hope that he will survive to leave from choice.

Janet

The last child I shall mention illustrates the pastoral system in breakdown. Later attempts to retrieve the situation came too late, and at the time of writing the girl's future is still uncertain.

I should perhaps mention that Janet was not in my tutor-group. I became involved with her problems as a class teacher, and it was in fact the class situation rather than the tutorial situation from which most of her problems arose. Had her tutor not had to confront so many departments the outcome might have been more satisfactory.

Janet is a highly intelligent girl in the top stream of the third year. Towards the end of her second year she began to show signs of a reaction against school, and during her third year set about defying the system at every point. She failed to hand in work, turned up for lessons without books, and finally began walking out of lessons. Behaviour like this had occurred in individuals in the lower streams of the school, but was unheard of from a child in the top stream, and a panic reaction began to set in. Teachers were asked to report on her, and the reports were fairly consistently bad, with the exception of her English and History teachers, who reported that her work was of an exceptionally high quality and her behaviour odd but tolerable. She had not walked out of these lessons.

What disturbed those responsible for her was the apparent detachment and calculation of her behaviour. She was not disruptive in the usual sense of being noisy or violent, but she was unusually determined to carry her rebellion through without revealing her motives.

It is worth mentioning at this point the immediate forces at which her rebellion was directed. A comprehensive school is still a controversial entity, especially in a 'mixed' authority which retains some grammar schools, and great store is set by the academic achievements of the brighter children. The comprehensive must prove itself, and therefore the top streams are regarded as an investment in the future of the comprehensive ideal. The teachers these children get therefore tend to be those who are likely to be most rigorous in their approach and most rigid in their expectations of behaviour. Even those who regularly teach the whole spectrum of ability develop a sensitivity with regard to brighter forms, which causes outbreaks of nerves when the children do not conform to expectations.

Faced with someone like Janet the instinctive reaction of the institution is to expel the deviant for fear her rebellion might spread, and this in fact was suggested. Even a small investigation of home circumstances indicated that Janet was a fairly mixed-up child and the fact that two teachers could tolerate and even enjoy teaching her would seem to suggest that personal relationships were at the root of her problem. Such reasoning was successful in keeping her in the school at first. I and another of her class teachers pointed out that her behaviour was no worse than that of some other children in the school, and that anyway there was nowhere for her to go. She got on quite well with her classmates (whose sympathy with her problem did not help her cause with those in authority). Sending her to a grammar school would have meant sending her to a place whose tolerance of her oddities would have been less than at a comprehensive. And, as was later proved to be the case, no comprehensive would take on a girl who could not be accommodated within a school such as ours with an excellent record with difficult children.

Threats were issued and for a while Janet seemed to be trying to conform. After a while, however, relationships broke down with some teachers and she became more withdrawn and more determined not to submit to authority. As a last resort it was suggested that for the rest of the year she could go to those lessons she liked and spend the rest of her week in the recently established Coaching and Counselling Unit. This she refused to do.

Possibly she felt she had committed herself too far for such a compromise, or felt, wrongly, that the Unit was only for backward children. More likely she just resented attempts to 'get through' to her. Her intelligence combined with total mistrust of most adults makes her almost impossible to establish contact with, except on her own terms. At this point her mother, to the school's great relief, decided to remove her, and as far as I know has not yet succeeded in placing her at another school.

There are no easy answers to problems such as Janet's. But at least the school must attempt to avoid obviously wrong answers, and resist the temptation to pass the problem on. The school's final offer was in fact a very generous one, but for someone as sensitive and aware as Janet, it involved a kind of labelling which she could not accept. It also came at a point where tensions had built up which could not be resolved without either the child or her teachers backing down. Earlier action on a personal level, possibly through the Unit, might have de-fused the situation sufficiently for the girl to sort herself out.

In any case a school must be more self-analytical in its approach to children who seem to represent a threat to its authority. I am here speaking of the school as if it were a person, but those who run a school do have a kind of identification with it, and quite rightly, since it is a measure of their commitment to the job. There must be checks however to ensure that in the concern for institutional self-preservation, humanity is not lost; that the problems of each child are dealt with sensitively and in the full knowledge of that child as an individual. The person on whom this responsibility falls first is the tutor. He, like a good defence counsel in a court of law, must always have the best interests of his client at heart.

It may seem that I have placed too much emphasis on the small proportion of disturbed children and not enough on the routine matters which affect the majority. These are the things that the school is good at. My job here is made easy by constant support and good organization. It is when one feels that one does not have the support of the school and that the best one can do with intractable problems is to avoid disastrous decisions for as long as possible that being a tutor is most difficult. I have described specific cases to make a general point. It is put in another way by E. H. Erikson in *Identity, Youth, and Crisis,* and emphasizes how serious our job as ordinary teachers is:

> Teachers, judges, and psychiatrists who deal with youth come to be significant representatives of that strategic act of 'recognition', the act through which society 'identifies' and 'confirms' its young members and thus contributes to their developing identity, which was described at the beginning of this book. If, for simplicity's sake or in order to accommodate ingrown habits of law or psychiatry, they diagnose and treat as a criminal, as a constitutional misfit, as a derelict doomed by his upbringing, or indeed as a deranged patient a young person who, for reasons of personal or social marginality, is close to choosing a negative identity, that young person may well put his energy into becoming exactly what the careless and fearful community expects him to be – and make a total job of it.[1]

The role of the tutor is not something which can be summarized in a few sentences. There are no well-defined points at which his responsibility begins or ends, and thus he can only try to respond sensitively and promptly to a situation when it arises. He is at the focal point of a child's school-life; the person who provides liaison between subject-teachers, housemaster, parents, and the school's hierarchy. This sounds, and is, a fairly daunting responsibility, but it can also be one of the most interesting and rewarding aspects of a teacher's work.

[1] Erikson, Erik H., *Identity, Youth and Crisis* (Faber, 1968; paper, 1971), p. 196.

7 The Possibilities of Counselling

by C. James Gill

Among the organizational possibilities now open to schools is that of appointing one or more 'counsellors'. Whether a separate counselling service is set up or not, the school has to ask itself to what degree its central pastoral organization is to be counselling-orientated. It is important that a school neither rejects the notion out of hand, nor merely takes a counsellor on board without considering the implications for the school's whole pattern of work. The work that trained counsellors are doing is inevitably affecting even those schools that do not have separately identified counsellors; and those that do are finding subtle changes of approach throughout their whole organization. The development of counselling in British secondary education is adjusting perspectives. Schools that have appointed counsellors are most successful if they see the new appointment as supportive, an additional tool available for the pastoral system.

C. James Gill developed one of the pioneer counselling courses in this country, and here he puts the work in context.

No matter how conscientiously house staff, heads of years, tutors, careers staff, and co-ordinators of guidance pursue their tasks there is bound to remain a diffusion of concern for individuals throughout the whole staff in any school that accepts personal development as a goal. There would, no doubt, be considerable reluctance on the part of most members of staff to give up their pastoral activities, since they regard them as an essential element in good teaching and obtain from them a great deal of personal satisfaction. When, therefore, a proposal is made to recruit a trained counsellor to a staff, they frequently see it as a threat to their own pastoral role; they then go on to the defensive and argue that every teacher is, or should be, a counsellor.

As with the view that all teachers are teachers of English, there is cause to regard every teacher as a counsellor. Good teachers have always talked over personal difficulties with individual pupils and helped them to make decisions; counselling in this sense is not new. What is now under discussion is the appointment of suitably trained men and women as members of staff, charged with responsibility for counselling pupils and with time and space in which to do it.[1] English specialists brought a new dimension to the teaching of English without detracting from the contribution all teachers make to the use of

[1] Schools Council, Working Paper No. 15, *Counselling in Schools* (HMSO, 1967). The National Association for Mental Health, *School Counselling*, Report of a Working Party of the NAMH (1970).

English; counsellors with skills in the field of inter-personal relations can bring additional resources to the provision of care and guidance without disturbing the relations that already exist between staff and pupils in schools where pastoral care is accepted as a major responsibility.

Teachers in positions associated with care and guidance have a concern for keeping an eye on the all-round educational attainment, conduct and discipline of the pupils in a house, year, form or tutorial group. In the exercise of his disciplinary role a tutor is constantly making judgements; in his concern for a pupil's progress he frequently gives advice; his 'counselling', more often than not, is likely to be directive. When dealing with young people there is a big temptation to take the line, 'If I were you I should do so-and-so', thus taking responsibility, on the strength of what might be suitable for us, for persuading others to follow a certain course of action. For example, a boy whose work was deteriorating in his first year in the Science Sixth admitted that he had never wanted to continue with science; he had really, at thirteen, aspired to enter the Church and was more interested in the humanities. In earlier years science was his strong subject; he took the advice of his teachers and faithfully followed the track laid down for him, but at seventeen he could no longer tolerate the prospect of taking science at university; his motivation weakened, he became anxious, his work suffered. At thirteen he had been too reserved or too shy to tell anyone what he wanted to make of his life. This is not unusual. If, at the time the decision was made, the boy could have had the benefit of non-directive counselling, he might have explored his true inclinations and his potentialities in more depth before making a choice. Of course some pupils may be too immature to make sensible decisions, and there are factors such as maintaining a balance in the size of classes and in numbers taking certain subjects which may preclude pupils from following courses of their own choosing. Nevertheless, if they are to learn to stand on their own feet young people must be given genuine opportunities to make choices and to take educational, vocational and personal decisions of real importance to them.

The terms 'non-judgemental' and 'non-directive' occur in counselling literature.[1] In brief, the counsellor's purpose is not to judge a client but to accept him as a person of worth; not to

---

[1] See, for instance, Rogers, C. R., *Client-centered Therapy* (Houghton Mifflin, New York, 1951; paper, 1965).

give answers, but to assist the individual to find his own solutions to his particular problems. This does not mean that in accepting a person, a counsellor necessarily finds his behaviour acceptable, or in seeking an individual's own solution a counsellor never puts forward possible alternatives. To exercise sensible choice young people need to know their own strengths and weaknesses, their growing interests, abilities and skills in relation to the present and possible future situations at work, at leisure, in the home or in the community at large. Of these two areas of knowledge – that of the environment and that of the self – schools usually find knowledge of the outside easier to transmit and safer to handle, yet, in the process of growing up, so much depends on self-understanding and the ability to manage oneself.

Counselling is client-centred. The counsellor tries to grasp the personal meaning to his client of what is said and seeks to understand how the client perceives and interprets his experience. We are all inclined to respond to our own perceptions of what is going on in the outside world, and this determines our behaviour. In the relationship between counsellor and client it is therefore important for the counsellor to attempt to understand the client's framework of reference, to try to see through his eyes. This understanding or empathy is one of the essential qualities in an effective counsellor. To reach this level of communication the counsellor must have carefully observed the physical and social backgrounds of the young people who are his clients, whether working-class or middle-class, from slums, high-rise flats or well-to-do suburban houses. The counsellor must also listen totally: he must be adept at reading between the lines, at noticing what is not said as well as what is said, and he must observe the non-verbal communication – the tone of voice, facial expression, set of the body and gestures – to gather the feeling associated with what is said. If he can then in his responses to the client communicate this understanding, possibly by reflecting back a feeling of anxiety, depression, hostility, rejection or failure, the client recognizes that the counsellor 'is with him', and he is then the more inclined to pursue the exploration of his own feelings, or the significance of his particular problem, situation or predicament. A client will also talk more readily and frankly of his experience as he sees it if he feels secure, and through this verbalization he can begin to clarify his problems and come to see his way to a solution, or learn to live with a situation that cannot readily be remedied. If he feels threatened, in the sense of not being understood or not being taken seriously, or being unfavourably assessed or judged by the counsellor, the client may defend himself, become aggressive or cover up. Under conditions of acceptance, in which he meets an adult not seeking to blame him but prepared to listen and respect his confidence, he is likely to respond to the warmth of the relationship, and, feeling secure, explore in depth with the counsellor what is troubling him. But he will the more readily be sincere, open to all his experience and to the possibility of change, if he perceives the counsellor to be similarly sincere. These qualities of understanding (empathy), acceptance (non-possessive warmth), and sincerity (genuineness or congruence), have been found to be those most productive of effective counselling.[1]

Not all clients are suffering undue stress, serious indecision, emotional disturbance or maladjustment: some young people seek information on what are apparently quite trivial matters but which nevertheless worry them, and they may feel too shy or awkward to discuss them with a parent or class teacher. Those who fail to form friendships or establish good personal relations may benefit from the experience of a simple relationship in which they can talk honestly with an adult, without fear of being rebuffed or hurt, and this may give them enough confidence to try again outside the counselling relationship. For some boys and girls one or two interviews suffice; others need continued support over a long period, and for a minority, referral to outside agencies may be advisable. The counsellor, therefore, has to be able to respond differently in different situations, according to what is most appropriate; and it is perhaps in his identification of need and his resourcefulness of response that the trained counsellor can best supplement guidance given by other members of staff. An investigation of the work done by trained counsellors in twenty-five schools showed that nearly half the interviews dealt with personal problems or decisions, slightly more than a quarter with educational decisions, and the remainder with vocational matters. Of these three areas, teachers would probably feel most competent in educational guidance and least competent in personal guidance, while agreeing on the value of preparation and training for those engaged in careers work. Since the individual as a whole

[1] See Truax, C. B. and Carkhuff, R. R., *Towards Effective Counseling and Psychotherapy* (Aldine, Chicago, 1967): an account of research into the effectiveness of counselling.

person is concerned in all these decisions, there seems to be a good case for having someone on the staff particularly well informed and skilled in personal guidance.

There is no mystique in counselling and no miracles should be expected. Client-centred counselling is simply what the term implies – the boy or girl concerned is central to it. The aim is not to pass on a determined quota of external information, or to preserve the ethos of the school, or to secure conformity to the needs of society, although all these may be inextricably involved in whatever decision, course of action, or behaviour-change emerges from the interaction between client and counsellor. We cannot develop in isolation from our fellows, and we must seek individual fulfilment that gives satisfaction both to the individual and to society.

If all this sounds theoretical and far removed from the harsh realities of the classroom, teachers are asked to examine their own experience, to think of the lessons that have given them satisfaction and to consider the relationships with pupils that have not only been most rewarding to them as teachers, but have somehow yielded an unexpected growth in the boy or girl involved. Every teacher has had these experiences; they will bear analysis in the light of what has been described as good counselling practice.

Let us turn to practicalities. A counsellor sees individual pupils in a 'counselling interview', and he therefore must have a room where they can be fairly quiet and free from interruption. In Stoke-on-Trent, for example, where the appointing of trained counsellors has been taken further than in any other LEA area, the aim is to provide each counsellor with a unit including an interviewing room, a room for a part-time secretary, and a waiting space. It is essential for counsellors to have the full support and confidence of the heads of schools, and the head must try to ensure that the role of the counsellor is clearly understood by staff, pupils and parents. At first, most pupils going to the counsellor will probably be referred by members of staff, or will arrive at the counsellor's room at the request of outside agencies or parents. After a counsellor has been at work in a school for a time, the general experience is that more pupils refer themselves than are referred by others.[1] Pupils can make their own direct or written requests for appointments,

[1] See Thompson, A. J. M., *An Investigation into the Work performed by some trained Counsellors in English Secondary Schools*, Unpublished Report to the Social Science Research Council (University of Keele, 1970).

and an agreed procedure for dealing with them is worked out between counsellor and staff. There is obvious sense in a counsellor completing an appointment slip which has to be agreed and initialled by the teacher taking the lesson from which the pupil will absent himself while attending an interview. Some lessons are more important than others to the teacher; some are less attractive than others to the pupil. Counsellors are also available at times of the day when pupils are free from classes and when they may call to see the counsellor briefly without an appointment. If, however, a counsellor gives up too much time in breaks and lunch hours, he might weaken the informal contact with colleagues in the staff room that is so essential to the success of a counselling service. When counsellors make contact with parents, either in school or at home, to maintain the principle of confidentiality they do so with the agreement of the boy or girl concerned unless there are quite exceptional circumstances.

A theoretical discussion of confidentiality raises more difficulties than are usually found in actual practice. If a young person talks to a counsellor on the understanding that what he says will be treated in confidence and not divulged to anyone without his agreement, confidentiality must be respected; otherwise the counsellor's usefulness in the school will soon be undermined. If pupils themselves approach the counsellor for help they are usually willing for him to seek further help if need be from, say, their parents, the head of the school, or a member of staff. If the client introduces information into the interview relating to events likely to bring the client into danger or to do serious damage to the school – such as pregnancy, a decision to run away from home, or the use of drugs – the counsellor, exercising his judgement, may decide to tell the client that he is prepared to do anything he can to help, on condition that the client agrees to his passing on the information to other people if he considers it advisable. Not a few teachers are worried because they suspect some pupils will take complaints about the staff to counsellors. This does happen, but by no means as frequently as teachers appear to expect. If conflict between a teacher and a pupil causes distress, learning difficulties or hostile behaviour, there is a good case for providing a means of having it talked over with someone else if the pupil does not have sufficient confidence to approach the teacher concerned. Counselling will normally aim to bring about this direct approach. After shedding some of the emotion involved in the original conflict, pupils may themselves decide to talk it over with the teacher, or they may ask the counsellor to speak to the teacher about it first, or they may ask to see the teacher with the counsellor. These are potentially difficult situations, and there is an advantage if the counsellor has had experience of teaching and knows intimately, at first hand, the problems of the classroom. He will also know what feedback from counselling sessions is most useful to the head and members of staff, or as a contribution to discussions on the curriculum and organization of the school. Much can be passed on without a breach of confidentiality.

Whether his difficulties be inside or outside the school, the aim is to help the client to resolve them for himself, and with increasing maturity, to face similar difficulties in the future with more self-reliance. Yet it is not always as simple as that. Young people frequently find themselves in situations which cause them stress, and it is true that if they learn to deal with the situation and to tolerate the stress they mature in the process. For one or more of a variety of reasons, however, such as quarrelling parents, bereavement, inability to make friends, learning difficulties, obsessional fears and depression, they cannot control the situation and may find the stress intolerable. At these times talking is not enough: they can see their position with clarity; they want someone to do something about it. In cases such as these the counsellor can more readily intervene to reduce the stress if he is working within a team that includes supportive members of staff within the school, and social workers, psychologists and medical services outside the school. Long-term therapy is not at present either within the competence of the one-year trained counsellor or within the role expected of him in schools, although some courses of training place more emphasis on therapy than do others. His colleagues will certainly expect him to 'assist with seriously disturbed pupils and those whose behaviour is disruptive in the school. It is therefore essential for him to know when referral is advisable to the Child Guidance Clinic or the school psychologist, or when to enlist the help of the school welfare officer or the child care officer, so that having dealt directly with those cases within his competence, he can collaborate, when required, with colleagues in outside agencies.

His training prepares the counsellor to administer and interpret a range of psychological tests and interest inventories; individual tests of intelligence are still reserved for use by trained psychologists. The interpretation of test results to young people requires tact and skill, especially where the aspirations of pupil or parents are unrealistic. Cumulative records, too, assume importance in his work, for he is concerned with personal development and interested to chart its progress in individuals. The amount of detail to be included in cumulative records, where they are best stored, who has access to them, and how they are to be kept up-to-date are matters for decision by the head and staff; the keeping of records gives extra work to the staff and they should be made as useful as possible to the staff and readily accessible. In addition, the counsellor usually keeps any notes of a confidential nature in his private papers.

Where the counsellor puts his major effort will depend on where the school sees its priorities. At points of change and possible discontinuity the counsellor can be of assistance – say, in the transfer from primary to secondary schools, when some pupils might be under stress and at risk in their new setting, or in discussing possibilities with young people trying to make up their minds about optional courses, or whether to leave school in the fifth year. This range of possible involvement may appear too wide for one person to cover adequately. Is it very much wider than that of a headmaster or headmistress, or of the head of a subject department who happens to be in charge of a house?

In most secondary schools, certainly in schools of six hundred or more pupils, there is sufficient work for a full-time counsellor. By counselling full-time the role conflict involved in attempting to be both an accepting person as a counsellor and an assessing person, exercising authority and securing discipline as a teacher, does not arise. Confusion in the minds of pupils, too, can be avoided if the counsellor is not directly responsible for discipline. As an adult in the school the counsellor of course cannot divest himself of authority or a share of responsibility for the general discipline of the school. Common practice is to refer serious cases of ill-discipline up the staff hierarchy to the head of house or the head of year, or beyond, depending on the nature of the transgression. The advantages of omitting the counsellor from this hierarchy will be readily recognized once a school undertakes the quest for the cause of the pupil's divergence from the norm instead of using its disciplinary sanctions to secure conformity. For some pupils, too, there is an advantage in going to someone who is not a teacher to discuss matters of deep concern; having entered into a relationship in which confidential matters are explored in a counselling interview, a pupil can break the relationship and be spared the possible embarrassment of meeting frequently in the classroom, as a teacher, the person in whom he has confided.

Yet there are obvious gains from working with young people in groups. Groups give a welcome change from the rather exhausting face-to-face interview, the counsellor keeps in touch with teaching, sees young people relating to one another, and meets and gets to know more pupils quickly. Most counsellors in fact spend time each week working with groups – possibly discussing such subjects as personal relationships and problems encountered in growing up in a modern society, as part of the curriculum work in social education. In group guidance there is a high information content and the group is usually led by a teacher acting as chairman. If classes can be broken down into small groups, say of eight to twelve, or at most, fifteen members, group counselling may develop out of group guidance.[1] In group counselling the focus is on individuals in the group and the interaction between members of the group, not on the counsellor. The counsellor facilitates the exploration of common problems, and in finding that others have similar difficulties to one's own there may be a growth of self-acceptance and self-understanding. Apart from the saving of time, group counselling when skilfully handled can be very effective. For most people, however, it presents more difficulties than the individual interview, and it would be wise for counsellors to move to it through experience of group guidance and individual counselling.

Increasing attention has been given to group work since the first counselling courses were started. One-year full-time university courses were started at Keele and Reading in 1965; Exeter and Swansea introduced courses soon afterwards, and there were in 1971[2] at least ten courses on counselling, or containing a large element of counselling, in universities, colleges of education and polytechnics. The university courses recruited between twelve and twenty experienced teachers each year, the average age being in the middle thirties. Nearly all the teachers were seconded on salary by their employing authorities. The content varied from course to course, but all

---

[1] See Jones, Anne, *Counselling in Practice* (Ward Lock, 1970).
[2] Hamblin, D. H., and Watts, A. G., *Training Courses for School Counsellors* (Careers Research and Advisory Centre, Cambridge 1970). Gives details of courses and how to apply.

placed a good deal of emphasis on psychology, especially on personality theories and developmental psychology, and also on the theory and practice of counselling. Through visits and through talks from personnel actually engaged in the services, the students gained first-hand knowledge of outside helping agencies such as the Child Guidance Clinic, social services, educational psychologists, child care officers, school welfare officers, and the Youth Employment Service. All students had (supervised) counselling practice in schools. Considerable attention has been given to practical preparation for counselling, and some of the courses have developed role-playing and simulation exercises and the use of audio- and video-tapes. Practice is also given in the administration and interpretation of a range of psychological tests and interest inventories and the use of cumulative records. Through group discussions and other forms of group interaction, and sometimes through being counselled themselves, the students gain in self-awareness and in a knowledge of how others perceive them. This is important for those whose work will be to listen sensitively and to enter into the perception of others in counselling interviews.

As we move towards a more open and a more caring society, the resources available for guidance and counselling in schools will increase and decisions will be required on whether to provide courses of training for those concerned with pastoral care, or for full-time counsellors, or both. It would seem sensible to provide for both and to plan short part-time courses in counselling skills in addition to the one-year full-time courses. In fact it would appear that all teachers could gain from the study of counselling theory and the practice of counselling skills.

8 Reaching Home

by Patrick McGeeney

The Plowden report[1] marked the ostensible conversion of the British education system to recognition of the existence of parents. Since then no school has admitted to anything less than 'a good relationship with parents'. Too often the change has been merely marginal, or has been a change of stated aim alone, while practice has remained the same.[2] The duty to inform parents, the necessity to gain full information from them, and the hope of developing their interest in the school have recently become well-documented themes. The care of the pupil is impossible without a working relationship with the home. But how? Practical steps are required that cover such diverse matters as the form of a school's letters and the running of the reception office. Here Patrick McGeeney surveys the range of possibilities open to secondary schools.

Headteachers cannot avoid a relationship with parents. In the tone and style of their remarks they define the kind of relationship envisaged. Here, for instance, is the head of a London secondary school, firmly dug in behind the ramparts of traditional authoritarianism:

> I am the professional and I have been appointed on the assumption that I know how to run my school properly. Given the slightest encouragement they will want a PTA, and they tend to get run by the busybodies who want to tell the professional how to run his business. Imagine, for instance, a patient–doctor association!'[3]

Second, the commanding officer giving out routine orders, prepared to offer only token concession to changing custom and convention:

> It's a parent's duty to attend parents' meetings. We stand no damned nonsense about this. It's their job and the prefects stand by the door to check. We tick them off on a register as they come in and, if they don't come, I send for them the next day to explain the reason why.[4]

Finally (in the noticeable shift from the first person singular to the plural), the outward-looking invitation to partnership:

> However much your son or daughter may kick against authority (and there's nothing especially modern about that: everyone does it at some stage; it's part of growing up), you are more influential in his life than anyone else can be. That is why we value your attendance at parents' evenings and in the PTA. There is still a feeling expressed by some parents that the school knows best and should be allowed to get on

[1] *Children and their Primary Schools* (HMSO, 1968).
[2] For a recent history of the subject see McGeeney, Patrick, *Parents are Welcome* (Longman, 1969), and chapter 9 of *Head of Department*, Marland, Michael (Heinemann, 1971).
[3] BBC Third Programme: *Parents Are Welcome?* 1969.
[4] Dr Rhodes Boyson, *The Times Educational Supplement*, 1969.

with it. We ourselves never take that attitude. .... In my experience, discussions with parents are often most profitable when views have seemed most divergent.[1]

The issue then is not whether parent–teacher relations are necessary, but what sort of relationship is likely to be in the best interests of the children. And certainly research[2] confirms one's hunches that, where a relationship is seen to be warm, friendly and encouraging, the ground is better prepared for the growth of mutual trust and understanding. The problem of course is not as simple as that: parents also view the relationship from differing standpoints.

> 'You don't gain anything from going up there. All they can tell you is how he's getting on. I mean, if he does his best, that's all he *can* do. If your child hasn't got it in him, he can't do it, can he?'

> 'Oh, yes, we know Miss Potter socially, and there is a very free communication between us.'

> 'We cannot speak too highly of Quennevais School. The PTA flourishes both as a money-making agent and as a two-way vehicle for ideas. The Head is firmly in the saddle as a policy-maker with the firm backing of his staff, but there is an openness to parents' views which is refreshing.'

In this respect, what successive education reports of recent years have emphasized is the professionals' need to be aware of the sociological dimensions of their task.

Family and social class are the most powerful environmental influences upon a child's social, physical, emotional and cognitive development.[3] The consequence is that children from manual worker homes are at a disadvantage compared with children of non-manual workers at every stage of the educational process. The former, even at the same level of measured intelligence, are more likely to deteriorate in performance; proportionately fewer pass the 11-plus; more leave school at the earliest permitted age; and fewer gain access to Further and Higher Education. This is because the way a child deals with each experience, including those he encounters at school, is strongly conditioned by the values, attitudes, and beliefs of his neighbourhood subculture.

> The middle-class family is said to be child-centred, future-oriented, and interested in achievement and mobility. It teaches children to respect

[1] Mr Rogers, Head of the Dixie Grammar School, Nuneaton, in a letter to parents of new pupils.
[2] Argyle, Michael, *The Psychology of Interpersonal Behaviour* (Penguin, 1967).
[3] Craft, Maurice (ed.), *Family, Class and Education* (Longman, 1970).

property and to value neatness, thrift and punctuality. The lower class family, on the other hand, is described as adult-centred, present-oriented, and interested in enjoying life with extended family and peers. It teaches children to admire toughness, physical prowess, generosity, and practicality.[1]

By their mode of social control, the quality of their language and their way of thinking, all parents are, in the broadest sense of the term, educators. What the professional teacher has to recognize is that, as the parents are – wittingly or not – already participants in the process of their children's learning, they may as well be invited to become partners, in the hope of influencing them. To influence others you have to know them. Hence the need for parent-teacher co-operation.

If this may seem to be a statement of the obvious, it is worth noting that it took almost a century of state education in this country before any official enquiry was undertaken to find out what parents thought of their children's schooling. The Report[2] – the only large-scale research we have concerning communication and relationships between parents and secondary teachers – had this to say about face-to-face contacts generally:

> In the national survey among parents who had children in maintained primary schools, carried out for the Plowden Committee, 8 per cent had had no real talk with the head or with the child's class teacher. . . . In the present enquiry in which the children were in the third, fourth or fifth years of their secondary schools, 37 per cent had had no real talks with the head or any of the child's class teachers at the sampled school.

One is prompted to ask why, if it is possible to reach so many parents at the top of the primary school, the same cannot be achieved at least during the first year of secondary schooling. It is in fact possible. Mr Willcock, Head of the Minsthorpe Comprehensive School, writes:

> In this predominantly mining community, a very large percentage of the children are from the homes of unskilled or semi-skilled workers. During the first year we meet at least one parent of each child. This year 96 per cent accepted our invitation. . . The other 4 per cent were visited at home.

The initiative must come from the teachers, not merely because so many parents feel they are interfering if they go up to the school uninvited,[3] but because the problems at the secondary

---

[1] Herriott, R. E., and St John, N. H., *Social Class and the Urban School* (Wiley, New York 1966).
[2] *Young School Leavers*, Schools Council Enquiry 1 (HMSO, 1970).
[3] ibid., para. 170.

stage are specialized, and unless the staff identify and bring them to the notice of parents they may not even be aired.

Parents should be captured at the outset, when hopes are high and curiosity strong about the aims and purposes of secondary schooling. One mother describes the reception arrangements at the Creighton School, Muswell Hill:

> In the July before my son went to the school, they held a meeting for parents *and children* – and guided tours round the school. Then a letter to say that a child already at the school would call on each new child during the summer holiday and arrange to meet them and go with them on the first day.

As the tone suggests, first impressions are important; and for this reason alone the initial contact should be sufficiently interesting and informative to make parents want to come again. They are unlikely to be absorbed by a platform recital of administrative procedures or by a lecture on educational theory. The former can be provided in a prospectus: information about school buildings, members of staff, the house system, courses of study, meals, homework, absences, reports, uniforms, and the like – with the minimum of negative and prohibitive rules and regulations. Theory is more easily understood through observations of practice. The advantage of an invitation in July, before entry, is that it can coincide with an end-of-session display of work and activities. What the parents need to be told is the importance of parent–teacher co-operation; that parental interest does affect educational achievement; precisely and unequivocally the arrangements for contacting the staff; and an indication of how they can give support and encouragement at home. Above all, they need to meet the person who is to be responsible for the pastoral care of their child.

House tutor, year tutor, or form tutor – what matters is that the pastoral caretaker should be knowledgeable about the pupil concerned. 'Half the parents of 15-year-old leavers were anxious to be told more about how their child was getting on.'[1] At many schools, to ensure that discussions with parents are meaningful and relevant, a file is kept on each child throughout his stay. Right from the start, information given by parents and teachers is recorded. After each interview, the group tutor sets down on paper some observations, which are re-read just before any subsequent interview. This goes into the child's file, together with examples of his work in English, Maths, Art and other subjects, so that when parent and teacher meet, the

[1] Schools Council, *Enquiry 1: Young School Leavers* (HMSO, 1968).

exchange is centred upon evidence of what the child has learned.

Where, as seems to be the common practice, only one evening is set aside for individual consultation, the time factor will be a major problem. One Middlesex school advised: 'Since some teachers may have as many as a hundred parents to interview it would be appreciated if you could arrive as soon after 7 p.m. as possible, and to limit your interview with each teacher to not much more than five minutes.' Why should they be asked to arrive all at the same time? Perceptiveness and patience are bound to flag in circumstances where some unfortunate teacher – and parent – would still be there (on the above calculation) in the early hours of the morning. At the Creighton School: 'Interviews are held on different evenings in three successive weeks from 6.30 to 9.30 p.m. Interview lists are placed in the school entrance hall and parents have to visit the school prior to the meetings to sign for the times they require.'

It is a further economy of time where it is left to the group tutor to recommend whether parents need to be passed on to a particular subject tutor.

The difficulties of establishing personal contact will be particularly acute in large schools where some of the parents live a considerable distance away. An ingenious solution was hit upon by the staff at the Woodroffe School. The Head, Mr Pearn, informs parents that:

> We have divided the staff up into a number of teams, and each team will be allocated to one area – Lyme Regis, Charmouth, Thornecombe, Marshwood, etc. With the kind support of the heads of local schools, a room will be made available at regular intervals throughout the year and the staff team will be in attendance there during the evening so that you may discuss any problems you may have with them. If there is any question of detail which any individual member of the team is unable to answer, detailed notes will be made of your problem and a full answer sent to you by post without delay.

Mr Pearn adds, concerning the fact that not all pupils are reliable deliverers of messages from school: 'We have a notice board system in the town and the local villages on which copies of all letters and notices are displayed.'

The reluctant parents will have to be approached more directly. Home visiting is one possibility, though this will be unacceptable to some teachers – and, in any case, not every teacher will have the tact and skill to undertake this. With the development of school counselling services, some schools are extending the role of the counsellor to include special responsibility for home and school liaison. The advantage here is that the person who does the home visiting has the time and the expertise to establish links with the appropriate social and welfare agencies. Better use, in fact, could be made of these specialist agencies surrounding the school. In the West Riding, for example, Mr Beedleston, Senior EWO, initiated (in co-operation with a local head) an experimental scheme of visits to the homes of children entering a particular secondary school.

> Upon reaching the home, I explained that I was the Welfare Officer for the school, and as they had just had a boy or girl just started there, I wondered if there had been any problems:
>
> Does the child like the school?
> Has he/she settled?
> Are there any teachers the child does not like, and if so why?
> Has the school had any effect on the child such as feeling tired, etc?
> Does the child like school meals?
> Has he/she any health defects?
>
> By this time most parents had asked me inside, and I quickly saw what type of home the child lived in. This led me to ask if there were any older or younger children in the family, and what facilities the child had to do homework and to study with other children about.
>
> After this, the crucial question was what was the parental attitude to education. Were they interested in the child staying on after the statutory leaving age? It was surprising what was learned even about older members still at school. In every case I was received with courtesy and many said what a good idea it was, as it made a personal contact between home and school, and that they would be glad to see me at any time if a problem arose. I stressed, however, that if anything of a serious nature occurred, I should expect both parents to visit the school with me to thrash out the matter with the Head.
>
> All the information gained was handed to the Head and discussed with him. The intention was that upon my next visit I could discuss these notes with the parents – and also any notes provided by the school staff. This gave a background picture of each child which was useful for guidance.

The key question to arise from these personal contacts is what kind of support and encouragement can be given at home; in particular, how can the less education-oriented parent be induced to participate. The Head of Strode Secondary Modern School, in an attempt to provide some answers, appointed a Home Education Organizer, Peter Preston. The title is significant, for the starting point is the assumption that 'The children's leisure time may be regarded as a huge, largely unused, educational resource demanding the co-operation of parents and teachers.' There is space here for only a brief outline of what has been achieved. First, hobbies: begun in school and continued in the home with the help of parents, children made kites, go-karts, rag dolls and so forth, the products being set up for exhibition (ten were arranged in one year) before being presented by the children to the local Centre for the Mentally Handicapped. The most valuable outcome of the discussions centring upon the exhibitions of work was the opportunity for parents to exchange views among themselves and with the teachers on source materials and the difficulties of encouraging and sustaining their children's interest. Second, school visits: parents were invited to accompany the children to places of interest, giving information and advice where they could, and learning how to utilize an outing to guide their children's interest purposefully. Third, residential courses: parents have the chance to look round the residential centres and to hear from the warden and his staff firsthand information about the activities offered – again, a point of entry to the child's learning activities. Fourth, holiday activities: an extension of term-time hobbies and visits into the vacation, by means of a booklet suggesting activities and outings, and a Know Your Town Quiz, to be completed by the end of the holidays. Fifth, with remedial pupils, reading: introducing pupils and parents to the local library, the publication of 'Book Guides', encouraging parents to borrow and to read 'set books' along with the child, and books of playlets to be read *en famille*. The larger context of all this has been the restructuring of the curriculum on the basis of work that 'flows over into the home'. Before going on to discuss this more fully, some consideration needs to be given to one aspect of secondary schooling which is of central concern to the majority of parents: the relevance of the curriculum to their children's prospects of finding a suitable job after leaving school.

Once again, the *Young School Leavers* Report offers useful comment: 'Parents in general would themselves also have valued more information about jobs and careers and advice about their children's capabilities so that they could be of greater help to them in deciding on suitable work.'[1] Working-class parents tend to have a lower level of occupational aspiration and educational achievement than the ability of their children would justify, a point which is underlined by Dr Douglas: 'The low expectations of the manual working class parents may reflect the real difficulties that many talented pupils have in attempting to enter the professions when they lack

[1] *Young School Leavers*, op. cit., p. 126.

skilled advice and encouragement from their parents and schools.'[1]

Equally, some children at the other end of the social scale need to be protected from the pressures of over-ambitious parents who are unrealistic about the potentialities of their offspring. As one Head reminds us:

> Parents of potential candidates for higher education places have had to be convinced that their children were worthy of the chance; the safe apprenticeship or good office job represented the peak of their ambition. Other parents, on the other hand, encourage children in wild dreams: a career as a vet for a girl who 'just loves animals' (but has little academic ability and does not like science) is our annual nightmare. Careers guidance in the normal sense is a non-starter in conditions like this. It pre-supposes a reasonable equation between ambition and ability.[2]

Sensibly, some heads give supporting information outlining scholarships and awards, and the requirements of different Further and Higher Education establishments, and of careers that might eventually be followed. (At my daughter's school, parents are invited to be available to give advice about their own jobs to pupils.) Mr Rivers-Moore, Head of Havant Grammar School, issues a table of statistics interpreting the national proportions of successful university applicants in each A level subject. And Mr Redfearn, of Ecclesbourne School, duplicates a five-page document, *GCE Qualifications Needed for Certain Courses and Professions*. Knowle School, Darwen, is one of the many schools which arrange a Careers Evening to meet the local youth employment officer and personnel officers from firms in the area. Mr Bosomworth, Head of the Walbottle Grammar School, aware that some parents are reluctant to allow their children to stay on after fifteen, has compiled an *Information Sheet for Parents; the* 16+ *Question – More School or Work?* in which he compares the long-term career prospects of early and late leavers. To enable the parents to understand the financial commitments, simulated case-studies are given, illustrating the allowances that would be received, at 16-plus and 18-plus, assessed on parental income. Rightly, the assumption is that a child's future course of study and subsequent career are important enough to warrant joint consultation – in contrast to the practice of such schools as the one which peremptorily

---

[1] Douglas, J. W. B., Ross, J. M., and Simpson, W. R., *All Our Future* (Peter Davies, 1968).

[2] Poster, C. *Headship in the 1970s.*

forewarned that: 'The decision must rest with the staff, who know your child's ability.'

Parents will more easily encourage their children to stay on if they can appreciate what their children are being taught. Some schools set out to explain the nature and scope of the curriculum: in newsletters to parents or through demonstration lessons. The English Department at Crown Woods School, London, mounts evenings in which both demonstration lessons and simulated lessons with parent 'pupils' are seen by large parent audiences.[1] The account included on page 144 of similar work at Renistone Comprehensive School in the sciences gives working details of how success can be achieved, especially by encouraging parent participation. Another approach is instanced by Calving High School, which mentions: 'Illustrated talks by heads of department on recent developments in the teaching of their subjects, and coloured slides and taped commentaries by pupils and staff. ... Our next project is a 20-minute movie of work in the Science Department.' The implication here is that the complexities of the curriculum can be put across to a wider audience if translated through the mass media, a point which is illustrated by the popularity of television programmes showing the research projects of competing teams from various schools. This also adds weight to the argument that the curriculum should be relevant, purposeful and practically useful. The material prepared by the Schools Council Humanities Curriculum Project, for instance, on *War, The Family*, and *Personal Relationships* impinges upon the lives not only of the pupils but of their parents too. A strong case can and has been made for the view that the community-orientated curriculum is the only approach likely to engage the involvement of parents and other members of the community in educational priority areas.

> Parental involvement and support for curricular enterprises would probably be enhanced by a socially relevant curriculum, in that their own experience, occupations, insights and so forth would be material evidence. The mysteries of the school would be, in part, replaced by a substance well-known to the parent.[2]

We need to cut the knot of O-level strangulation before teachers, pupils, and parents can speak freely and relevantly about what needs to be learned.

[1] For a fuller account, see pp. 85–87 of Marland, Michael, *Head of Department* (Heinemann, 1971).
[2] Eric Midwinter: *Curriculum and the EPA Community School* (Liverpool EPA Project,) Occasional Paper 6.

A start can be made with the subjects in which the parents' own experience, occupations, and insights provide the material evidence – as at the Paddington Comprehensive School (the base, incidentally, of the Liverpool EPA Project). Patricia Griffiths, Head of the Home Management Department, is worth quoting at length:

> The whole of our scheme of work is based on the home, and wherever possible we refer to individual practices regarding home making, house purchase, family life, and so on. We also encourage the pupils to invite their parents, sisters, aunts, grannies, to come into the school to share meals, to listen to talks, or even just to take part in class. In addition, we organise assignments to include the care of senior citizens who come into the school from nearby tenements and homes, and the care of children brought to school by at first their brothers and sisters, but now more often by their parents. In the local area, we have involved ourselves in luncheon club activities, a local restaurant, nurseries, and individual homes.
>
> I personally have taken children to my own home (particularly helpful with Chinese and West Indian children who are trying to cope with learning about British life and institutions when they themselves go home each evening to China and the Caribbean) and to restaurants in small groups. They have also taken my husband and me to their homes.

According to Mrs Griffiths, there is an

> Ever-open door to the school – parents, friends and passers-by are encouraged to come and look round. At our Open House – fairly regular open days and evenings – there are no particular activities or displays. All staff continue normal teaching. Parents can come in, look around and join in classes at any time from 1.15 p.m. to 9 p.m. (to allow shift workers to come along).

Inescapably, the most important message conveyed is the sort of atmosphere which pervades the school.

This is the central point to be grasped concerning home and school liaison – its educational significance. The relationship a head envisages with parents will reflect his attitude towards the pupils within his charge. It seems hardly likely that a head who addresses parents defensively and suspiciously, and insists upon rigid rules and control of entry, will be any different in the way he speaks to children – and the irony is that this attitude tends to provoke the very hostility such heads most fear. At the Paddington School, on the other hand, the pupils are given the chance to learn, by example, that there is really little to fear and a great deal to be gained by a free and open exchange of views. The objection is sometimes made that, if closer parent–teacher relations are fostered, some pupils will

Science for parents

by J. M. Nicholson, Renistone Comprehensive, Sheffield

I suppose few subjects in the school curriculum have seen such radical changes in teaching methods during the past fifteen to twenty years as science. The apparatus and equipment, the emphasis on practical work of an investigatory nature the experiments themselves are foreign to today's generation of parents.

They, for the most part, handled little more than accumulators and magnets in physics and Bunsen burners and test-tubes in chemistry. Biology tended to be a glorified nature study with the emphasis on collection rather than experiment.

It was with this in mind that the members of our science department decided to attempt a different kind of open evening. We decided not to have static exhibitions of exemplary work, with spick and span pupils carefully rehearsed to demonstrate the latest piece of apparatus. We wanted the parents to experience, as far as possible, modern science teaching at first hand.

The function had been mentioned in a termly letter from the headmaster, but we knew that if we left it at that we could expect no more than twenty (the number we had at another parents' meeting on science two years earlier). Each member of the science department, therefore, undertook to advertise the event among three or four of the forms which they taught. Invitations were duplicated with a reply slip to indicate the number expected. Forms were regularly reminded of the evening (their initial reaction to the idea of their parents actually doing experiments was enthusiastic—and at times, hilarious.) Reply slips came in steadily, and finally, there were 200 parents almost equally divided between the lower school (first and second years) and the rest of the school.

We had arranged for seven laboratories to be manned and by including three students who were with us on teaching practice we provided two members of staff to each laboratory. Our three laboratory technicians stayed behind for the evening to set out apparatus.

Three labs were equipped with senior work and a handful of older boys and girls stayed behind to help parents with the experiments. They were instructed, as far as possible, not to demonstrate but to encourage parents to do things for themselves. In the chemistry laboratory parents made crystals of sulphur, did acid-base titrations, measured rate of reaction by iodine clock and gas syringe methods and investigated the reactions of potassium iodide.

In the biology lab they did a variety of experiments on the themes of heart, blood and digestion, including examining their own blood under a microscope. In the physics lab they measured acceleration using trolleys and ticker tape and a linear air track and also tried out various electronics experiments.

The other four labs were given over to lower school science. We use a series of worksheets in the lower school and in each lab worksheets were available for parents to use themselves. In the chemistry lab a 'class' of 30 parents went through a simple experiment in which calcium is added to water, the hydrogen tested and then the mixture is filtered and expired air is blown through the filtrate. In another lab they were taken through a series of experiments designed to illustrate, in the parents themselves, variations in a living organism.

In a third lab they made chromatograms from various mixtures of inks and dyes and in the fourth a wide variety of first and second-year experiments were on view, mainly on the theme of energy changes. Parents could try them out for themselves.

The second half of the evening followed the more usual line, with coffee and biscuits, a display of books for sale, a talk by the head of science followed by questions to a panel of science teachers, and finally informal conversation.

An example of involving parents in school activities. Reprinted from *The Times Educational Supplement,* 16 July 1971.

resent what may appear to them to be a restriction on their natural desire for independence. This is less likely to happen where they are included in the relationship, particularly if they are encouraged to take the initiative in inviting adults to parti- cipate in the work of the school. Young people can best learn what is implied by a responsible and mature relationship if they are given some responsibility in decision-making appropriate to their age, and if the teachers they encounter are themselves mature in their personal approaches to others. At the Creighton School, the Sixth Form are represented on the Parents' Associa- tion Committee; and at the Woodroffe School, parents and pupils are given the opportunity to help formulate school policy on certain matters: for instance, the committee 'with representatives from the Parents' Association, the Governors, the staff, and boys and girls to look into the whole matter of uniform'.

It is perhaps appropriate to end where we began, with a head defining his relationship with parents. Mr Pearn, Head of Woodroffe, in his circular letters to parents, provides a model of maturity and responsibility to staff and pupils alike:

> The greatest single problem faced by every school in the country is that of communication between parents and school. Parents have always been welcome here and we have always invited you to make an appointment should you wish to have a private talk with me or any member of staff. Far too often, however, the very children who need most help are those whose parents we have not met. If it is impossible for you to come to the school we will willingly visit you, but I cannot overstress the importance of personal contact. . . . Partly the problem is that parents are too modest and feel that this is a matter to be left to the teachers. In fact, your children's lives are too important to be handed over to any professional, however skilled or devoted he or she may be.

9 Keeping in Touch[1]

[1] This chapter is based on an article I wrote for The Home and School Council, published in December 1970.

For the secondary school, the written report is indispensable for the educational care of the individual pupil, and no extension or new shaping of other aspects of a school's way of creating a relationship with parents is likely to make it obsolete. It is arguably far more important in itself than the report in a junior school for at least two major reasons: firstly, size, atmosphere, and the pupils' relative maturity are bound to create a more distant feel for parents than they will experience in a good junior or infant school, and, secondly, the range of specialist teachers with whom a pupil will work creates the need for a handy way of bringing reactions together. However much a formal report may seem at first glance to be part of the school ritual of the past, it is in fact a crucial tool, capable of great development and flexibility. However, like so many other aspects of the way our schools are run, a school wishing to scrutinize its reporting system, or the headteacher of a newly reorganized school making a fresh start, will find precious little to guide them – except the memories they can scrape together of previous schools. There is, surprisingly, a recent book devoted to the subject,[1] but it is vague, platitudinous, and based on very little observation or research and even less fundamental thinking. The subject has apparently seemed too mundane for articles or studies, even in, for instance, the Department of Education's quarterly *Trends*. The Advisory Centre for Education have produced a useful folder of examples, which, however, soon went out of print. It is, though, odd that a decade in which 'good communications with parents' has leapt suddenly into everyone's mouths as a desirable aim, there has been no methodical survey or account of good practice.

This chapter is my personal survey of the ground, based on my own experience (which has included helping to re-shape the reporting system for a comprehensive school of 2,000), my observation of other schools, and some sampling of parents and pupils. Most valuably, though, I have been able to make a careful scrutiny of report forms from some three hundred secondary schools collected by the Home and School Council, together with a sample of memoranda and instructions to staff from some schools, many helpful explanatory letters by headteachers, and even a number of actual reports in photocopy. This sample survey was self-selected in that the examples came only from schools (and a few parents) who were members of the Home and School Council and wished to respond to the

[1] Keating, Leslie, *The School Report* (Kenneth Mason, 1969).

secretary's invitation. My definite impression, though, is that the reports I studied were fairly representative, ranging from the most conservative to the most fully and recently revised.[1]

There is no escaping the two central facts: the vast majority of schools are plodding through a regular ritual in a time-honoured way. In this, a staid form is sent out according to a rigid routine, embodying a grid of percentages, class sizes, grades, and positions in class, which are followed by per-functory phases of vague generalization. The more both the figures and the words are analysed, the less they reveal. The firm overall impression is of take-it-or-leave-it distance. There is no feeling of communication, certainly not a two-way flow. This is not to deny that *care* is put into such reports (much of the averaging, totalling, and so on must take hours), but there are serious limitations to the value of the whole exercise.

On the other hand the second fact is equally clear: a smaller number of schools have carefully considered the real needs of parents, pupils, and teachers, and have assessed the practical possibilities open to them. Many of these revisionary schools are comprehensive. This is not surprising, for the largish compre-hensive school with a wide ability-range, especially if it has a well-developed pastoral system, runs into reporting difficulties on almost every count. (It is surprising, though, how many of such schools are nevertheless perpetuating patently in-adequate systems.)

Throughout the secondary phase, reports should act as moments for calm and full assessment of all the aspects of a pupil's school life so that the parent has as full a picture of it as possible (this is an elementary right). Secondly, this picture is useful for subject teachers as it forces them to stand back for a moment and see what is happening; other teachers who have pastoral responsibility also need such information in a some-what formal way if their care of the individual is to be as informed and pointed as it should be. Even the pupil needs this opportunity to look at himself through the teachers' eyes, yet apart from the tension of last night's homework. By the end of the first year in the secondary school, the pupil is taking a real interest in what is written about his or her work. One purpose of this mutual knowledge is remedial: steps can be taken to make particular improvements, but only if the report pinpoints particular aspects with some descriptive skill.

At the heart of the whole reporting question is the problem,

[1] An earlier survey was done by Albert Rowe for *Where* No. 17, 1964.

which some schools are exploring vigorously, of standards of reference. Any comment (or grade summary) is in fact, or by implication, *comparative*. What needs to be quite clear, but often is not, is what standards of comparison are being used. The most common map reference, as it were, is the teaching group. This, for instance, has usually been so in grammar schools, many of whose reports still picture the individual in a competitive class position for each subject. Such a comparative standard makes sense only if the composition of the teaching group is well defined and well understood by parents. It is obvious that even in a highly streamed situation there will be overlap in ability between groups,[1] and that the degree of overlap will vary from subject to subject. This undermines the 'form position' basis – even if its heavily competitive stress were to be acceptable. It is equally certain that in many schools parents frequently do not understand class nomenclature, and with the more complex and flexible option patterns of older classes this is becoming more difficult. Furthermore, the extensive introduction of the teaching of some or all subjects to mixed-ability groups in lower years suggests further objections to that basis of comparison.

Some schools endeavour to compare the pupil's present with his past attainment 'in terms of his own ability' – an attractive notion, but one which has its own dangers in suggesting an early ability assessment within which the pupil may be trapped. This is most common in mixed-ability teaching. Many schools 'band' pupils into groups of classes of broadly parallel ability, and they compare only within such a band. The danger here of reports reinforcing a multilateral organization only half-hidden by a comprehensive label is very serious. Some schools compare over the *whole* ability range – and in a fairly comprehensive 'comprehensive school' this could be the same as comparing with the nation's expectations of a certain age-group. The worry that this will depress the lower-ability children is partially answered by highlighting *effort* as a separate aspect, angling the comments suitably. This problem of the standards of comparison is one which a school must explore thoroughly. It can then look at the mechanics of the job.

There are six main areas of decision for a school to consider in formulating its reporting procedure. They are interlocking,

[1] cf. Diagram 3,3 in *Comprehensive Education in Action* (NFER, 1970), which shows that in one seven-stream school pupils of a certain level of ability were in each of six of the streams!

and by no means mutually exclusive. I suggest that by considering each in turn a school can shape a procedure which fully reflects its broader policies, and which meets the needs of today:

(a) Timing;   (b) Format;   (c) Grades;
(d) Comments;   (e) Tone;   (f) Feedback.

(a) Timing

The timing of a school's reports has far more importance than might at first appear. The traditional pattern was one report a term for each pupil, and this had much to recommend it. It recognized the reality of the termly teaching unit; it was frequent, and it related to the 'termly position' which for many schools was the measure of progress. This simple scheme, though, is rapidly becoming more varied, and frequency is being sacrificed, rightly I think, to effectiveness.

Firstly, many schools have dropped back to two a year, and the first is sent home not for Christmas but halfway through the spring session. This helps to smooth over the already ridiculously exaggerated end-of-term run-down, and, most important, allows the reports to be issued and considered while the school is in session. This facilitates effective parental feedback, and provides the opportunity for staff to consider the pupil's whole report. One of the major questions to be asked of a report is 'What use is made of it?', and there seems more chance of a full consideration when it is not caught up in the school holidays.

Once the termly cycle is dropped, it can be seen that there are even more significant possibilities for flexibility. Sometimes further changes are made in the interests of better report-writing. One school with 'vertical' tutor groups staggers its reports to achieve a high level of frequency, and the opportunity for the tutor to write with the concentration possible if only a few are being processed at once. The Headmaster of that school explains:

> Reports go out every second term of a child's school life and are staggered across the year. Thus, the Fourth and Second have Reports at Christmas and in July, and Third Year in the middle of the Spring Term and the Fifth Year in the middle of the Summer Term. This means that each House Tutor has only about seven Reports to write at one moment in time which enables the kind of Report that I have sent you to be written regularly.

The detail and care in the reports would seem to show that such a staggered system does help.

But, of course, these advantages would not be gained in an age-based school. Staggering can be used, though, for more important reasons than merely spreading the work-load. A small number of schools have asked themselves exactly when is the best time for a pupil to be reported on. The answer is that each age in the school has a different need. Some schools argue, for instance, that there is a great need for parents of first-year pupils to have a rapid reaction from the school, perhaps not long after the first half-term. Other schools have seen the special needs of pupils in their examination year (the very end of the spring term is arguably too near to June examinations for major criticisms). One school has staggered its reports in an attempt to relate them to the real dynamic of the pupils' lives, thought of as a continuous progress through the school, not as a repetition of seven similar years. The scheme is:

Year	Term	Special function
1	Autumn – second half	Description of response to new learning situation
1	Summer – end	Full report
2	Summer – early	Full report
3	Spring – first half	Full report, specially angled to consideration of choice of options for fourth and fifth years
4	Autumn – second half	Description of response to new courses and groupings
4	Summer – second half	Full report
5	Spring – first half	Pre-examination considerations
5	Summer – end	Leaving Certificate

and the sixth and seventh years follow a similarly varied pattern.

Most of such schemes reduce the total number of reports. I now feel that far from causing a drop in significant communication, such a cut leads to better real reporting. This is especially so when 'partial' or 'interim' personal reports are encouraged. Some schools report only on certain of the pupils:

> In this school we have two examinations a year. In January everyone in the school is examined and reports are issued to boys in the Fifth Form and the Upper Sixth (since these are the G.C.E. candidates) and to those other boys in the school (usually between 10 and 15 per cent of the total) whom we feel deserve reports because their work is either extremely good or very unsatisfactory. At the end of June we have a second examination for all boys who are not taking the G.C.E. and after this every boy who has taken the exam is given a report.

Although there seem to be certain dangers in this – for one of the functions of a report is to focus on the 'middle' pupils who have not been so noticeable – the notion of special reports for certain pupils from time to time is valuable. Too often really critical remarks come to parents as a bombshell after long silences. Other 'partial' approaches recognize that not only do the needs of different ages and different pupils vary, but also different subject disciplines have different reporting needs. Here, for instance, is a specimen report for the English Department of a school which is outstanding for its careful consideration of reporting:

Dear Mr & Mrs Brown
Autumn Term 1969: *CSE English Assessment*
CSE English is a two-year course that bases its final grading on continuous assessment and a final examination. Continuous assessment means that at the end of every term Mary is given a mark for the work done in that term. These end-of-term marks all count towards the final grading at the end of the two years. The marks are based on quality of work and effort. Obviously, if a student has not done all the work that has been set, this must be taken into account. We use five marks: A B C D E. A is good, C is average.
We thought you would find it helpful to know Mary's mark for the Autumn Term, 1969.
It is B and we make the following remarks:
She fails to produce a lot of her work for marking. We must have this to show to the examiner.
If you would like to discuss Mary's progress with us, please make an appointment to see us at the school. If this is not convenient one of us will come and see you at home. If neither of these is possible perhaps you would like to make any comments at the bottom of this letter. We would be only too pleased to read them.
Yours faithfully
Head of English

I have no doubt that the days in which all the pupils of a secondary school are reported on in a standard way in every subject at the same times in the year are nearly over. Flexibility in timing to spread the teachers' load, shape the report to the particular subject and pupil needs, and relate them to other aspects of school life, will lead to a far more varied pattern.

(b) Format

The single-sheet report still dominates British reporting. Its virtues are cheapness as well as ease of storage, postage, and

handling. Many schools demand the actual report back for
filing – but this is indefensible: parents must be encouraged to
keep their copies. Others allow the report sheet to be kept, and
transfer merely the grades on to various forms of internal record
cards. This allows a supplementary confidential, frank, col-
league-to-colleague comment to be added, but is basically unsatisfactory unless a full record of the comments to parents is
also kept.

Ingenious use is made by a large number of schools of
various forms of report books. At their simplest these are
merely a bound-up set of reports that will see the pupil through
his school life. One advantage which is argued by some is that
teachers see earlier reports as they fill in the latest, but this is
countered by others, who maintain that this inhibits freshness
of comment. A stronger advantage is that there is ample space,
which a number, but by no means all, schools exploit, for a
clear explanation of the system, grades used, and so on. (A
variant on this kind of report book is the kind with carbon
paper and duplicates: the top copies go home, and the carbons
build up a cumulative record. This is not really a book from
the point of view of the parents, and has very little, if any, advantage in convenience from the point of view of internal
procedures.)

To me the report *book* is depressing. Occasionally, of course,
it is valuable to look back, but the need to flick through the
earlier reports before reading the latest is irritating, the whole
book begins to look bedraggled, and it is hard to change the
format or even style of commenting as the pupil gets older.
Added to this is the fact that the book is kept at school, not by
the parents.

The problem of the school's keeping a copy is being solved
in an increasing number of schools by the use of NCR (no
carbon required) paper: this can be bound up in pads of any
number and sheets of any size. The top copies can be printed
in the normal way, and are interleaved with duplicates. Provided a backing card is kept handy to put under the duplicate
and prevent the impression appearing farther down the pad,
there are no difficulties in use. This facility makes it easy for
school and parents to keep copies, it is capable of variations in
format, and it seems to me to have out-dated the report book
idea. The layout and wording of the report page is most
important. Firstly it should have the right air of attractiveness
– too many reports are merely daunting. Only a handful of

schools have ventured into coloured ink or away from the rectangular grid, yet the results in improving the image are clearly justified.

The layout also dictates the teachers' comments: many forms allow as little as 2 in. × ¼ in. for these, and even treble this is inadequate. By printing *all* the possible subjects, of which only a few are actually used, space is wasted, and even the grid pattern itself is wasteful. Some schools, wishing for a variety of reasons to keep to the single-page multi-subject format, have produced more pleasing layouts which encourage rather than inhibit effective comment. A few schools supply folders in which the sheets can be kept by parents.

It seems pretty clear, though, that the traditional single-page format is inadequate for the job which many schools want of their reports. These schools are increasingly turning to 'slips'. This system has a number of variants, but its essence is that each subject teacher is given pads of specially printed slips (which can be in duplicate and may be of NCR paper). The teacher enters the pupil's name, his or her subject responsibility, and teaching set indication. The teacher then adds his comments and 'posts' the completed slips to the form teacher or house tutor, who assembles all the slips for each pupil, adds his own general slip, and staples or clips them into a folder for issuing. As one headteacher put it: 'We find the system very efficient, but more expensive than report books.' It is also rather more complex in its administration, and needs a good design if the final stapled-up bunch is not to look scrappy. Many schools would not feel that this system would be viable for the whole school, but it has great advantages, especially for the older option-organized classes:

(a) There is a vastly increased space available, though briefer comments need not look lost.

(b) Unlike conventional multi-subject report sheets, slips can be filled in by teachers where and when they like (at home, in the art room while looking through pupils' paintings, etc.). This is a great help, and avoids the staffroom muddle and panicky rush that is otherwise inevitable.

(c) Where there is a range of subject possibilities, packs are tailor-made for the individual's choice of subjects.

There is also, of course, the possibility that the cover may carry a suitable explanatory letter.

A few schools have completely replaced the whole method of each teacher reporting via a central document to the parent. The need for internal reporting is so great in a comprehensive school, and the dissatisfaction with conventional reports so strong, that each teacher sends a full and entirely frank report to the tutor, who then writes a continuous letter based on these, adjusting the precise comment to his grasp of the needs of the pupil and the particular family.

My own belief is that in the comprehensive school no one format suits the whole school. Graphic design and printing techniques should and can be at the service of the school to produce the appropriate format to encourage good reporting. For instance, the position and emphasis of a grade box in relation to the comment space can be varied. There is no need for the grade to precede and dominate the comment: it can be placed to the lower right-hand side of the comment space, and thus be presented as a subordinate check only. There is concrete evidence from experience that the format is one of the major factors influencing the quality of comment.

(c) Grades

By 'grades' I mean any numerical or letter system which attempts to summarize all or part of a pupil's school life. A sample of today's reports show that almost all use some form of grading, and the methods include: (i) marks in percentages (raw or standardized, for exams and/or class work); (ii) letter or number grades for attainment, which are often standardized to a normal distribution over a class, group of classes, or the whole year; (iii) positions in a ranking across a single class or a group of classes; (iv) letters or number grades for 'diligence', 'effort', or whatever – normally unstandardized and frankly subjective.

A few schools have no grades of any type for certain years at least, and a somewhat similar number have a battery of number grades, analysing aspects of a pupil. The following explanation from the back of a report best illustrates this analytic approach carried to an extreme:

Explanation
   These assessments are based on the teachers' observations over a period of the pupil's work, attitude and ability in class. They give a more complete profile than is obtained from the usual assessment based on performance in terminal examinations, though they may be sup-

plemented by various tests. It is intended that they should be used to find and develop a pupil's strengths rather than to emphasize weaknesses.

The five-point scale is applied to the whole of a year group in which there will be approximately 5 per cent in the A (excellent), 20 per cent in the B (good), 50 per cent in the C (average), 20 per cent in the D (below average) and 5 per cent in the E category.

The abilities assessed are as follows:

1. Knowledge
   The ability to memorise the facts connected with the subject, topic or activity.
2. Understanding
   Ability to apply the facts learnt. Powers of deduction. Ability to recognise problems and choose appropriate means to solve them.
3. Skills
   Acquisition of skills applicable to the particular activity or subject, e.g. ability to write grammatically or spell correctly, to calculate, use tools correctly, the techniques of painting or drawing as opposed to the creative or imaginative side.
4. Originality
   Powers of creativity and original thought. Initiative.
5. Neatness
   How the work is presented. Layout, order, arrangement, etc.
6. Oral
   Ability to take part in discussion and express a point of view.
7. Co-operation
   Ability to accept others, to pool knowledge and work co-operatively in groups. (This also includes attitude to authority and readiness to obey or take command if required.)
8. Perseverance
   Conscientiousness. Progress over a period. Persistence, etc.
9. Self-Understanding
   Realistic self-understanding and self-acceptance. Self-disciplining when required by needs of others or an activity. Self-forgetting, curiosity and enjoyment.

I consider that such grades are far harder to interpret than teachers seem to realize. One justification that is often stated for grades is that they avoid empty comments of the 'Satisfactory' type. My definite impression is that comments following grades are usually actually inhibited by the grades. It is staggering how often in schools up and down the country a grade which by the report's own printed definition means, for instance, 'below average' should be duplicated in precisely similar words. A second motive for using grades is that they are more objective and precise than verbal formulas. The precision, though, is often illusory, for attainment or effort are not *that* easily assessed. In many subjects the validity of a single grade is very dubious; many of the teaching aims (e.g. to inculcate a sense of the past in history) are difficult to grade, and others are too diverse to simplify. (The seemingly logical answer to this is to subdivide, but one report which I saw totally baffled the reader by subdividing English into eight sub-divisions, and mathematics into four.)

For all these reasons grades on their own, or merely supplemented with minimal conventional phrases, are surely inadequate. Yet they have their definite value in some cases according to subject, age, and function of report, in balancing the comment, by giving it, as it were, a bench-mark to which the comments can refer. One needs, therefore, to look at the advantages and disadvantages of each method of grading.

(i) Marks and (ii) Grades

Unstandardized marks are strictly meaningless. A parent has no means of knowing whether 65 per cent, for example, in geography is good or bad unless he knows the mark range for that subject on this occasion. Comparison between subjects ('Well, at least your English is better') is dangerous, as the mark range in the subjects may differ. Marks, whether for course work or an examination, can be shown to have these basic statistical flaws, yet schools still present them, and they have an entirely spurious air of certainty and clarity for parents. As one head states in his instructions to staff: 'Parents tend to attach undue importance to a mark without understanding the variations in marks that may occur from subject to subject.'

If marks are to be used, they must be standardized, probably in each subject according to a normal distribution curve (though there are objections to this also). Even then unrealistic significance tends to be attached to marginal differences, and it seems better to convert into, say, a five-point scale (A–E or 1–5). Many would argue that these also should be distributed so that 10 per cent have A, 20 per cent B, 40 per cent C, and so on. In many schools the actual marks are not revealed, but the emphasis placed on the broad grade alone.

(iii) Positions

Whether or not class positions are included obviously depends on the fundamental teaching outlook of the school. Only a rigidly streamed school, with a promotion/demotion system, would contemplate working out positions. This debate is too huge and fundamental for this book. Ranking in positions does seem to be dying out, and among the least informative reports are those which include a 'class position'. Recent analysis of ability overlap in streamed schools confirms the meaninglessness of such classifications.

(iv) Diligence Grades

Many schools retain these, presumably on the grounds that they balance the emphasis on marks or attainment grades. Many schools distribute these grades according to a statistical normal curve, though it is difficult to see why diligence in each teaching group should follow a normal curve. Can there not be whole classes that are making good effort?

If grades are to be used it is common sense that the report must have a clear printed description of how they are arrived at and the significance of the teaching group nomenclature to which the grades refer. This is not always easy to do; indeed it can be easily misunderstood within a school. Many reports attempt this description, but it is often sketchy and poorly worded.

My research suggests that as a profession we underestimate the clarity, objectivity, and effectiveness of words. Grades may be useful as subordinate checks, but they convey precious little as compared with a good verbal description.

(d) Comments

Report comments have often been mocked, and often still deserve it. The advice of many headteachers is sensible as far as it goes: 'For instance in the past I have come across "does little homework" and I cannot help feeling that a parent would be justified in asking why something is not being done about this by the teacher concerned.' This raises a number of points. The final suggestion is certainly true, but I should not like to see such comments banned for this reason. Similarly, it is sensible not to put a comment if a teacher really has nothing to add, but disappointing if after half a year's teaching there really is nothing.

Most comments are vague ('John has worked well', 'Rather weak', etc.), and the language is usually drained of any colour, concrete imagery, or personal phrases. This is presumably a result of poor format, hurry, and an emphasis on 'This is a formal document'. Years of experience seem to have knocked the descriptive power out of the teachers' writing. Effort and attitude, which from one point of view would seem elusive to pin down and almost undefinable, stubbornly remain the most commented on aspects of a pupil's progress. It is curious how reluctant teachers seem to be to analyse a pupil's growth in skills, concepts, or intellectual aspects generally. Yet broad moral exhortation seems a disappointing substitute for the essential professional art of skilfully pinpointing remedial steps. If you compare, say, two actual fourth-form reports in art, there is little doubt which is the most helpful:

> Angela works well.
> Vicky's textures are good, but her proportions need care.

Barked commands like 'Must improve!' are too common. Although it is no doubt true that 'more effort' would help, it is one function of a report to specify ways in which effort could most profitably be used. I have not seen many comments which seem to me as helpful as the following diagnosis of a first-year pupil's English:

> John enjoys the stories we read together, follows them carefully, and understands even the most difficult. He is lively and humorous in acting, joins in keenly in discussion, and asks questions that show a thoughtful reaction to language. So far his writing has been poor as it lacks ideas, is badly punctuated, and does not sound right when read aloud. His own reading also needs encouragement.

Such a description should interest parents and offer points on which they can work.

(e) Tone

I have already implied that the tone of many report forms – that is, their basic printed material – is impersonal. Indeed it is usually distant and often borders on downright rudeness:

1. Parents are responsible for the care of Report Books when in their charge.
2. The Report Book, after completion of each report, must be shown to the Parent or Guardian, and after being signed by him must be returned to the Form Master.

Others couch the information in the form of an introductory letter, and use language which is clear but also relaxed, courteous, and inviting. After the cold and crude bureaucratic instructions of many schools' reports it is a joy to read one which can say: 'We are pleased to send you. . . .' Am I eccentric in thinking that the tone of the printed matter should be warm?

(f) Feedback

Many schools expect evidence of receipt by the return of a small perforated strip at the foot of the report or some such device. An increasing number of schools, though, are doing what is now common in junior schools (see, for instance, *Should Parents Report Too?* by Lawrence Green, in *Where?* 2, Spring 1965), extending this to a request for full comments by parents. My own experience and the figures for response which I have seen from other schools suggests that this is a facility which is much appreciated. The system sometimes involves a special space on the basic report, but more successfully a separate sheet. The real trouble is that such comments are of value only if queries are answered, and comments seen by the teachers concerned. To do this requires administrative care, and not all schools can manage it, certainly not for every report.

Related to this is the linking of reports to parents' evenings. A few schools actually hand reports out personally at a meeting. An increasing number time meetings so that they follow the issue of reports, and thus the report provides a basis for the discussion.

Interim Reports

Whatever the frequency and spacing of regular reports, some form of intermediate communication is required. For one thing, too often a crisis explodes on parents in the form of a highly critical comment on a main report without any early warning signals. Many schools have developed routine documentation to assist in this process. In one boys' school, for instance, subject teachers have packs of duplicate slips on NCR paper:

MONTGOMERY OF ALAMEIN SCHOOL

May I draw your attention to the fact that your son's progress is being hindered because:

1. Homework is irregular in its return.
2. Homework standard is unsatisfactory.
3. General standards and approach to work are unsatisfactory.

Perhaps you would like to ring the school and make an appointment to see his Tutor.

Tutor...............................

Date:

A teacher who is worried posts the slips to the office, who send one copy home and the other to the tutor.

This system, and others like it, has the virtue of ease, but has a somewhat mechanical feel and can result in a shower of unrelated slips arriving at a home. Other schools have developed a system of communication out of the old homework books. Such books were often printed by schools with double page for each week, and ruled space for each day. Pupils were then able to use the book for noting down their homework. More recently the book has been seen also as the easiest and most readily available mode of communication between interested adults: subject teachers, pastoral figures, and parents. To achieve this the page has simply been re-ruled to allow space for remarks, and, most important, a place at the foot for the parents' and the tutor's signatures. The aim of such a device is to encourage the teachers to jot down special praise or details of any failure *at the actual time*. This is then seen by the tutor and parent fairly soon, and each can build up a picture of current progress.

Such systems certainly have difficulties: the central question is whether the effort involved is justified by closer participation and care of the pupils. It is at least open to question whether troubles can occur merely over the system itself, and the struggle shifts from caring over essentials to nagging over the books. If a school is not careful the neatness and completeness of such a book becomes the real goal, rather than recording the actual progress in learning. It is also obvious that unless parents have the purpose and working of the book explained carefully they ignore it or regard it merely as a piece of red tape. It is impossible to solve this problem completely, but here is an example of the inside cover of the homework record book of another school, called a 'Day Book', which has attempted to make the purpose of the book clearer to parents:

AN INVITATION TO PARENTS:

An important purpose of this Day Book is to help pupils in the sensible planning of their work. It has also a second valuable purpose: to help you keep in regular touch with the school.

1. On the facing page you will find your son's or daughter's subject **timetable, homework schedules,** and the name of his or her subject teachers, and tutor.
2. In the rest of the book a double page is taken for each week; the left-hand showing the actual work to be done at home, and the right-hand side the week's Merit Marks and Order Marks.
3. The central section of each page should be used for remarks by any of us who are concerned with the pupil's progress. **Please feel free to write replies, or mention other matters that concern you.**
4. More personal or lengthy matters, which would not be suitable for an open Day Book, should be raised in letters – to the subject teacher if only that subject is concerned, or, more generally, to the Tutor.
5. At the foot of each double page is a space for your signature: **please do not think of this as just a routine.** We ask you to sign it as a message to us that your son or daughter has completed the work as far as you can tell, and that you are satisfied that the assignments for the week correspond to the pattern shown on the timetable on the first page. If you are in doubt do not sign. Inform the Tutor of your doubt.
6. The Head of House will be pleased to see you by appointment concerning the general progress of your son or daughter if you will write or telephone the school.

PLEASE USE THIS DAY BOOK FULLY

I think that on overall balance such a device *is* worth the trouble, for, used sensitively and efficiently, it can help to keep parents in the picture and encourage everyone concerned to keep a careful and positive eye on progress.

Conclusion

I do not think that anyone familiar with recent research findings on parents' need for communication, anyone with children at school, or anyone who has considered the various aspects of a school's work would regard the majority of present school reporting systems as adequate by professional standards. On the other hand there now seems to me to have been a sufficient number of thoughtful experiments for a school to be able to devise a pattern and establish a procedure and tradition of report-writing that really does help the close pastoral care of pupils.

10 The Supporting Services

by Denis Ince

Until recent years the teacher in the English educational system carried out the pastoral side of his teaching role as best he could with whatever resources he could muster. Today, however, he is able to receive help and support from a wide range of agencies and organizations which are vitally concerned in the welfare of children of all ages. These bodies are many and varied. Some are national. Some are local. Some are statutory. Some are purely voluntary. But as all of them are involved in child welfare, they can be of great help to the pastoral organization of a school, and it is an important task to make sure that the school as a whole is in close working touch with these organizations.

This means that knowledge must be diffused throughout the school, clear procedures for contact and referral must be devised, and good personal contacts established. This unity of purpose can be splendidly seen already in such organizations as the Haringey Pastoral Association, which brings together teachers and workers from the whole range of supporting services for regular meetings on aspects of their work. A school-based example of this is the 'fraternal lunches' held at Mount Pleasant School, Birmingham. Once a month the school invites representatives of all the related organizations in the area for a lunch-time meeting at the school. The representatives include the clergy, housing and neighbourhood community leaders, the youth service, the police, and all the social services. On each occasion one gives a short talk on some aspect of the work.

The range of relevant supporting services is now vast, and Denis Ince surveys them and their possible contributions to the school.

The Educational Welfare Service

With the passing of the 1944 Education Act, local authorities were given new powers and responsibilities in regard to the welfare of children of school age. Subsequent minor acts in 1948 and 1953 specified the kinds of welfare services which were to be provided by local authorities, for instance the provision of clothing, footwear, school meals, and bus fares for children in need. With the increase in these welfare services for school-children, local authorities started to appoint educational welfare officers to organize these welfare services effectively. These new educational welfare officers gradually replaced the old school board officials, whose job was primarily one of checking up on children's absences from school.

Today, the educational welfare officer, though still having the duty of ascertaining the reasons for school absences, now has other duties which concern the whole welfare of children.

He must ensure that every child of school age is adequately clothed and shod, is receiving a school meal daily if family circumstances necessitate it, and is having free transport to and from school if he lives beyond a certain radius of the school premises. He also ensures that parents receive certain maintenance allowances if they are entitled to them in respect of their child or children. Thus the educational welfare officer is in a position to bring material benefits to the child to enable him to make best use of the educational facilities of the school. Because he has to visit parents in their own homes, the educational welfare officer is very well placed to act as a link or a bridge between the home and the school. Through his contact with parents he can develop a good *rapport* with them and through this he can discover their needs, their worries and their tensions.

Some teachers, especially those who have specific responsibilities for pastoral care, for example housemasters in large comprehensive schools, undertake home visiting to meet parents and discuss their children's progress (or lack of it) with them. The degree to which teachers should undertake home visiting is very much a controversial issue, and this is not the place to state the arguments for or against. It is true to say, however, that those teachers who have undertaken home visiting have usually found it to be a most helpful and rewarding experience, since it has given them the opportunity to gain revealing insights into the children they teach. Most of these teachers however, will also admit that at times they have met with parents who have been completely unco-operative and resentful of what they consider to be an interference into their private lives by the school. At other times too they have met parents who have been apathetic, who have cared little about their children's well-being and who have rebuffed their efforts to help them.

But the majority of teachers do not visit parents in their homes. It is to them that the educational welfare officer can offer most. He can frequently give teachers information about the home environment of children, and can often supply a clue which will suggest the reasons for a child's errant behaviour or erratic progress. And this is of immense value; for even today many teachers appear to be completely unaware of the very poor social conditions under which many schoolchildren live. This lack of knowledge is understandable, for, as Josephine Klein has shown so vividly in her book *Samples of English*

Cultures,[1] many teachers do not come from the same social backgrounds as the children they teach. Some teachers still do not realize that many school-children live in cramped and over-crowded houses or flats, where there is scarcely any privacy and a complete lack of personal possessions. Only recently the writer of this chapter met a fifteen-year-old school-boy who was regularly punished by his teachers for not doing satisfactory homework. These teachers obviously had no idea that the only quiet place the boy ever had to do his homework was on a park bench with the aid of a failing gaslight. The boy was too proud ever to admit this fact to the teachers.

Thus the educational welfare officer can do much to help the teacher to understand better the social needs and social handicaps of the children he teaches. In addition, the educational welfare officer can also bring to the attention of the school medical officer those children who may require special educational treatment, because of some physical or mental disability.

Though he can help the teacher in so many ways, the educational welfare officer is not always readily welcomed into some schools. This is perhaps because his role is not clearly understood. He is still regarded by some headmasters and staffs of schools merely as an attendance officer – someone who chases the truants and nothing else. This reluctance to co-operate with welfare officers may also be attributable to their present lack of formal professional training. (A local government committee is currently making recommendations for a professional training programme for educational welfare officers.) In many cases, too, the educational welfare officer has far too big a case-load for him to give a great deal of attention to every case referred to him

But much could be done by the schools to make more effective use of the welfare officer, by encouraging him in his role and making him feel more a part of the school. This could be done in a variety of ways, as is done already most effectively in some schools, by inviting him to participate in the various school activities and social events, for example, sports days, open days, PTA meetings, school visits and excursions, speech days, and prize givings, and also by inviting him to sit in on case conferences when housemasters and teachers discuss children who are causing anxiety and concern.

[1] Klein, J., *Samples from English Cultures* (Routledge and Kegan Paul, 1965).

The educational welfare officers can, with encouragement from the schools, provide an excellent service which will not only help the teachers to carry out their teaching functions more effectively, but which will have lasting benefits for the children.

School Social Workers

As has been shown in the previous section, the Educational Welfare Service is a steadily developing area of pastoral work with school-children. A few local authorities, however, have attempted somewhat more ambitious schemes and have developed a rather different approach. They have experimented with the idea of having a professional social worker attached to a school or to a small group of schools located close together. These professional social workers have been given a wider brief than the educational welfare officers, though they do undertake many of the duties performed by the welfare officers. Very briefly, the school social workers investigate (at the request of a head-teacher) all those cases where it appears that a child is not gaining any great benefit from school. Thus they look into cases where a child's behaviour is giving cause for concern, where a child is either constantly unpunctual or absent for no good reason, where a child appears undernourished or not properly clothed or shod, where the child is making very poor progress at school, where the child is suspected to be in moral or physical danger or suffering from neglect. This is by no means a complete list, but it does serve to indicate the kind of case that the school social worker might have to undertake. In certain areas where there is a high immigrant population the school social workers have the added task of making contact with the parents of immigrant children to explain to them some of the intricacies of the English educational system.

Schemes such as these have not been in existence for a great length of time, and as yet it is difficult to evaluate their degree of success. There is no doubt that they do provide a very useful and necessary bridge over the gap that exists between the teachers and the parents. In schools where they have been employed, social workers have been able both to supply much useful information to the teachers, and to give valuable help and support to the parents. But the scheme has had its short-comings. Because the social workers are 'attached' to schools and are not 'part' of them, the necessary *rapport*, understanding, and trust have not always fully developed between the teaching staff and the social workers. This has not been helped by the social workers' having a very high case-load, which has reduced still further the amount of time they can actually spend in the school, making and developing positive relationships with staff members.

The scheme also has tended to suffer a little from a lack of 'feedback'. For instance, the school would refer a case to the social worker, who would make a preliminary investigation. After this the social worker would perhaps pass the case over to the appropriate social-work agency for further necessary action by them. All this would take time, and during this period, the school would hear nothing. Weeks might pass before the school was informed about what action was being taken. In such circumstances it is inevitable that doubts and misgivings about the scheme would arise, and the teachers would feel some reluctance to refer further cases to the social workers.

As yet, only a very few local authorities are experimenting with this type of scheme. Undoubtedly this concept of pastoral care has much merit in it, and once these practical difficulties are smoothed out, the scheme should be of great benefit to both teachers and children alike.

Teacher/Social Workers

Another way of extending pastoral care is by means of the teacher/social worker. This is a concept developed by Maurice Craft (Senior Lecturer in Education at the University of Exeter) when he was Head of the Department of Social Sciences at Edge Hill College of Education. Very briefly, the concept consists of having in the school a qualified teacher, who has had some social-work training and who has special responsibility for organizing and carrying out pastoral care within the school. The teacher/social worker operates in three main spheres. Firstly he makes contact with the parents of children in their own homes. This is felt to be very important, since many parents for a variety of reasons do not make contact with the schools. Though the teacher/social worker will primarily visit the parents of children who are experiencing some type of problem or difficulty in the school situation, it is not intended that he should visit these parents exclusively. He will also make contact whenever possible with the parents of children who are making good or satisfactory progress at school. In doing this he is liaising with them, informing them of the work the school is doing, answering any questions or queries which the parents may have, and in general, trying to bring the parents to a closer and clearer understanding of the school and what it is trying to do for their children.

The second aspect of the role of the teacher/social worker is concerned with the early detection of signs of delinquency or maladjustment in children. Because of the nature of their training these specialist teachers will be on the alert for signs in children's behaviour which indicate that they are experiencing social and emotional difficulties which could lead to maladjustment or delinquency. By recognizing these symptoms early enough, and by taking the necessary remedial action promptly, it is hoped that many children will not be allowed to develop unhappy, anti-social or delinquent tendencies.

The third aspect of the teacher/social worker's role is that of developing close co-operation with the agencies concerned with the welfare of children. The teacher/social worker knows that he has only a limited amount of time, and limited resources, with which to help young people. Therefore he builds up good working relationships with the members of the other social-work agencies in the area, so that he can call upon them for their expertise and knowledge. He comes to know what each of these agencies can offer in the way of specialized help and support to children in need. Thus when he is faced with a particular problem he knows at once whom he can turn to for assistance.

Working in these three ways the teacher/social worker can be most useful to the headteachers and the staffs in schools. It has been argued in some quarters, however, that the roles of teacher and social worker are largely irreconcilable, as one role has authoritarian overtones, while the other puts great stress on a permissive attitude. While not denying this apparent dichotomy, the organizers of the Social Work Course at Edge Hill College believe that certain of the fundamental principles held by social workers are invaluable for the teacher in the school. The syllabus of the course reflects the importance placed on these social-work principles for students in training. Three of the main social-work principles which are stressed on the course are:

(a) Acceptance

Just as the social worker sees each of his clients as an individual worthy of respect and attention, so should the teacher view each child in the school as a unique individual whose behaviour reflects to a large extent the influences of the social forces around him.

(b) Non-judging Attitude

In the same way that a social worker 'accepts' his clients in a non-judging way, and concerns himself with developing a helping relationship with the client in order to help him to 'face up' to his problems, so should the teacher be able to develop significant relationships with individual children, so that he can help them through any social, emotional, or educational difficulties which may encompass them.

This non-judging attitude, implying as it does a high degree of *confidentiality*, may be difficult for the teacher to practise, especially in those schools which are organized in a highly formal or authoritarian pattern.

(c) Self-Awareness

Just as all social workers in their training are made aware of themselves as people, by coming to understand the bases of their own particular beliefs, motivation, attitudes and values, so also should teachers come to an understanding of themselves. The development of self-awareness is crucial if teachers are to be sensitive to the needs of the children in the schools.

Medical Services

The physical health and well-being of the child is central to his educational development. Obviously the child who is short-sighted, or the child who is partially deaf, will be hindered in his educational progress unless his particular debilities are recognized and attended to. Similarly, the child who is undernourished, or poorly clothed, or lacking sleep, or suffering from some medical ailment, will not gain full benefit from his time in school until these shortcomings are remedied.

The teacher, therefore, should always be looking carefully at the children in his charge to ensure that their physical health is good. If he has any doubts about it, he should refer the child through whatever channels have been established in the school to the School Medical Service, so that the necessary help can be obtained.

In most cases, where the physical health of the child is involved, the parents will be only too willing to assist the school in its efforts to provide suitable medical attention for the child, but it is by no means uncommon for parents to be apathetic or indifferent towards their children's physical condition. In such cases, it may be beneficial to obtain the help of either the school nurse or the health visitor.[1] Both school nurses and health visitors (who are often based at the school clinic) are usually trained to relate easily and in a friendly and sympathetic manner with parents. Also they are usually regarded by parents as 'persons wishing to help', and not looked upon with suspicion or alienation, as a teacher might well be in a similar situation. Two simple examples will illustrate this point.

One day, during a routine health inspection of children at school by the school nurse, a girl was found to have lice in her hair. As is the practice, the girl was excluded from school until her hair was found to be clean. When the girl went home at lunch-time and reported this fact to her parents, the father immediately rushed round to the school and created a disturbance. He blamed the school for the incident, ranted at the class teacher and the head, and refused to be placated. The school nurse, remembering this incident at a later health inspection when she had to exclude another girl for the same complaint, this time went round personally to the girl's home to chat with the mother, and explain in a simple way the reason for the girl's exclusion. She was also able to discuss with the mother the best ways in which to clear up the head lice. Because she acted in this way, the nurse was able to allay the embarrassment which the mother felt about the exclusion order, and thus she did not feel hostile to the school. She was also able to reassure the mother, to soothe her anxieties, and by means of her practical advice ensure that the girl made a very speedy return to school.

This is just a simple illustration of how appropriate liaison between the school and the home can do much to prevent upset and anxiety. A more dramatic example concerned a girl in a comprehensive school who was suffering from a cleft palate. The teachers in the school were concerned about the girl, since she was beginning to feel isolated from her fellow

[1] The role of the Health Visitor was defined by the Jameson Committee in 1956 as being a health educator and social adviser. She concerns herself with not only the physical needs of the family, but also their psychological and social needs. She is invariably a qualified nurse who has received some social-work training.

pupils. The school contacted the parents and asked them if they would let the girl have an operation to rectify the cleft palate. For reasons best known to themselves (either through indifference, indolence, or for other reasons), the parents did nothing to arrange for the operation to take place. The more the school tried, the more reluctant the parents appeared to become. Finally the health visitor was called in. She visited the parents, but she too was rebuffed. However, through her contacts with the local hospital she persuaded a hospital doctor to approach the parents and point out to them that they could have legal proceedings instituted against them for neglect if they continued to take no action with regard to their daughter's condition. This was enough for the parents, and they agreed to the necessary operation for their daughter.

It is in ways like this that the school nurse and the health visitor can be of great value to the teacher in the school. In some areas the health visitor, because of her frequent visits to the homes of children in the area, can help the school with information about social conditions or events within the homes which can have adverse effects on the educational progress of the children. It is important that the teacher should know when a child is faced with an emotional crisis in his home – for instance, illness of parents, unemployment of father, husband living with another woman, drunken parents, father a heavy gambler, father in prison, so that the teacher will not impose on the child a burden which he is not able to support.

Obviously a health visitor will not divulge this kind of very confidential information lightly. Therefore it is incumbent upon the teacher, who is concerned about the well-being of the children in his charge, to develop a professional relationship with the health visitor – a relationship which is based on mutual respect and trust.

Another important aspect of medical help available to schoolchildren is the School Psychological Service. This is a very important area since it is highly likely that the teacher will at some time or other come across a child who is experiencing emotional problems which are reflected either in behavioural difficulties or poor academic progress or both.

During the last forty years, since the late Sir Cyril Burt pioneered the first School Psychological Service in London, most Local Education Authorities have established similar organizations in their own areas. Though the form of the psycho-

logical services differs slightly from area to area the general
pattern of provision is similar. The School Psychological Service
is usually based in either a Child Guidance Clinic, or a Child
Guidance Centre, and its chief personnel are one or more
educational psychologists, a psychiatric social worker[1] or generic
social worker, a number of teachers skilled in remedial teaching techniques, and often a speech therapist. The service also
makes use of doctors skilled in the treatment of psychiatric
disorders.

If a teacher suspects that a child in his class may be in need
of the help of a psychologist or psychiatrist he or she should
discuss the matter with either the housemaster or tutor concerned or the headteacher. Then the permission of the parent
must be obtained before any further action is taken. This permission is vital, since very little can be done for the child by
either a psychologist or a psychiatrist unless the parents are
willing to be helpful and supportive. Obtaining the permission
and support of the parents can be difficult, for many parents
react with great hostility to any suggestion that their child
should be seen by a psychologist or a psychiatrist. Great care
and tact is always needed in such cases. Some headteachers
contact the parents by letter, inviting them to come to school
and discuss their child's progress with them. Others approach
the parents by visiting them in their own homes in the evening,
or whenever is suitable. This latter course is not always successful, since in the evenings the child himself or other people may
be in the family home and this can make discussion rather difficult. Another approach is for the psychologist himself to write to
the parents and invite them to visit the clinic to discuss their
child with him.

This is probably the least successful way, since parents may
become alarmed and very apprehensive to receive a letter
about their child on writing paper headed 'School Psychological
Service'. They may also experience practical difficulties in
finding and visiting the Child Guidance Clinic on a particular
date and at a certain time.

The generic social worker or psychiatric social worker can
do much to allay the fears and anxieties of both parents and
children. These workers can also do a most useful job in counselling parents who have a child who is in need of psychological
or psychiatric help. They can explain to parents the advisability

[1] A Psychiatric Social Worker is a social worker who has undertaken
special training in psychiatric medicine.

of special educational treatment for their child, they can explain the types of special treatment which are available, and they can explain in terms which parents can understand and accept what is meant by such words and phrases as 'educationally sub-normal' and 'maladjustment'. These social workers can also provide the teachers with much help and advice in their pastoral duties by sitting in on case conferences, when housemasters and teachers discuss the progress or otherwise of children who are experiencing emotional difficulties or creating behavioural problems. In listening in at these case discussions, the social workers (and the psychologists if they are available) can offer much practical help and guidance to the teachers.

The Social Services

Before the recent reorganization of the social services took place[1] each local authority had within its administration a Child Care Department. The child care officers who operated from these departments were often a source of help to teachers in the fulfilment of their pastoral duties.

Today, however, with the gradual absorption of most of the social-work agencies into local, unified, multi-purpose Departments of Social Services, the specific role of child care officer is being phased out. The duties and responsibilities of the child care officers are being assumed by generic social workers who, as their name implies, have a much wider brief than the former child care officers.

Children come into the care of the local authority in a variety of ways. They can either be committed 'into care' by the Courts as being 'beyond parental control' or 'in moral or physical danger', or 'in need of care and protection'. Or they may be in short-time care by the local authority because of some temporary breakdown in the family home – for instance the mother is ill and there is no one to look after the children. Children 'in care' will either be living in small local-authority homes or with foster parents, and many will have undergone traumatic emotional experiences. All of them will be under the general supervision of generic social workers. It is important that teachers work in close co-operation with the generic social

---

[1] The reorganization of the social services has taken place as a result of the implementation of the main recommendations of the Seebohm Report, *Report of the Committee on Local Authority and Allied Personal Social Services*, Cmnd 3703 (HMSO, 1968).

workers and establish good working relationships with them so that the children who are 'in care' will be able to develop to the full – mentally, physically, emotionally, and educationally.

The generic social worker has much important and confidential information about the child which will be of great value to the teacher. Likewise, the teacher will have much invaluable information which will greatly assist the generic social worker in his or her work. Although the school will be asked to supply periodic reports about children in care, there is a need for teachers and generic social workers to be in personal contact so that meaningful and helpful information can be passed from one to the other. (People are usually prepared to be far more frank in their speech than in their writing.) Confidential information will only be shared if there is mutual trust and professional regard.

There is one particular point to which it is likely that in future much attention will have to be paid by both teachers and generic social workers. This concerns foster-children who become eighteen years of age while still at school. As a child now attains his majority at eighteen, foster-parents will no longer be able to receive any allowance for a foster-child once he has reached that age. Thus it is possible that when this happens strain or tension could arise in a foster-home between foster-parents and the child. It is clear that there will be a real need for close relationships to be established between the teachers, generic social workers and foster-parents, so that the child may be helped through this possibly tense period of his life.

The Probation Service

Whenever a child on probation is attending school, the headmaster or housemaster will be called upon to furnish the probation officer with periodic reports (usually monthly) about the child's progress and behaviour. At times also the probation officer will visit the school to discuss the progress of the child with the teachers. These are useful occasions for developing good personal relationships between the probation officer and the teachers, for both have information about the child which will be useful to the other in their professional duties.

It should perhaps be mentioned, however, that some probation officers are reluctant to visit the schools, since they feel that their presence there might have an adverse affect on the child who is under a probation order. The probation officer can also be of use to the teacher in that he (like the health visitor, the educational welfare officer and the generic social worker) is in contact with parents in the neighbourhood and is aware of the family and social problems which face some of the children in the school. He can also be of practical help, in that he can often ensure that children on probation attend school regularly.

Juvenile Liaison Officers

Juvenile liaison officers are serving officers (either men or women) of the police force, appointed by chief constables in many large towns. Very briefly their task is to *prevent* children becoming delinquent rather than to apprehend children who have performed delinquent acts. By the very nature of their task they are most willing to co-operate with the schools, especially in cases of persistent truancy. This is because the persistent truant has been shown by experience to be highly likely to commit some delinquent or anti-social act. If the headteacher or housemaster brings to the attention of the juvenile liaison officer children who are persistent truants, the officer will usually visit their homes to discuss with the parents the reasons for the child's absences. In many cases this has proved to be a most effective method of stopping persistent truancy.

Because the liaison officers are very much concerned with the prevention of delinquency they are always ready to help the schools to organize displays and exhibitions concerning police activities. Much valuable work in this sphere has already been done in an effort to show children that the policeman is a 'friend' and not an 'enemy'.

The Careers Advisory Service

The Careers Advisory Service is designed specifically to help young school-leavers to find suitable employment when they come to the end of their period of full-time attendance at school. The careers officers who carry out the duties of the Careers Advisory Service are employed either by the local education authorities (in the majority of cases) or by the Department of Employment.

Though the careers officers are often hampered by too large a case-load, they can do much valuable work in helping young people, not only to find employment which is both suitable and satisfying, but to widen their thinking about the world of work. They are anxious to work in close co-operation with the careers teachers in the schools, and the school counsellors if such persons have been appointed. Where such close co-operation exists it is often possible to organize highly effective 'Careers Conventions', which are most helpful both to young school-leavers and to their parents.

The Youth Service

The youth leader is a person who often knows a great deal more about the needs, hopes, fears and ambitions of children than do the teachers in the classroom. This is because the experienced youth leader has been specifically trained to build up good personal relationships with young people – relationships based on trust, respect and shared confidences. Because the boy who goes to the youth club goes there of his own free will (no one makes him spend his time there), he is usually more relaxed, more open, and therefore, more likely to express his feelings than he is in the school situation.

Teachers therefore can learn much from youth leaders about the children they teach. Contact between teachers and youth leaders is usually very easy to make, for many youth leaders welcome teachers into their clubs as part-time workers, on either a voluntary or a salaried basis. Increasingly, too, many secondary schools are developing their own youth clubs or have youth wings attached to the school premises. In the latter case there will usually be a member of the school staff acting as youth tutor. Where this occurs, contact between the staff and the youth leader is relatively easy and straightforward to make, and much useful information about the children can thereby be exchanged.

Voluntary Organizations

So far, this chapter has concerned itself with certain statutory services which support the teacher in his pastoral role. There are also, however, various voluntary organizations which give valuable help to the teacher. It is not possible to mention all these voluntary bodies, but two very important categories come immediately to mind – the religious denominations, and the National Society for the Prevention of Cruelty to Children.

Throughout the ages religious bodies have been actively concerned (and still are in many cases) with the education of children and young people. Most ministers of the churches (of all denominations) are only too ready to help the teacher in any way possible with the fulfilment of his pastoral role. The minister is usually well acquainted with the people in his parish or area, and has probably seen generations of the same family come and go. He is thus well able to offer the teacher much relevant help and information about children who may be causing anxiety at school. He is also in many cases readily accepted into the family home, should there be strife and disharmony there. Teachers concerned with developing their pastoral role should try to develop close contacts with religious ministers in the area of the school, and elicit their support.

The National Society for the Prevention of Cruelty to Children, as its name implies, is very much concerned with the welfare of children. Though it does not have any formal contacts with the schools, at various times teachers have made use of its help and resources. Through informal and personal contact between NSPCC inspectors and teachers, parents whose children appear to be undernourished, or suffering from ill-treatment or various forms of neglect, including poor attendance at school, have received a visit from the NSPCC inspector. He has often been able to help and advise the parents without necessarily having to threaten them with prosecution. This type of help and support is much valued by teachers.

Conclusion

This chapter has been concerned with outlining briefly the work of some of the main social-work agencies through which the teacher in the school can receive help with his pastoral duties.

These agencies, and the people who work in them, are most anxious to be of help and service to children. Because of this they are also very keen to co-operate with the teachers. But it is *co-operation* they seek. They do not wish to be told by teachers what they may or may not do. If the teachers and the social workers can work together, then the promotion of good social welfare for children will be greatly strengthened. In the promotion of a good spirit of co-operation it is the teachers who should take the initiative. It is they who should make the opening moves. The teachers should welcome the social workers into the schools, should share confidences and trusts with them, and make them feel at ease in the world of education. If this can be done, then teachers and social workers can pool their resources, their skills, and their expertise, and thereby help children in every way possible.

11 Patterns of Care

Six case-studies

Introduction

Although considerable reference has been made in this book to school examples (and all have been drawn from actual schools), the approach so far has been analytic and generalizing. In this chapter I shall look at a number of schools' pastoral organizations in a little detail.

The case-studies are not intended to be studies of all aspects of a school, and they are certainly not objective evaluations. It is depressing how few school studies have been done.[1] I have chosen a few of the schools which I have myself visited for study. I have specifically enquired in as much detail as possible into the main organization, but, of course, my descriptions do not include all the aspects of the school. They concentrate on the factors I judge to be directly relevant to my discussions of pastoral work. The length of each section is related to the number of generalizing points I feel able to deduce from the pattern – and should in no way be taken as my judgement on the 'interest', still less of the 'success' of a particular school or its pattern. The schools are all anonymous, and certain details have been varied to make identification less easy. It is important to realize that in most (though interestingly not all) of the schools there was a continuous if jerky series of changes going on. If a description had been attempted at an earlier or later time a different picture might have been drawn.

I am very much aware that my visits were limited in time and depth. These are sketches from the outside, not thorough-going case-studies. Much of my information was gleaned from questioning senior staff, and no doubt reflects their views, which are naturally partial (although I was impressed by their honesty about difficulties and flaws).

The picture seen from inside might well seem different to that which struck me. Nevertheless, I found the visits thought-provoking, and the pictures seem to me to contribute to an understanding of the problems and possibilities of pastoral organization.

School G

School G is a boys' secondary modern school of 1,100 on the outskirts of a county town which has a high professional and

[1] The bibliography on page 229 lists all those available. The extended study by Elizabeth Richardson is the most valuable.

middle-class population. The area admits only some 15 per cent to grammar schools, and thus the intake of school G covers a large ability-range; it includes a wide rural intake as well as a high proportion of pupils from the town itself.

The present headmaster took over five years before I visited the school. He had been very dissatisfied with what he had found: a centralized administration in which all knowledge and power seemed to be with the headmaster alone; a seemingly slipshod and uncontrolled school, with little drive or pride; a fairly high level of corporal punishment; and only a mediocre relationship between boys and teachers. The system was the traditional one of form masters of streamed groups, and the form master normally changed each year. Occasional public canings and frequent bus-queue rows seemed symbolic of the régime.

The interest of the newer system, which had been worked out over a number of years, is that in the headmaster's words the school had 'replaced the cane by the tutor'. That is not to say that corporal punishment has been formally or completely abolished, but that knowledge of the pupil and a very close tutor–pupil relationship has made it seem a crude and inefficient sanction, and whereas before it was used widely and frequently, now it is used only centrally and rarely.

For subject teaching, as for first-year pastoral purposes, there are eight parallel mixed-ability groups, plus two remedial groups with differentiated curricula: one of 'semi' and the other of fourteen 'fully' remedial pupils. For the eight main groups a third of the week is spent on 'humanities', five periods on French, four on games and PE, two on music, two on art, four on science, and six on maths, which is setted.

Further up the school the timetable has 'separated out', with more subjects and more setting. The Middle School (Years 4 and 5) has open-access options for most of the pupils, but a third of the age-group, as it were 'below the bar', have less choice and more integrated studies.

The diagram on page 186 shows the main organization. At first glance the pastoral pattern may look fairly conventional, but there are a few significantly effective points.

(i) Reception and Primary-Secondary Continuity

First-year pupils are received into houses (basically two groups a house), but have a separate and defined 'first-year' life. Not only are their tutors' rooms grouped in a recognizable 'first-year'

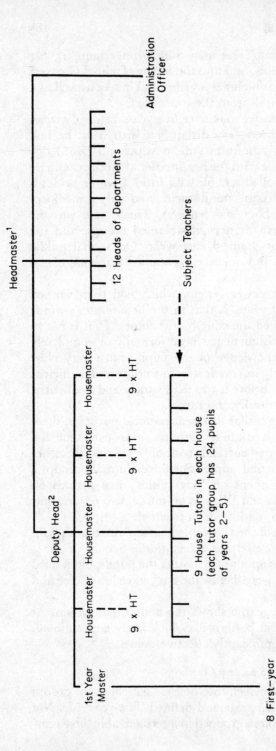

THE ORGANIZATION of
SCHOOL G

Administration
Officer

Headmaster[1]

12 Heads of Departments

Subject Teachers

Deputy Head[2]

1st Year Master | Housemaster | Housemaster | Housemaster | Housemaster

9 x HT | 9 x HT | 9 x HT | 9 x HT

8 First-year House Tutors + 2 Remedial Group Tutors

9 House Tutors in each house (each tutor group has 24 pupils of years 2–5)

[1]HM also curricular planning; timetable–making; examinations administration

[2]DH also day–to–day routine;

area of the school, but also their tutors are responsible in the first instance to a 'First Year housemaster', whose responsibility is solely for the entire first year. Thus he is a link-man, responsible for establishing relations with the feeder primary schools on the one hand, and for passing on his pupils to the main body of the houses. In rank he is equal to the main housemasters, and naturally takes his place at their weekly meeting.

In this year the 'remedial' pupils are withdrawn from the houses for registration and pastoral purposes into two special groups. It is hoped, and thought, that this provides an easier induction for them, and helps them to take their place in the normal house tutor groups from the second year onwards. It will be noticed, also, that this provides a strong element of the 'horizontal' which it seems every 'vertical' system craves. (cf. page 69.)

(ii) Method of Grouping

Pupils from one house are placed into the kind of vertical group described on pages 52-5, but in this case ranging over years two to five only. In this school the system of bringing these ages together is felt to help maturity and behaviour, break up homogeneously difficult adolescent groups, and create a network of different types of relationships within the small group. It is thought by School G that the sight of the needs of the younger pupil can help the older, just as the sight of the pupil/teacher relationship of the older can help the younger. Certainly I gained the impression that these groups were remarkably well socialized and easy to handle.

(iii) Size of Groups

The method of grouping in School G relates very closely to an important decision: almost all staff are pressed into a tutorial and almost every room, however apparently unsuitable, is used as a tutor room. The result is that tutor groups are only twenty-four strong – well below the national norm. Not every school can find the space for this, but it is a central act of faith in staff (as I discuss in Chapter 4) which permits a different style of 'tutoring', especially in relation to the vertical age range. The two decisions combine to encourage individual relationships rather than dragooning. Linked with continuity and good internal communications, this encourages an extremely close knowledge of the pupil by the tutor. All those points combine to warrant my describing the school, and this is the final feature which I should wish to highlight, as one of 'tutor supremacy'. It was, for instance, quite clear that the senior staff would not deal with a pupil unless the tutor had been consulted; indeed normally the tutor would actually be present.

One structural difficulty will be seen from the diagram on page 186. A subject teacher wishing to contact the tutors of his pupils potentially has all but the first-year tutors to contact. Even in a house-based mixed-ability second-year group, say, he has nine house tutors. A very convenient NCR slip system makes this easier, but no one would deny the drawback. The school is satisfied that it is a price worth paying for the undoubted advantages of this structure, but it is a high price.

School H

School H is an eight-form-entry mixed comprehensive school in a down-town area of a large city with a high immigrant population (60 per cent), and almost no 'grammar' children. It was created from an amalgamation ten years ago, and had moved into purpose-designed and generous buildings some years before I visited it.

Teaching in the first two years is largely in nine pastoral units per year, though groups are split two into three for science, and French is partially set in year 2. Year 3 sees full setting for maths, French, and science. A notable feature, related to language problems, is that of the seven periods of English in the first year: six are staffed with *two* teachers to each group. They work in the one room to a common, jointly planned programme. This is continued less lavishly, i.e. for only two or three of the English periods, in years 2 and 3. There was a fairly low rate of staying on into the fifth at the time of my visit, and the middle school offered open-access options to all but seventy ex-remedial pupils, who had a unified 'Social Education' course for most of the week. Thus the pastoral unit in the fourth year was not a teaching unit. This seems to be virtually impossible to achieve in any school offering choice, and it seems probable that it would be a poor ambition anyway, for by mid-adolescence the pastoral relationship is probably better cleared of teaching tensions. The very few sixth form pupils are largely doing repeat first-level examinations, and one tutor is able to have oversight of the small group.

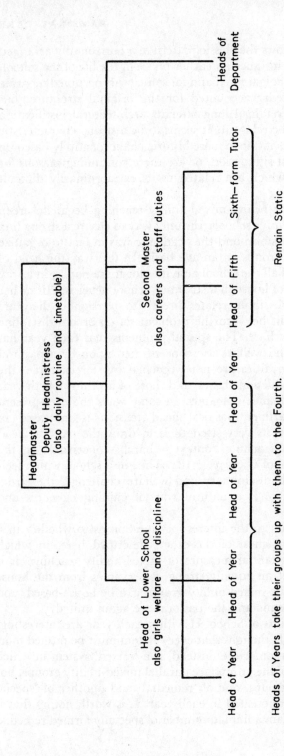

Headmaster
Deputy Headmistress
(also daily routine and timetable)

Head of Lower School
also girls welfare and discipline

Second Master
also careers and staff duties

Head of Year   Head of Year   Head of Year   Head of Year   Head of Year

Head of Fifth   Sixth-form Tutor

Remain Static

Heads of Department

Heads of Years take their groups up with them to the Fourth.
Normally 7 Form Teachers of mixed-ability groups (30)
plus 1 'Remedial' and 1 'Special difficulties' (15–20)

SCHOOL H

School H shows the classic pattern of a horizontally arranged school. In this instance an earlier phase in the life of the school, when it first amalgamated and for some years occupied separate sites, undoubtedly accounted for the original structure, but this has been retained long after its architectural justification has ceased to be relevant. It seems to be a strong characteristic of the school. Is it due to mere historic chance, entirely based on the earlier split-site period, or are there continuing reasons for its existence, which are related to its extraordinarily difficult intake and area?

It seems that before mixed-ability teaching began to creep into comprehensive schools, the only way to ensure a strong link between the pastoral and the academic was in fact to organize the linking of groups on an age basis. In this way the head of year is head of all the school activities for those pupils, in a way that the head of house in a streamed school never is. His or her concern with discipline relates directly to oversight of the year; there is no split between the problems of classroom discipline and general welfare. The special problems that each year has in guidance and welfare are concentrated upon by a pastoral head whose loyalties are not wrenched by, for example, the needs of his induction classes, and those of his third/fourth-year vocational guidance demands. In some ways the ever-present head of department/pastoral head tension is increased in this pattern, as its very strength is to draw the pastoral head into the class teaching context – barely conceivable in the pattern of School G on page 184. Thus in a school which feels it has a major disciplinary and welfare challenge, the struc- ture shown here is a natural way of gaining closeness and control.

This leads on to the interesting question as to whether in a school, such as most of the others described here, in which there is a substantial measure of mixed-ability teaching, it is possible to get an equally strong cohesiveness from the house system – for the mixed-ability groups can be house-based, and thus the academic and the pastoral are again united.

The base units of School H within each year are interesting, for it is so easily thought that every system must be pushed to its logical conclusion. Here, instead, is a 'mixed' system in which the majority of the groups are parallel mixed-ability groups, but two smaller groups, one of 'remedial' and another of 'special difficulties', are created in each year. It is worth noting that it is easier to retain a limited number of specially formed remedial groups at the tail of a batch of mixed-ability groups in an age-based linking than it is in a house system.

All age-based systems face the decision about the year heads: should they rotate – and stress continuity, or should they remain static – and stress expertise? (cf. page 67.) School H has put knowledge of the pupil first, and so year heads follow through as far as the end of the fourth year. It will be interesting to see whether the raising of the school-leaving age, with everyone staying into the Fifth, will lead to the Fifth being included in the rotation also.

My impression was that this school had about as difficult an intake as any I have seen. I am not in a position to assess how well it copes with its problems in all respects, but I did get the very strong feeling that it was one of the most relaxed schools I visited, with a very low level of tension. (The headteacher felt there was probably not as high an achievement as might be possible.) It seemed that this fact was at least to some extent accounted for by the close academic/pastoral links of the school.

School I

You can swoop down by car to School I, from the amazing hillsides of Derbyshire into a small valley town, its mill industries of the past now in serious decline. The school has the most staggering views in those directions of the distant areas from which a large number of the pupils come each day. Once a small-town grammar school, its old buildings still retained as one of the new comprehensive school's houses, School I is now a five-form-entry mixed comprehensive.

The diagram on page 192 shows the main points: vertical tutor groups for years 1–5 grouped into four houses. The curriculum is fairly standard, but has some significant deviations. The first years, for instance, start a six-period-a-week integrated humanities course, dubbed 'Man', as well as a two-period 'Personal Relationships' course. As pupils are taught in the first year in four house-derived mixed-ability groups, plus a remedial one for most subjects, there can be a little house liaison, but the vertical tutor groups reduce this by creating a vertical pastoral unit different from the teaching groups.

This is one of the most strongly house-oriented schools that I have come across. It has been found possible to group the

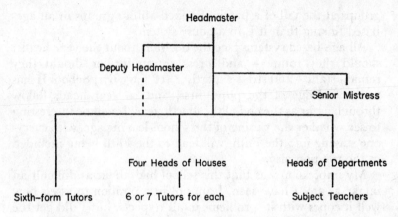

SCHOOL I, five—form—entry mixed comprehensive, small country town

tutor groups for each house in a geographical unit. The entire guidance and counselling system, including careers guidance, is based within the house, and the heads of these houses, each with about 160 pupils, have great power. They seem to relate almost directly to the headmaster. The senior mistress, although an admirable and sympathetic woman, therefore seems very awkwardly placed to me. The role of her predecessor was 'walking around telling girls off'. The present holder of the post has created a role which is something nearer to that of a counsellor for girls. The building up of the housemasters has also had a curious effect on the position of the deputy headmaster. His role is officially concerned with 'school matters', discipline, and staff and pupil duties. This creates conflicts, for there seem to be almost no 'school matters' left after the elevation of the house roles to such a degree.

It will be realized that having four houses in such a small school reduces the pupil case-load per house to well below the usual average – in this case only 160 pupils per house. This means that the heads of the houses really do know their pupils closely. It was very noticeable to me, though, that this produces another effect: each housemaster has only six or seven tutors for whom he is responsible. These really are small, closely knit working teams. Tutors stay with groups as long as possible, and it is thought that 'weak tutors are helped by the system'. They are consulted on all disciplinary matters, take a large part in careers advice, and are clearly well briefed and active, covering all aspects of school life.

It was interesting to see the school at lunch, in house dining-rooms. The vertical groups break up into 'family group' tables, with about eight pupils of all ages. A sixth-form pupil comes back, not only to her own house, but actually to her old tutor group. It is noticeable that in this pattern, the sixth-former who has separated off from the house to join peers feels a stronger continuing loyalty to the house, for there are still pupils *within* the house groups who have grown up alongside him or her. The 'return' of the sixth-former to supervise a table was not in itself unusual, but when combined with vertical groups provided a very real link, as the 'table' of six or eight were all not only from the sixth-former's house but from his or her own actual tutor group.

Heads of houses carry the responsibility for maintaining close links with the contributing primary schools. This is made easier by geographical recruitment to the houses. This means that each has a defined and reasonably limited catchment area and group of schools. Among the advantages of this system are the easy settling in to the school, the possibility of effective liaison between house and primary schools, and the practical point for a scattered community of making transport for house-based activities so much easier. However, there was some fear among senior staff lest the already limited social mix of the rural communities had been hardened by the restricted entry to the houses.

Some of the pastoral features of School I were clearly characteristic of its relatively small size – especially the use of heads of houses as senior staff. Other points might be of general application – especially the very small size of the houses.

School J

It would be difficult to find a greater contrast between the environment of School I and that of School J. Though mixed, and similarly putting great stress on a house organization, School J is hemmed in by blocks of flats, an anthology of every style since the 'thirties tightly packed together on the inner edge of a down-town area of urban decay. The school, originally built to serve the housing estate, now draws from a wider catchment area as the families in the original flats have grown up. Enjoying a very high reputation in the area, the school has an eight-form entry, which used to include a slightly higher proportion of able children than the proportion of the neighbourhood. The intake represents a considerable challenge, being intellectually far below the national average, with a very high proportion of deprived and disturbed children, and an immigrant population of some 25 per cent. In its foundation days in the 'fifties the school had been allowed by its LEA to 'attract' as good an intake as it could. It had therefore used the devices of strict control, academic emphasis, tight uniform policy, and a determined public image in its struggle for a 'good' intake. This achieved, the school found itself faced simultaneously with an increasingly rapid drift of the more able and ambitious families from the area to the outer suburbs of the town, and the authority's determination to impose a strict banding policy. Thus the school looked on with impotent bafflement while it received annually a smaller share of an anyway declining top-ability band.

Like many comprehensive schools of the 'fifties, this school was organized in 'houses' in a building which offered no possibility at all of any geographical grouping – not even any house heads' rooms. The school was originally tightly streamed, though by the time I visited it the middle school had worked the familiar changes from classes to courses, and in fact only the vestigial remains of even the separate-course system ('commercial', 'academic', 'technical') remained, as an open-access option system had gradually been introduced. Years 1–3, however, were still streamed, and Years 4 and 5 were grouped for pastoral care into course-biased groupings – for example A.1 for a particular academic range of option possibilities, or 'technical' for boys following a technical 'package' for sixteen of the thirty-five periods.

Thus the academic organization was very near the traditional streamed system, except that the fourth- and fifth-year pastoral groups had only a tenuous relationship with the teaching units. When talking to the senior staff about the pastoral arrangements, I was struck by an oddity of vocabulary that took a little time for me to actually identify. I realized that it was the phrase 'house system' that was puzzling me. Most schools will talk about 'houses', but this self-conscious use of 'system' indicated the structural fact that the house organization was indeed a separate parallel 'system' running up through the school but not actually part of the main structure, rather in the way the plumbing system of a building is recognizably separate from its load-bearing structure.

At this point it is necessary to look at the hierarchy in the diagram opposite:

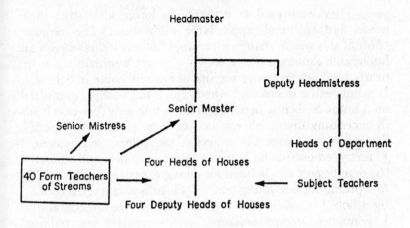

SCHOOL J

It will be seen that the structure is unusual in having at the top a head plus three – even in the pre-1971 Burnham days. In fact the senior mistress, who was markedly less senior than the senior master, was paid on an old Grade E. The senior master had evolved out of an old 'senior *house*master', i.e. one of the housemasters paid more for developing and co-ordinating the pastoral care. His predecesor had also been 'careers master', and this too was inherited as an integrated part of the role, but there was no specialist careers teacher. Thus the senior master was recognizably 'head of the house system'. There was not the close and direct contact between house heads and headmaster of school I, and the effect was to reduce markedly the status of the intermediate pastoral heads compared with that of those in other schools I visited, as well as to push the head to a position in which he was very much out of contact with the pastoral reactions.

The senior mistress was out on the usual limb. Girls' discipline, with house heads and deputies supplying continuity, seemed inevitably a matter of summary action. Like the senior mistress in School I, as she had nobody responsible to her, she had little effective place despite considerable personal ability.

The position of deputy head of house was unusual in that the holders of these posts had a real part in the house, having virtually complete responsibility for the pupils of their house in the first two years and the pupils of their own sex in the third year. They were paid at a markedly lower scale than their heads, but still had appreciable allowances. The positive effect of this was to reduce what would otherwise have been an intolerable case-load (i.e. $1,300 \div 4 = 325$ approximately) by nearly half, not far above the size of a whole house in School I. It is interesting to consider whether in a large school organized on a house basis it is better to achieve tolerably low case-loads by increasing the number of houses or by putting in deputies. There are two prime advantages of the system used by School J: firstly, co-ordination between houses is easier, and secondly, the deputy post can be used for giving experience of leadership to a promising but young teacher. One disadvantage shown up by School J is how to divide the work. Here the horizontal split I mentioned seemed unhappy, as a hand-over was required when continuity was desirable, and families could be split between head and deputy. A better arrangement, it was being felt, would be a simple division of cases vertically up the school, with the head of house having ultimate responsibility.

There is no vertical line under the deputy heads of houses on the diagram because there the line stopped: day-to-day care was normally in the hands of 'form teachers' of the streamed groups. They seemed, though, to have no structured part in the organization. This is a clear example of the way in which old models (the single-order school in which the form teachers refer directly to the headteacher) are awkward when used with other elements (in this case the separate 'house' system). The form teachers had no one to brief or lead them, and there was an uneasy and unclear relationship with the pastoral care of the house staff. They in their turn had inevitably drawn away from the day-to-day figures, who had no formal relationship with them.

The role definition of the senior staff that resulted from this gave considerable difficulty. The deputy was in charge of the timetable, day-to-day routine and cover for absent staff, and the old role of generally holding the fort. Academic records and responsibility went with this job. The senior master was in charge of boys' discipline, oversight of the house staff, attendance of pupils, careers, and extra-curricular activities. The senior mistress was responsible for academic standards of the first two years, girls' discipline, and various sundries like visitors and student teachers. It can be seen that a form teacher concerned about, say, a second-year girl looked to the deputy for home-work timetables, for example, the senior master for attendance, the senior mistress for disciplinary help, and the house for 'welfare'.

This is typical of the problems of running streams against houses, but School J had an unusually separated house system. The heads and deputy heads of houses were clearly devoted and extremely hard-working, and the advantage of the separatism seemed to be that just because they were not part of the power structure they were able to be counselling-orientated, and to take a deeply personal interest in the cases which came their way. It is doubtful, though, if this was a fair price to pay for severing the function of the intermediate pastoral heads from that of the daily pastoral figures. The cost could be seen in the press of pupils needing to see the house staff, and apparently in the way cases reached the house staff only when already acute: there was no integral relationship between the ordinary and the severe in school J.

School K

It would have been possible for School J to have developed an age-based pastoral system, but for School K, which I shall describe in less detail, there seemed no choice available to the headmistress. Its size, she felt, demanded an age-based arrangement. She had had considerable experience elsewhere before being appointed to start this new comprehensive school in an area that had little or no contact with surrounding districts. Her previous headship had been in a large but closely knit town. The area of School K was mainly rural, and had an immediate past of clearly defined tri-partite organization. The LEA had decided on a three-tier system with First and Middle Schools – all of which would feed into one very large High School at thirteen. This would be a sixteen-form-entry school: although it is not as big a school as School L over all, it has the largest form-entry of any I describe – twice as large as School J.

Thus the school had a very strong horizontality imposed on it. The headmistress, who had a year to plan it and at that stage had very little opportunity for consultation, soon dropped the idea of houses, for she argued that there would have had to have been too many. Teaching was to be largely in pastoral units, and she reckoned ten houses would have been needed. Instead she devised a simple but striking pattern to give large year-groupings as the main split, each led by an intermediate

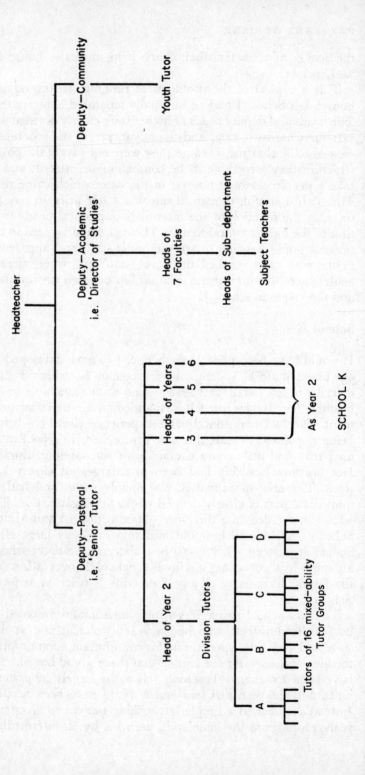

Headteacher

Deputy—Community
— Youth Tutor

Deputy—Academic
i.e. 'Director of Studies'
— Heads of 7 Faculties
— Heads of Sub-department
— Subject Teachers

Deputy—Pastoral
i.e. 'Senior Tutor'
— Head of Year 2
— Division Tutors
— A B C D
— Tutors of 16 mixed-ability Tutor Groups

Heads of Years
3 4 5 6
As Year 2

SCHOOL K

pastoral head, but with 'Divisions' breaking down these further, and the division tutors interposing a responsibility layer, which is very unusual. This system would seem to have certain disadvantages of communication, but on the other hand it creates small intimate cells which seem ideal for staff training and support. The five year tutors (i.e. for years 2–6, as the age-range starts at thirteen) look to the deputy head as senior tutor. It is interesting to compare this arrangement with an alternative solution I found in a sixteen-form-entry 13–18 urban down-town school. There the head of year was supported not by a subordinate hierarchy, but by *two* teacher-counsellors in each year.

One of the most interesting points about School K is that it has two main planning committees: the Academic and the Pastoral. At first glance this arrangement may seem to militate against the close liaison which I have argued is so necessary. However, the year tutors sit on the Academic Committee alongside the faculty heads. The Pastoral Committee also has interesting representation. Its constitutional composition includes as well as the year tutors and senior staff, one elected 'lay tutor' (i.e. a tutor with no division or year responsibility), the youth tutor (whose responsibilities are directed towards evening activities), and the head of the PE and Recreation Department. Thus it will be seen that pastoral decisions have a broad base of views – especially as heads of faculties have the right to attend, and frequently do.

Here, then, is a pattern which takes the base-unit, a mixed-ability, single-age group, as the centre of the school for pastoral and teaching purposes, and has constructed the rest of the organization to give the tutor the strongest possible support. The tutors have been given considerable responsibility, with their division head as a leader and co-ordinator. It was this headmistress who, when she studied my list of tutor roles on page 75, spoke approvingly of her system requiring the label 'Tutor Rampant'! The possibility of a counsellor had been considered, but the school reckoned that the case-load would have been well over 300, and that this would have been too high. Even more forceful, apparently, was the argument that the function was anyway embodied in the role of the tutor.

Working in a largely inward-looking community, and with no separate youth provision, the school has been able to look actively towards community work, and the youth tutor and a deputy with broadly 'community' responsibilities devoted considerable and successful time to this.

School L

Like School G, School L stood high on the outskirts of the suburbs, approached by tree-lined roads, and surrounded by well-kept suburban detached houses. This, though, was the largest of the schools I sampled: an annual intake of 360 boys and girls (thirteen-form-entry), spanning the ability and social-class ranges fairly representatively, and drawn from a cross-section of housing, from local-authority flats to professional houses. Another house-based school of the 1950s, with no architectural attempt at even house heads' rooms, the school had six houses (interestingly reduced from the eight with which it opened), each led by a house head at an old Scale C (new Scale 4) only, and with a deputy (who had no extra pay) of the opposite sex, with only minor responsibilities.

The diagram shows that this was one of the few schools to use its senior assistant in other than a sex-based discipline role. Since the early days of the school (though not from the start), the triple hierarchy had clear functional divisions, and it seemed that even in the pre-1971-Burnham days the ex-senior assistant, called 'Director of Studies', despite his lower salary had broadly equal status with the deputy head:

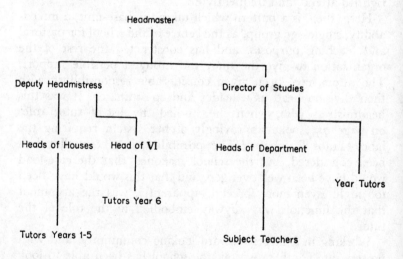

SCHOOL L, thirteen—form—entry suburban mixed comprehensive

Originally a streamed school that had worked through banding to a large measure of mixed-ability teaching, the school had consciously chosen mixed-ability house-grouped single-age tutor groups as the basic pastoral unit, as a way of combating the stratification of ability streaming and to produce some social cohesion. The tutors (two per year per house) are clearly part of a team led by the head of the house, and there seems a high level of delegation of concern down to the tutor. On the other hand it was admitted that the leadership of tutors was harder than the departmental leadership of the same people as subject teachers. The level of tutor involvement in, for example, subject choices for the middle school was impressive, but there still seemed a tendency for action at the more senior levels to be taken with less reference to tutors, than, for instance, in School G.

The heads of houses each had additional responsibilities in the school, some of them (such as 'staff duties') of a markedly disciplinary nature. This gave them power and standing, especially as this was associated with the delegation down to tutors of much of the routine administration. This status was said to have both advantage and disadvantage. The voice of the pastoral view of the school was clearly heard at the top – through, for example, weekly meetings chaired by the headmaster, but also attended by the Deputy, Director of Studies, and Head of Sixth Form. On the debit side, though, co-ordination and leadership of such powerful figures was difficult.

Unlike in School J, there was a separate 'careers master' responsible for liaison with the Careers Advisory officers and for specific advice. Although he endeavoured to work closely with the houses, it was noticeable that to a large degree his existence drew off vocational discussion from the rest of the pastoral system. He worked almost entirely directly with pupils, and only rarely with other teachers.

But this was not the only aspect of guidance that was substantially drawn off. Educational guidance was pinpointed in the third-year preparation for fourth-year choices. It is an interesting example of the need in 'vertical' schools for 'horizontal' components that under the Director of Studies were year tutors. These were chosen from the house tutors (and paid extra). Their original brief was to look after promotions and demotions in the streamed situation, and to keep an eye on streams (which, of course, cut across houses and departments) that needed attention as a group. The most important of these was the third-year tutor, dubbed 'course adviser', who assisted the Director of Studies in educational guidance. At the time of writing this major educational guidance was moving back into the hands of the house heads and their tutors, with the year tutor merely as co-ordinator of the supply of information and the collation of figures to establish suitable set sizes.

This, however, is at the heart of the problem of house organizations: their relationship to the academic structure. School L, while seeming to have a marked split at the top, also had an even fiercer one at middle-management level. A horizontal division of responsibilities among senior staff is in most circumstances more likely to produce equality of concern among all. In School L the split at the top was more apparent than real, as it appeared there was very close integration of planning. Heads of houses, on the other hand, had handed vocational guidance to the separate careers master, and very much educational guidance to the year tutors and course advisers co-ordinated by the Director of Studies. Discipline and welfare remained with the houses. This split was sharpened by the complexities and ingenuities of the curriculum-planning and timetabling, which were not devised in consultation with the heads of houses. The recruitment to those posts was markedly different to that of the heads of departments, and, to seal the divorce, weekly planning meetings were run separately for both groups of middle management.

Here was a hard-working and well-run school, with very good co-ordination between the day-to-day tutors and their team leaders, the heads of houses, but with a sad division between those teams and the curriculum organization.

12 Conclusion
The Quality of Care

Many people would look at the sub-title of this volume with apprehension, for to some 'organization' is not compatible with 'real' care. Some believe that 'care' is too human and personal to be organized. Others feel that merely to organize is probably itself sufficient. Still others, as I mentioned in the Introduction, consider that care can be overdone and that the current pre-occupation with it is unnecessary. The thesis of this book is that what we have come to call pastoral care is the essence of a school, and that the structuring of the school is the key to its success. In this final section, I shall draw the strands together to attempt to define the other ingredients in the elusive 'quality of care'. I shall also describe some aspects and procedures which have not fitted in conveniently earlier.

The bogey of the inhumanity of efficiency needs scotching first. There are still many who believe that you cannot be 'efficient' if you are to offer true care, and there are even those in schools who would claim the reverse. They flaunt their inefficiency as a badge of the real quality of their care. The hard fact is that efficiency is useless unless it is humane and sensitive – indeed it is hardly truly efficient unless it is. But humanity is not possible in schools without efficiency. In many a complex comprehensive school insufficient pre-planning is put into, for example, mastering the timetable complexities. The head of department who said of one school 'Much of the first three weeks is taken up with slotting pupils into classes' was echoing a dismal truth of wider application. This sort of muddle hardly helps humanity or close pastoral care.

It is important also to face the criticism of size – and its presumed impersonality. I hope that the possible procedures which I have outlined show that size is no barrier in itself.[1] Undoubtedly the fear of size still lurks on the outskirts of the educational scene. In fact the larger comprehensive school frequently has a far more detailed knowledge of the individual pupil than the smaller, supposedly more intimate one. This kind of statement is not susceptible to proof, but anyone who has had the opportunity to compare schools will have realized that size is a less significant criterion than organization and spirit. The Chief Inspector of a very large rural and urban authority declared that the most detailed and knowledgeable reports on pupils who required referral to outside agencies in that authority came from its largest schools. A parent whom I know well and had boys at both a large comprehensive and a

[1] Two important research studies have confirmed this. (c.f. Ross, 1972.)

traditional-sized grammar school found the former knew the boy at that school much better than the latter. This seemed to be a result both of the atmosphere of the smaller school, which clearly felt boys were interesting only when they were 15-plus, and also of the organization. At times of family crisis the smaller school was totally unable to respond; the larger had the necessary past information and a real relationship with the family embodied in a definite pastoral structure.

Those who speak of the fear of size make much of the atmosphere of a school. This is an intangible matter to which it is difficult to give adequately sensitive attention in a book of this sort. However, all the procedures which we have surveyed are compatible with a warm personal atmosphere – indeed the efficient procedures allow and foster warmth. Even love must have method.

It is tempting to say that the manner of the head is the starting point. Certainly, even in a large school the manner and style of the head is a major contributory factor. Patrick McGeeny's quotations on page 134 illustrate this. I know of one whose characteristic image in my memory is of his fumbling down in his pocket for change for a small boy's dinner ticket, and another who is remembered for standing six feet away from any door and looking for a pupil to appear to open it. It is not unrealistic or 'soft' to say that the courtesy and warmth of senior staff, together with their attention to personal details, are important factors in the pastoral atmosphere of a school. There is a mini-thesis to be written on the wider implications of talking over a desk or from an easy chair to easy chair, or of showing someone personally to a door, or dismissing them from a chair of office. Such differences are extremely important in their effects on any organization.

Those who fear size overlook one important advantage of size: like the collegiate university as opposed to the small isolated college, or the market town as opposed to the tiny village, the community is made up of various interlocking circles of knowledge and relationship. As a pupil comes to the double swing doors of the larger school, he may well meet an adult whom he does not know. That is not impersonality, but life. The adult may be a teacher, parent, student, visitor, workman, or inspector. How the two get through the door is a significant experience. In the smallest secondary schools I fancy I detect a very definite routine acceptance of others, and very few real greetings. In the large school, as in the large

village or small town, there are *real* greetings from pupils
to teachers who they know well but haven't seen for some
time.

A final important point about size. One of the unnoticed
aspects of the abolishing of selection was that in the separate
'selective' and 'non-selective' (which is, of course, merely a
typically British euphemism for 'selective' according to less
acceptable criteria), even the most sensitive and thoughtful
teacher and school could hardly help having norms at the back,
or even the front, of their minds. Because of the extension of the
continuum, the comprehensive school can less readily have a
norm, or type pupils against the expected pupil 'material' (that
awful give-away label). Instead, the large school is obliged to
think of individuals, and must organize for individual help with
no expectation of norms. A headmaster of a three-form-entry
grammar school was able to say quite confidently that a
particular problem had not been spotted 'because we don't
expect the boys to have those kinds of troubles here'. It is
inconceivable that the school with the full range of pupils could
become so complacent or so blind to reality.

The Community

Two sections of the book have looked explicitly at the technical
problems of relating a school to its parents. More generally,
though, the book embodies the notion that quality of care for
the individual pupil is most likely to flourish within a school
that has a coherent attitude to the world around it. I hope this
has come through even in such technical sections as the structural discussions of school organization.

The school has been seen in England as in a tradition of
'specialness'. This puts it apart from many other institutions,
and gives it an 'authority' that expects to rule on everything.
It is arguable that the further-education tradition of 'account-
ability' has much to offer to schools. The tradition of 'the school
versus the rest of society' is deeply entrenched – but surely
fading. The metaphors of the battlefield come too easily to the
lips. In the past the school has been a kind of fortress – turning
blank walls (except for the occasional brandishing of a flag or
trumpeting of success) to the hostile outside world. It is important to realize that this affects not only its external relationships – the drawbridge was rarely lowered – but also its
internal relationships: leaders and men operated as in a state

of siege, with peremptory commands, routine drills, and blind obedience!

This view is fading, and many authorities are building and planning schools which have specific community relationship. Perhaps the best known of these is Laurence Weston, opened in Bristol in 1959 by Cyril Poster, who had a vision of a 'community school'. Such devices as a shared library, evening-session activities arranged by an Activities Organiser, a Community Council, and a play centre symbolized the involvement. As Cyril Poster said[1]:

> There were some early misgivings about the presence of adults on the school premises. It was felt that they would be a distraction to the pupils, or that the adults would be disinclined to use a library that required them to mix with numbers of young people. From the outset no difficulties were encountered and a free and natural use by young and old was achieved.

Not every school will want or be able to sense its immediate local community as specifically as such a school, but all will have more vigorous and understanding pastoral care if points of contact with the community are devised. It is important, for instance, to look carefully at the physical provision for parents and visitors. It is difficult for many teachers to realize how the special *school* atmosphere can reduce a competent visiting adult to insecure nervousness, especially if he or she is a parent worried or just uncertain about his or her child. The actual entrance to many schools is difficult to find – frequently side doors look inviting but prove to be locked, and main doors when found offer an array of apparently equally openable glass doors cunningly arranged so that only one actually yields to a push. Foyers frequently confuse, with no clear decorative or architectural feature to indicate the correct next direction. Notices are either absent or embody the favourite school word 'report': 'Visitors should report here'. The actual reception is often by an overworked clerical assistant, who has to drag herself from typewriter or telephone switchboard to answer the enquiry. All that accomplished, the visiting parent all too often then has to wait in awkward, unprivate, and uncomfortable conditions.

It is essential to close and practical relationships with parents to survey the approaches to the school, to make sure that routes are clear, notices sensible, reception areas practicable and comfortable, possibly with pupils' work on display as a point

[1] For a full account, read *Community School* by Cyril Poster (Macmillan, 1973).

of interest. The receptionist's skills are as necessary in the secondary school office as in the plushiest business concern. Obviously such arrangements, or the links with parents described in Chapter 8, are not in themselves sufficient, but they can assist a change in attitude towards making the pastoral care related towards the community.

Attendance at School

Obviously the sheer fact of whether pupils attend school or not, and if so how regularly and according to what pattern, is a basic pastoral concern. Teachers have always accepted that frequent absences are a clear sign of a pupil's not succeeding, and they probably also readily admit that irregular attendance is a bad sign for the future. However, they may not realize how serious it is. In the first place it is much more widespread than is often thought. The National Child Development Study has shown that the average child loses a full year's schooling by the time he or she is fifteen! These figures (based on 17,000 children born during a single week in 1958) show both class and regional differences. If 'good' attendance is an average of no more than half a day off in a week over the year, the following differentiations are clear:

Home Social Class	Percentage of 'good' attendance
Middle class	87
Skilled and semi-skilled	79
Unskilled	71
Regions	
South, South-West and North Midlands	85
East and West Riding and North West	78
Wales	76

Such averages disguise the actual effect of absences. A very interesting study by Shirley Hase into the attendance pattern of matched pairs of children in an urban comprehensive school[1] concluded that 'Irregular or broken attendance, especially one to two odd days or half days each week, appears to be more damaging to educational progress than longer periods away.' This study showed that a much higher absence level was associated with the pupil in each pair who did not succeed in school – even though he or she was of the same measured ability on entering. Here are two typical pairs from the study:

[1] 'Is Under-Functioning in School Related to Non-Attendance?' *AAM Journal*, Volume 22, Number 2 (Summer 1971).

Gregory and Paul

Gregory was in Group 7[1] for mathematics, English and verbal reasoning on entry. He started in the eighth stream, a remedial group, but was promoted to the seventh stream in the second year. He did a technical course in the fourth and fifth years and struggled towards CSE at a modest level. He nearly lost his nerve about two months before his examinations but was encouraged by all and persevered to the end of the fifth year. He had an elderly stepfather and an older stepbrother and sister. He was a cheerful, obedient, likeable boy who had some standing with his peers because of his excellent ability in swimming. He made the most of his limited ability and was away 57 half-days in four years.

Paul entered too with Group 7 assessments. He began in the ninth stream and continued in a remedial group until the end of the third year. By then he had lost the equivalent of one year's schooling and inevitably left with no qualifications in the summer of his fourth year. He was the middle boy of five children, all of whom were or are bad attenders. The parents have been summonsed from time to time to little effect. Paul suffered from asthma and frequent colds, usually supported by medical certificates. His health improved during the last year and he won a SA Gold Survival Award. His attendance, however, in that year reached an all-time low.

Absence in half-days					Total
Gregory	1st yr	2nd yr	3rd yr	4th yr	half-days
	1	20	25	11	57
	equivalent to 5 weeks lost.				
Paul	93	103	84	108	388
	approximately 38 weeks lost.				

(It will be seen that Paul had virtually one year's absence in the four he was nominally 'at school'!)

Sarah and Jennie

Sarah on entry was in Group 5 for mathematics and verbal reasoning and Group 6 for English. She was in the seventh stream until the end of the second year, when she was promoted to the sixth stream. She followed a commercial course in the fourth and fifth years leading to CSE and RSA, in which examinations she had some success. She is now completing a further year of commerce in the sixth form and is a school prefect. She was often commended for good work and a responsible attitude in the junior forms and was very helpful at organizing others. An only child, she has had a very successful career at school, always supported by a good family background.

Jennie was placed in Group 5 for mathematics, verbal reasoning and English. She was in the sixth stream for the first three years, and in the fourth year started a two-year commercial course, but left at the end of one year. She had a brother who had also left at the earliest opportunity. Her interest in school started to wane in the second year, and her absences reflect this. There were no consistent physical reasons for her absence: she was simply uninterested in any aspect of school life.

[1] Pupils were divided at 11 + by the head into seven groups, of which 7 was the lowest 5 per cent.

Absence in half-days   Total
Sarah   1st yr   2nd yr   3rd yr   4th yr   half-days
                     13   12   23   8   56
                     equivalent to 5 weeks lost.
Jennie   2   22   36   51   115
                     equivalent to 12 weeks lost.

These cases show that absence leads to further absence, as the pupil finds the return to the thread of activity less and less easy. As Shirley Hase summed it up in her study:

> The attendance record of each child requires constant and time-consuming attention by those responsible both in and out of school. When this supervision is insufficient or irregular, children can become lost to school, and, although sometimes present physically, mentally they have opted out and leave at the earliest opportunity. The cumulative effect of non-teaching increases the absenteeism through fear of being 'shown up' in class. . . . A difficult home background and lack of parental involvement are often said to be the cause of educational under-functioning but . . . it would appear that poor attendance is an under-estimated component of failure.[1]

An important NFER survey which attempted to identify the characteristics that made certain pupils 'allergic' to school certainly confirmed that 'allergy to school . . . is associated with . . . a greater incidence of truancy and delinquency and absences are condoned by parents'.[2] The mean difference in half-days absent in one year between the 'most industrious' and the 'least industrious' in comprehensive schools was that between 19·40 and 38·43, and the differences were especially great in social classes 2, 3 and 4. In other words pupil allergy to school was more differentiated by absenteeism in these social classes than in the highest and lowest. (The researchers comment: 'Perhaps home for the worst-off children is, on occasions, a less palatable alternative than school'.[3]) The assumption in the Hase study is that strenuous efforts to combat absenteeism will produce a greater level of success and thus in its turn a better level of attendance. Of course it is probable that to some extent at least, the poor attendance was a *sign* of the malaise rather than a cause of it. Possibly even the enforced regular attendance of Paul, Jennie, and their like would not have significantly raised their school performance. To some extent the NFER figures erode the hopes of the AAM survey quoted on page 208, in that by analysing the differences between

[1] ibid., page 19.
[2] Sumner, R., and Warburton, F. W., *Achievement in Secondary School* (NFER 1972), p. 35.
[3] ibid., p. 36.

allergic and successful school pupils by different type of school and by different social class, it has been possible to show that absenteeism does not correlate with allergy and failure equally for all types of pupil: a high or low social-class pupil can be allergic on a reasonably good attendance rate!

It is probable, though, that the greatest effect of absenteeism is felt by the 'middle allergic' pupils, and that a school with a high tolerance of absenteeism is feeding their allergy. There is a fairly high proportion of such pupils in inner-city schools, and a careful absence-check policy is essential.

The starting point is the definition of the role of the tutor, already discussed in detail in Chapter 5. He must regard the register and any pupil diary or record book as a creative (and not merely bureaucratic) routine. The vital point is that every absence not covered by a note should be followed up by a routine letter home from school. It is too easy for 'progressive' teachers who would go along with my plea for the flexible, friendly, and adult styles of relationship to see such a suggestion as retrograde. I should myself insist, however, that it is no kindness not to create a clear framework. The parents must know, and the worst fault of pastoral organization is to let absenteeism build up before it is spotted and the pupil and parent faced with it.

In a large school with a weak absenteeism policy, substantial differences between the rates of absence in different groups will become apparent. Indeed the regular monitoring of absence patterns is an essential tool of the pastoral head: substantial variations from group to group need looking into. Such care by pastoral heads will be reflected in the care the tutors give to their pupils. Complementing the attendance register, the school must also consider attendance at lessons. One of the difficulties arising from complex and varied group timetabling is that it is possible to overlook absence from particular lessons. A policy to check this starts with care over pupil lists. In most schools the lists of registration units are well kept, but in many, set lists are more haphazard. A workmanlike policy of heads of departments' issuing set lists before term is essential. Teachers must have a method of checking regularly. This does not necessarily mean 'calling' the register, but during the teaching session it is almost always possible to note the absentees. This in itself helps – for pupils respond to the knowledge that someone knows and has noted whether or not they are present. The next need is a simple system for subject teachers and tutors to be able to compare registers. Even in the small school, especially in urban areas, pupils are often marked present in main registration but do not turn up in lessons. The simplest method is a series of small chits, supplies of which subject teachers can keep in their 'mark' books. These can then be sent to the office for the checking of any doubtful absentees.

The pupil whose parents think he is at school should be at school. For many pupils a lax school attitude, policy, and procedure is an opportunity that may lure them into difficulties. A vigilant attendance policy allows warm and rewarding pastoral care to flourish.

Internal Communication and Records

The tradition of record-keeping and internal communications which is still dominant in secondary schools is the one that grew up in small, relatively homogeneous schools in which there was a high degree of continuity in terms of low staff turnover, curriculum repetition, and, usually, local social stability. This tradition relied on staffroom conversation, casual over tea or more formal at staff meetings, in which a single pupil could be reviewed by the entire body of teachers. Significant information, it was hoped, spread naturally, and enquiries by a particular teacher could easily be directed to the most knowledgeable colleague, who was 'just over there in the corner'.

I have indicated on a number of occasions in this book that I do not consider that this worked anywhere near as effectively as nostalgia strenuously protests that it did. A form teacher in a small girls' grammar school told me that it was virtually impossible to gather information on a pupil; she felt hampered, and regretted the lack of a system. A headmaster of a three-form-entry school told me: 'It's difficult to get co-ordination in the staffroom. A teacher doesn't know a boy's not doing his work in other subjects, and the Form Teacher doesn't hear until the end-of-term report.' In fact the end-of-term report was virtually the only method of gathering and disseminating information. Both these teachers were already feeling that even in the small, traditional, supposedly intimate organization, more formal procedures were required.

But even if it were conceded that such informal recording had been adequate, it is clearly not so in the comprehensive school. Apart from the growing social instability in urban areas and the depressingly rapid staff-turnover that is becoming the norm, the ambitions of the kinds of schools which I have described depend on records and formalized communication. In fact the effectiveness of all the care systems which have been described depends on the thoroughness of internal communication and record systems. It is important to realize that such systems are not passive receptacles. Efficient internal recording prompts action by collating and bringing significant facts to the right person's attention. Good record-keeping does not merely paper over staff changes, it also facilitates staff collaboration. It is, of course, vital to have full records at any moment when an intermediate pastoral head wishes to have additional support or advice from the senior staff of a school, or when the school needs to enlist the help of the supporting services described by Denis Ince in Chapter 10. The kind of regular pupil *Daybook* or *Diary* described on page 162 is a valuable part of the overall scheme.

In considering a record system there are four essential characteristics which need matching to the individual school's needs: (*a*) the form; (*b*) the siting; (*c*) the availability; and (*d*) the question of confidentiality.

The legal requirements of 'basic educational and medical' information obviously does not give sufficient guidance, any more than do the Youth Employment Service Regulations of 1950. Hayes and Hopson, writing from the point of view of careers guidance,[1] distinguish two main types of recording systems: cumulative and anecdotal. The second they see as 'supplements to cumulative records and not substitutes for them'. They are notes by teachers on any incidents in which they are involved that they consider significant. Their basis is the individual moment, and they do not attempt to generalize or to interpret.

A cumulative record in the view of Hayes and Hopson has the following requirements:

1. It should be unitary, i.e. not a multiplicity of reports.
2. It should if possible be self-explanatory. However, a manual of instructions should be provided so that teachers know how to process information and interpret it.
3. All those who are to work with it – headmaster, teachers, careers teacher, careers officer, and school counsellor – should co-operate in its design. This also involves training new teachers in its use.

[1] In Hayes, J., and Hopson, B. *Careers Guidance* (Heinemann, 1971), Chapter 9. This is an especially good section of the book and worth studying for further detail.

4. It should minimize the amount of clerical work that teachers are called upon to do.

5. Information should be recorded only if one of the designers can visualize a situation in which this might be used to make a decision. American investigators have found that as much as 40 per cent of the information on exhaustive cumulative records was ignored by counsellors who opted for certain key items.

6. It should show a complete picture of past development from the primary school upwards. At the secondary level this is not always possible, or if it is, the information will not be in the form required for continuous presentation, and may have to be summarised.

7. As it is designed for constant reference for diagnostic work and individual decision-making, it should be kept in a place readily accessible to all teachers.

8. All information should be free of evaluative comment and consist only of objectively reported facts.[1]

The last point is disputable. Certainly the tradition of British record-keeping involves subjective judgements, and I should not like to attempt to prevent these. It will be seen from their first point that they favour a 'unitary' system. This links with point seven, for many schools have a multiplicity of records stored in different parts of the school. For instance, one school had academic reports in the school office, health records in the medical room, and anecdotal and pastoral reports in the year head's rooms. Unification is essential.

There seem to be three main formats: card, book, or folder. The first tends to be too small; the first and second both seem inflexible, and do not permit other papers, such as letters from parents, to be kept together. My experience is that a single folder is best, provided, however, it contains standard printed and ruled cards. The cards then hold regular review information, and the folder also brings together copies of reports to parents and other documents. The skilled user soon makes his personal selection of points as he scans the card, and then flicks through the papers to pick up additional points.

Careers Guidance

The third of the interlinked trio of guidance (personal, educational, and vocational) has been discussed from various points of view throughout this book, notably in Chapters 1, 5, and 7. A school needs a coherent policy of vocational guidance which it can express through a variety of procedures. In the world of eclecticism, with its apparently unlimited range of

[1] Hayes and Hopson, op. cit., pp. 102–103.

choice, the adolescent is worried about whether he will fit –
even get – any job. In the world of such *apparent* choice this
worry extends to all – perhaps especially the ablest, who have
been considered by too many of us teachers as not needing
advice. The prolongation of dependence, which I described in
Chapter 3, has made this baffled worry a major strand of
adolescent life. In a differentiated and mobile world even the
meaning of work is difficult for the young. Simply they have
seen very few jobs. There are fewer jobs for them to see around
the home, television is not noted for portraying working
environments, and fathers often work in distant parts of the
town in incomprehensible jobs, the point and feel of which are
far from clear to their children. As Jerome Bruner puts it:
'The industrial revolution took the worker out of the home. Its
technological elaboration has made his work away from home
increasingly incomprehensible – to the worker himself, and
surely to the uninitiated young.'[1] Even more fundamental than
that, of course, the nature of *work*, not just particular types of
work, is less easy to absorb. In *The Experience of Work*[2] I myself
have tried to provide an anthology to help pupils explore the
relationship between life and work, and to share the experience
of work and what it means to the individual.

Meeting these needs, and relating the answers to the growing
individual, are major pastoral tasks of the school. As Leona
Tyler puts it in what is still the best book on counselling:

> Whether one is interested in the improvement of our society through
> the wide use of the talents of its citizens or in the development of the
> individual through the utilization of his most promising potentialities,
> the relationship between people and their jobs is of crucial importance.[2]

Despite the rising unemployment and the undoubtedly continuing trend that will make education for leisure vitally important,
this is still true. There is very considerable doubt about whether
we are succeeding at all well in this way. We can, of course,
never fully satisfy all customers. Indeed, it would be limiting if
we could, but there is evidence in plenty that in the field
of preparation for work we are markedly under-achieving.
Our 'report' would be: 'Tries occasionally, and can produce
good work, but does not have a grasp of the whole subject
and is easily distracted.' A comparison of the objectives of

---

[1] *Immaturity, Its Uses, Nature, and Management,* a lecture to the ICA, reprinted in *The Times Educational Supplement* (27 October 1972).
[2] Longman *Imprint* Books, 1973.
[3] Tyler, Leona E., *The Work of the Counsellor,* third revised edition
(Appleton-Century-Crofts, 1969), page 132.

fifteen-year-old leavers and their teachers revealed in *Enquiry 1*[1]
is one measure of the failure. Even in our cherished Sixth Form
there is evidence of dissatisfaction when you talk to students,
and a similar enquiry amongst sixth-form students found:

> While the majority (87%) of pupils felt that some of their teachers
> knew them well enough to give useful advice on how to improve their
> work performance, the proportion dropped to two-thirds for advice
> on careers and to just over a quarter for advice on personal matters.[2]

How can we look at careers needs in the school? The central
dilemma of school organization, which I referred to on page
84, is 'specialization' versus 'dissemination'. A junior school
is largely a disseminated organization – that is, responsibilities
are shared throughout the entire staff. A secondary school,
however, is essentially specialized, and it is noticeable that
junior schools are now introducing a marked, though small,
specialist element. As a school specializes, so it risks limiting the
breadth of impact. As it disseminates, so it risks losing knowledge and expertise. Vocational guidance is so important a part
of the school's pastoral task that it cannot afford to suffer
either of those risks. Both styles must be combined. In practical
terms that means that every teacher – especially in his tutorial
capacity – must have some knowledge and responsibility, but
that an expert is essential within the school to guide all.

In some ways I am against the concept of careers advice at all,
because it implies separation – all advice for the young should
be careers-orientated in that it should always have future life-
styles as a reference point. This means that as pupils join the
secondary school there should be a work ingredient in a natural
way in such subjects as science, mathematics, French, geography, history, and especially some of the newer 'humanities'
integrations. Later in the school, specific teaching must be
included. This should not be left later than the third year, and
might even start in the second. The teaching should certainly
not be aimed at the rapid choosing of a job, but should be a
more widely-based preparation for life.

Such lessons might be interpolated only occasionally in the
early years, perhaps by the careers teacher in tandem with the
regular teacher of another subject, or the tutor himself.

The basis of such lessons is simple. As the DES booklet for
teachers puts it:

[1] Schools Council, *Enquiry 1: Young School Leavers* (HMSO, 1968), p. 43.
[2] Morton-Williams, R., *et al.*, *Sixth Form Pupils and Teachers*, Volume 1
(Books for Schools Ltd. for the Schools Council, 1970), p. 232.

Many pupils often have very limited ideas of the ways in which adults earn a living and some of their ideas clearly reflect family prejudices which have never been questioned. A very proper educational task is to impart knowledge, to examine prejudice, to widen mental horizons, and there is ample scope for schools to educate their pupils through discussions about the way men and women earn their living in the adult world.[1]

These lessons would lead up to specific courses in years four and five. Here work would be studied in a carefully planned sequence, from self-assessment and types of work to modes of choice, methods of application, ways of training, and the work routine. Such a course would include information on further education and further qualifications as well as a broad look at the satisfactions and difficulties of work. All this would be seen as preparation for choice, for, as Pat Daunt remarked, 'Students cannot choose what they do not understand or understand what they do not learn.'[2]

A number of schemes for such programmes are given in chapters 11 and 14 of Hayes and Hopson's *Careers Guidance*. The organizational problem starts with the debate between separate lessons and integration. Integration helps to make sense of the study, but risks diluting it and not using expertise. Separate lessons tend, like all minority-time subjects, to sink without trace. That is why for the earlier years I recommended that the careers teacher should visit sessions in other subjects or in tutorial time. For the fuller programmes a special team is needed. At Woodberry Down School we have devised a 'Common Core Course' which avoids the minority-time trap of a small driblet of teaching every week. In it 'work' is part of a wider personal course which moves from simple psychology to sociology, and includes ethics, sex education, and understanding of the local and national community. Work is thus set in the matrix of life, and the course includes a study of advertisements,[3] the press, and society, and includes visits, films, visiting speakers, and discussions as well as research, reading and writing. The pupils in sets of twelve have six periods of 45 minutes each a week for a half term in the time usually given to English. The team, after half a term of preparation, move from group to group as the year goes on – thus the pupils have an

[1] Department of Education and Science, *Careers Guidance in Schools* (HMSO, 1965), p. 7.
[2] Pat Daunt, Headmaster of Thomas Bennett School, Crawley, 'Learning to Choose' (*CRAC Journal*, May, 1969).
[3] cf. my course for pupils *The Question of Advertising* (Chatto & Windus Educational, 1973).

intense flood rather than a series of driblets, and the teachers have the chance to repeat, and thus improve, their course.

It is important that the whole curriculum of the school is 'open' enough to permit real careers choice. This means that it must not differentiate too early or too fiercely. Arts and crafts, for instance, should not be taken away from the clever; languages should be neither imposed nor denied; sciences should not divide into separate disciplines in a way which creates barriers; there should not be sexual splits in the curriculum. Above all pupils should have access to a range of subjects. In the middle school this is particularly true of an option pattern, and there should not be 'package deal' options which once chosen tie the pupil, together with groups similarly motivated, to homogeneous vocation-orientated courses. (The vocational element can certainly be present, but the non-vocational subjects need not be linked: 'Building boys' need not do 'Building English'. Nor, indeed, should they even be 'building boys'. The vocational element should not dominate.)

But knowledge is not enough. The central question that I started by quoting from Erikson[1] needs answering in subject and career terms. As Leona Tyler aptly analyses it:

> A boy of 16 may be handed a test profile that makes perfectly clear what his pattern of ability is like, be informed about occupations in which such abilities are more applicable, and yet be totally unable to grasp the significance of these facts because of the network of ambitions, family expectancies, and self doubts in which he is enmeshed. It is more than information he needs; it is wise counselling.[2]

Counselling by tutor, intermediate pastoral head, school careers teacher, and visiting expert are all needed. However, when the pupil is coming up to making option choices in the third year, we often overplay direct career reference by linking choices too specifically to careers. Any teacher with experience of this process will know the situation when a pupil declares: 'I want to be a hairdresser. Should I give up history, or geography?'

In the early comprehensive days the desire to persuade pupils to stay on beyond the fourth year naturally led to a careers emphasis in the third-year choices. In fact, though, the emphasis should be on *subject* choices in this middle part of the secondary phase, when much of school should be directed to preparation for choice. The pupils are primarily choosing from

[1] cf. p. 2.
[2] Tyler, op. cit., p. 4.

the school menu, with one eye on self-knowledge and another on the needs of the walks of life.

Despite the emphasis I would put on careers work, indeed perhaps because of it, I am myself against a separate 'careers department'. Many experts would disagree. The Chairman of the National Association of Careers Teachers sees a *Department* as the organizational key:

> Secondary schools today are very often large and have a hierarchical career structure. In this situation it is absolutely essential that there should be a properly staffed and structured careers department, with a head of department paid on the same salary scale as the heads of the other major departments. Otherwise a teacher who specializes in careers work is going to have limited opportunities for promotion compared with the teacher who specializes in history or geography. Mr B. Hartop of the University of Durham Institute of Education told a recent Conference of the National Association of Careers Teachers that he believed that Careers education will have been fully accepted in schools when the head of the careers department can face the head of the English department in staff meetings on fully equal terms.
>
> The reason that it is essential to have a senior head of department for careers work is because this is the only way to get representation on the higher echelon committees of the school at which school curriculum and finance are discussed. Only in this way can the head of careers affect the curriculum (getting guidance sessions on to the school timetable), or get an adequate share of the capitation allowance. What some schools do is to appoint a head of department and then expect him to work wonders by providing guidance services for hundreds of pupils on his own. Just as there is a team of teachers in the academic departments, so there needs to be a team in the guidance department.[1]

I certainly understand the writer's motives, and sympathize with the experience which must have led him to demand a department with all its paraphernalia and staff. However, I consider it unnecessary in a school that places this work centrally, as I have described. Anyway I prefer schools run by function, not hierarchy, and resources dispersed by reason, not power politics. Harry Dawson's arguments strike me as being for tactics that should not be necessary if the overall strategy of the school is right.

I would rather see a 'Careers Adviser' who has, as it were, the whole school as his team, and the entire building as his department. (Capitation can be allocated as required.) Such a person advises all from the careers point of view. Here, as an illustration, is the job specification for the Careers Adviser at Woodberry Down in 1972:

[1] Dawson, Harry, 'How to Check the Careers Provision in Your Child's School', in *Where*, No. 67 (March 1972), p. 90.

Careers work should enable young people to choose a life rather than simply a way to make a living. This is rapidly becoming an accepted truism, which serves to remind us that in our culture one's job decision is 'the most identity-fixing choice that is made'.

If this is accepted, a number of principles follow for the work of a school:

   (i) 'Careers Guidance' is a very wide and deep process;
  (ii) It ought to permeate whole sectors of a school's pastoral as well as academic work, even though it surfaces recognizably only at key moments;
 (iii) It will certainly need to be a team operation;
 (iv) The process must be a continuous one, spanning the whole of a pupil's time with us, and not merely focusing on the decision moments. To do that is mere 'crisis counselling' without the necessary preparation;
  (v) Considerable knowledge and experience should be available in the school.

In Woodberry Down the careers work is co-ordinated by the Senior Master, who is Head of Upper School. It is, however, 'disseminated' guidance, rather than centralized in that the Houses, and their staff, are responsible for vocational guidance as an integral part of their personal and educational guidance, and have a vigorous tradition of careful careers advice. In addition the Second Deputy and Curriculum Co-ordinator will have a responsibility for developing the curricular implications of the philosophy outlined earlier.

This team is now strengthened further by the appointment of a Careers Adviser to develop all aspects of the work in a fully integrated way. The term 'Adviser' has been chosen deliberately to stress that it is certainly not envisaged that all the work should be centred on one person: this would be neither practical nor desirable. She will have the following basic responsibilities, though this list is not meant to discourage initiatives in any way that might help the pupils have a fuller and clearer idea of the implications of work:

(a) To build up his or her own knowledge by reading, courses, visiting, etc., so that there is substantial expert knowledge of all facets of careers guidance in the school;
(b) To advise the Senior Master on guidance procedures;
(c) To advise the Curriculum Co-ordinator, and with him the Heads of Departments, or the possible work implications of curriculum studies, and of the teaching of the necessary background for pupils' career decisions;
(d) To undertake direct class teaching of careers work;
(e) To liaise with the Authority's Careers Officers, and schedule their visits and interviews to the school (including the possibility of regular 'surgery' hours);
(f) To assist the Heads of Houses with advice as necessary;
(g) To brief staff (e.g. House Tutors) on aspects of careers advice as necessary;
(h) To be available to pupils either by referral by the House Staff or self-referral for specialist guidance;

(i) To maintain full information sources, display and access (in consultation with the Librarian);

(j) To advise the Librarian on the stocking of the Library with work in all its aspects in mind;

(k) To extend and maintain liaison with any outside bodies, employers or individuals that are relevant.

Of course, the Careers Adviser requires a good Headquarters, interview room, waiting room, book and pamphlet store, display area, telephone, and so forth. It is a good idea, though, to make sure that his work is not physically cut off. The Library should have links. The school bookshop should be an ally.[1] Classrooms should carry displays.

Good pastoral care must involve sensitive vocational guidance growing out of skilful teaching about the world of work We should not talk about 'the place' of careers in the curriculum, but about the need to make the curriculum fit the world – and that means permeated with the experience of work. We should not talk about 'vocational guidance' in isolation, but see it as permeating the whole of the care system of the school.

Partnership

The sociological and psychological evidence which I presented in Chapter 3 pictured a young person maturing earlier, staying at school longer, having many of the values of the adult world, but rejecting authority. His or her central concern is with self-identification, and even in the world of automation a concern with work is central. I have explored organizational ways of meeting such a young person's needs. The central question on which the earlier sections have focused is how it is possible to provide ways of caring and guiding, without cramping imposition, and how it is possible to give the necessary leadership and control without the pupil's loss of dignity – one of his most favoured possessions today. The key, it seems to me, is in our recognition of the maturity of the secondary pupil, especially from the third year upwards, but even in years one and two. The maturity may be partial; it may have lapses; it may be intermittent. But it is there. Our refusal to award the accolade of the recognition of the start of adulthood is based on an overplaying of adolescence, and our forgetfulness about adolescence in other cultures and other times. We lost a great

[1] See Davies, Marilyn, 'Paperback Bookstall', in *The Practice of English Teaching* (Blackie, 1971).

deal in putting full-time education in the place of the appren-
tice system. It is noticeable that when we do not grant adulthood, the adolescent endeavours to seize it, often choosing the
wrong handle. This is clearly seen in the habit of smoking. A
government survey showed, depressingly: 'There was little
evidence that schools that were doing most to discourage their
pupils from smoking were having much success either in the
short term or the long term.'[1] Any school-teacher could guess
the force that drives the young smoker to cigarettes. As the
report went on: 'Smokers differ from non-smokers in wishing
to achieve a certain kind of social maturity in the teenage
world outside the school';[2] 'Smokers seem impatient to grow
up.'[3]

No wonder that a child psychologist, speaking to a conference
at the Royal College of Physicians, suggested:

> We shall not touch the hard-core of the problem by moralizing or
> terrorizing. The moralistic attitude to drugs, drinking and smoking can
> never hope to succeed. By surrounding adolescents with the trivia of
> childhood we are inviting them to snatch at symbols of adulthood.
> Dr Hemming said adolescents smoked for 'support'. There was no hope
> of removing the support unless another was provided. 'If they are
> attracted to smoking because it seems to confer adult status, it would
> help if we drew them at an earlier age into closer participation in adult
> affairs. We have given them the vote at 18. Would it not be logical to
> give them the dignity of being treated as adults from, say, 15?'[4]

Many teachers might regard that as too glib by half, but if they
cast their mind to their observation of the secondary-school
pupil in his or her home – where they are far happier and more
relaxed than we teachers like to think – they would realize that
these are ingredients of maturity that do not show at school.
The much-vaunted residential experience, valuable as I agree
it to be, is often quoted as 'educating' young people into
maturity, and the far greater sense of pupils on various residential schemes is often commented on. I maintain that the
experience *releases* what is already there more often than it
inculcates a new quality. It takes the more relaxed residential
experience to show what school masks. Perhaps if the ideas of
Chapter 8 were more common, and teachers talked more often
and more fully to parents, this would be more generally realized.

The concept of 'institutional neurosis' has been accepted in

[1] Bynner, J. M., *The Young Smoker* (HMSO, 1969), p. 31.
[2] ibid., p. 57.
[3] ibid., p. 62.
[4] Reported in *The Times*, 1 June 1972.

the medical profession at least since John Russell Baron's simple
and convincing booklet in 1961.[1] His work showed that what-
whatever might have been wrong with a mental patient on
admission, this was eventually overlaid by a condition that was
a direct result of the environment of the institution itself. Is not
the same true of schools? Their setting, the problems of movement, the difficulties of wind-swept playgrounds, the approaches
forced on teachers by the pressures of school life, and other
well-known school features all combine to create the adolescent state we all deplore. In these conditions true pastoral
care is difficult. Working with other adolescents (between 14
and 21), John Bazalgette has stressed the need for 'working
alongside adults' – the one thing that our schools make difficult:

> The problem which has emerged as central has been to create ways in
> which young people can take a place in adult society, not creating
> special young people's areas in which adults can find a place, but
> finding ways of helping them to be alongside adults and to take a full
> part in an adult situation. To create special settings for young adults,
> no matter how enjoyable or well thought out these might be, is simply
> to split young people off into a world of their own, inevitably a world
> of unreality.[2]

However much we might agree with that, it is difficult to see
many ways in which school can be made into 'an adult situation'
even less how pupils can spend very much time 'alongside
adults'. Yet the basic thesis is clearly right, and every effort
must be made to increase the status of the pupils and work
towards a feeling of partnership.

One of the simplest ways is through the time-honoured but
usually rather weak School Council. Here is an acceptable
method of partnership. Why, though, have the efforts of most
schools in this modest form of participation and partnership
had so little success? Firstly, too large a range of ages have often
been asked to debate together; secondly, committee and
secretarial expertise have not been available; thirdly, little
real scope for action or decision has been allowed the Council.
My solution is to split the Council horizontally into, say, three
separate forums, with powers to convene plenary sessions as
required. Secondly, to give each a suitably chosen teacher as
'Permanent Secretary' – charged not to express his own views,
but to facilitate the Forum's expression of views and to assist
in passing these on to the correct quarters in the appropriate

[1] Baron, John Russell, *Institutional Neurosis.*
[2] Bazalgette, John, *Freedom, Authority, and the Young Adult* (Pitman, 1971).

way. I have found this a very successful move. Lastly, real issues must be debated by the bodies, and their recommendations acted upon wherever possible.

More than that, the staff must share a common attitude towards the pupils, one that will show itself throughout the day, that really conveys caring, and thus involves respect. Pupils of all ages feel the many slights of the day more than we recognize, and cherish their memories of co-operation and relationship. The matter is well summed up by this, which though from sixth-formers speaks for many in its views on the role of the tutor:

> The great majority agree ... in their dislike of either extreme, on the one hand a restrictive authoritarianism and on the other that permissiveness which seems to them synonymous with lack of interest and indifference.[1]

There is a myth that we have such a relationship, at least at the top of our schools. I doubt it. The public boarding schools sometimes do, but translated into state day-school terms, the situation is very different. Sixth-formers certainly do not feel their treatment is as equal as we feel it is – and they will say so in confidential conversation. That same research, for instance, reported: 'Some 10 per cent had detected no significant difference: "still the lord and master attitude", "they still don't listen".'[2] Frank Musgrove has spoken of American investigations as being in line with studies in this country 'which have shown adolescents belittled by their elders, regarded as a separate, inferior, and even threatening population, exposed to contrary expectations and demands from the general body of adults, and consigned ... to an ill-defined no-man's land'.[3] The Schools Council Sixth-Form survey found a core of discontent:

> 15% remarked that they were not treated in an adult enough fashion, and that they did not have enough personal contact with staff or that there was a lack of communication between staff and pupils.[4]
> Although the majority recognised differences between their sixth forms and the rest of the school, two fifths would have liked to see even bigger differences. The changes most generally desired were greater freedom of behaviour, less discipline and more privileges. Also

[1] Edwards, Tony, and Webb, David, 'Freedom and Responsibility in the Sixth Form', *Educational Research*, Vol. 14, No. 1 (November 1971), p. 50.
[2] ibid., p. 47.
[3] Musgrove, Frank, *Youth and the Social Order* (Routledge and Kegan Paul, 1964), p. 105.
[4] Morton-Williams, op. cit., p. 102.

wanted were better relations between staff and pupils with more adult
treatment from and closer contact with members of staff.[1]

Early leavers, when interviewed and asked to compare work
with their past schooldays were withering about relationships:

> You have more freedom – at school you can't talk or eat in class or
> anything. It's silly things really, it isn't as if you want to talk all the
> time or eat but you could if you wanted to and nobody would shout
> at you. At work they act towards you as though you are more grown-up.[2]

It is this aspect of schools that I have found most objected to
by the less able. One fourth-year leaver being interviewed by
his headmaster after having been caught smoking, replied to
the question 'Is there anything you like about school?' by
noting, 'Mr X's maths lessons, Sir.' Mr X was an efficient old-
time maths teacher. After a moment he added, 'Mr Y's drama
lessons.' Mr Y was an *avant-garde* teacher, who was vigorous,
but quite unlike the first. 'Well,' enquired the head, reasonably
rather puzzled, 'what is it you don't like then?' After a pondered pause, the boy replied simply, 'The school, Sir.' It may
be objected that such remarks are the perpetual moans of the
young. I do not think that this is entirely so, nor that they will
be expressed when something nearer human partnership is
available.

Nothing that I have written need be taken as a recipe for
'softness' or 'anarchy'. As a fourth-year boy in Leeds said:
'Strict teachers are for the best: they don't need to punish.'
By a 'human partnership' I do not envisage intellectual equality: the intellectual apprenticeship of the student is perfectly
compatible with a closer equality of relationship. Furthermore,
I am not arguing for abdication. I have had many complaints
from sixth-formers when for one reason or another a particular
teaching or pastoral relationship has slipped into laxness. One
group, for instance, complained rather ironically that their
own democratic discussions were getting nowhere because their
tutor was not keeping them in order! A subtle balance is recognized, and it is certainly not laxness that the students themselves demand. Research corroborates the impressions:

> The Form Master might be thought to represent a degree of pastoral
> care unsuited to the sixth-formers' new dignity. In fact, however,
> definitions of what he should do reflect clearly the desire for both
> independence *and* guidance.[3]

[1] ibid., p. 105.
[2] *Enquiry 1*, p. 139.
[3] Edwards and Webb, op. cit., p. 47.

The need for a gradually evolving and increasing partnership has been sidetracked in recent years by the 'democratic' movement, who, perhaps with excellent intentions, have wanted 'rights' for the young, but who have sought to get them by processes borrowed from union politics. This 'Children's Rights' movement essentially confirms adolescents as a separate sub-group. It tends to take the worst aspects of union power politics for models, especially the presumed worker/management dichotomy. I see this movement not as partnership, but as divisive and harmful in a school organized with pupil forums as I have described. The best interests of the teacher are met by identifying, and going as far as possible in meeting, the best interests of the pupils. Pastoral care need not be merely patronizing: it certainly requires the pupils' voices to be heard and registered if it is to succeed; but a strident 'Rights' movement is likely to damage it in a well-run school.

The quality of care depends on the quality of regard, and on a willingness to recognize the secondary-school pupil as already on the foothills of maturity. The ideal asks for the school to be a series of partnerships of different sorts:

> Young people must be provided not with separate, scaled-down versions of adult institutions, political, social and recreational, but admitted as junior partners into adult concerns: or as senior partners when they show their capacity to hold senior positions.[1]

Conclusion

In secondary schools today, we are all, in our piecemeal, amateur, and contradictory ways, creating a new kind of school experience. It will be an experience that is based on the realization that 'secondary schooling for all' means that a secondary school is not merely a preparation for life, but actually part of life. The American sociologist Professor Coleman has put it cogently:

> Changes have developed in the respective roles of schools and society. Now that society outside the schools has become rich as a source of information, but impoverished as a source of activity for the young, schools need to assume a new outlook. It is less important for them to transmit, as hitherto, vicarious experiences than to provide direct experience in the form of activities no longer available in the outside world.[2]

[1] Musgrove, Frank, *Youth and the Social Order* (Routledge and Kegan Paul, 1964), p. 157.
[2] MS report of Ditchley Foundation Conference 'Education and Youth Problems', February 19–21, 1971.

If this is to be so, the pattern of relationships will be the matrix into which the care will fit, and the relationships will change in four interlocking sets: with the community, with employment, with parents, and with pupils. In this book I and my contributors have tried to pay attention to each of these components. It is on the relationship with pupils that the final emphasis must be placed. In my introduction I quoted the persuasive words of Derek Morrell, and it is with a further reference to that important speech that I wish to stress the central point of this book:

> If there is positive reciprocity of feeling and aspiration as between the teachers and the taught, satisfying to both, there is a describable curricular reality; the teachers are contributing to the learning which is taking place, they are helping to create new realities. But if there is no such reciprocity, if there is total absence of mutual emotional satisfaction, the curriculum remains simply an idea in the minds of the teachers: it lacks reality, even though the teachers teach and the children go through the motions of scholarship activity.[1]

Most readers will recognize the force of the criticism that 'the curriculum remains simply an idea in the minds of the teachers'. The organization of pastoral care is concerned with creating an environment in which that 'reciprocity' can flourish. Too often the 'hidden curriculum', as the jargon now identifies it, is in contradiction to the best aspects of the ostensible curriculum.

The paradox of the school is that never before has close pastoral care been so important for the total well-being of pupils and society, and yet never before has it been so difficult to establish the best pattern of care. To do so, though, is the central challenge to the school today and in the foreseeable future.

[1] Derek Morrell, speech to the Anglo-American Educational Association, reprinted in *The Times Educational Supplement* (19 December 1969).

A Pastoral Reading List

This highly selected, and partly annotated, list of seventy-six books (plus two bibliographies and three periodicals) is planned as a basic reading list for an experienced teacher who wishes to consider in some detail the pastoral needs of a school and its pupils. The field is not evenly covered by published works, and thus even a selective list cannot be fully balanced.

There is now a large library of books on the broad social issues that lie behind the need for pastoral care, and a fair selection of these has been listed. The number of studies of the mechanics of school organization is still remarkably low – the subject seems to be regarded as too mundane for the academic and too remote for the teacher! The theory and practice of counselling has been well served, as, in recent years, have the needs of home/school relations – though in this last category the younger ages are covered in more detail.

In footnotes to the text full bibliographical references have been given for the sources of all quotations. Also a number of specific suggestions for further reading have been made where a particular book or article has seemed very closely connected with the point being made. Some of these titles are repeated here.

I have ventured to asterisk a selection from this full list as 'essential' titles for a starting point. (The place of publication is London unless otherwise stated.)

M. M.

The Social Background

CRAFT, MAURICE (ed.), *Family Class and Education – A Reader* (Longman, 1970): performance in school is related through a series of studies to aspects of background.

DALE, R. R., and GRIFFITHS, S., *Downstream – failure in the Grammar School* (Routledge and Kegan Paul, 1965).

FLOUD. J. E., HALSEY, A. H., and MARTIN, F. M., *Social Class and Educational Opportunity* (Heinemann, 1956).

FORD, J., *Social Class and the Comprehensive School* (Routledge and Kegan Paul, 1967).

JACKSON, B., and MARSDEN, D., *Education and the Working Class* (Routledge and Kegan Paul, 1962): a by now classic study of the relationship between background and the academic experience of grammar schools.

MAYS, JOHN BARRON, *Education and the Urban Child* (Liverpool University Press, 1962): based on the problems of central Liverpool, this discusses the work and problems of urban schools and their neighbourhoods.
The School in its social setting (Longman, 1967).

MUSGROVE, FRANK, and TAYLOR, PHILIP H., *Society and the Teacher's Role* (Routledge and Kegan Paul, 1969).

*MUSGROVE, FRANK, *Family, Education and Society* (Routledge and Kegan Paul, 1966): a challenging study of the family with emphasis on relationships with schools.

Comprehensive Schools

*BENN, CAROLINE, and SIMON, BRIAN, *Half Way There* (McGraw-Hill, 1970); Revised Edition (Penguin, 1972): a painstaking survey, which patiently and with understanding compares most aspects of the existing comprehensive schools. An invaluable though lengthy book.

BURGESS, TYRELL, *Inside Comprehensive Schools* (HMSO, 1970): although written for the layman, some chapters are among the best accounts of the reasoning behind such schools.

HALSALL, ELIZABETH (ed.), *Becoming Comprehensive* (Pergamon, Oxford, 1970): a series of case histories written by the headteachers of a number of schools.

HALSALL, ELIZABETH, *The Comprehensive School* (Pergamon, 1973): this is a detailed survey of the available research to discuss its practical implications. The author covers most aspects of school organization.

HOLMES, MAURICE, *The Comprehensive School in Action* (Longman, 1967): a fairly routine account of a typical comprehensive-school structure.

ILEA, *London Comprehensive Schools 1966* (Inner London Education Authority, 1967): obviously such a survey dates rapidly but the data on school organization and the work of departments is worth study.

MILLER, T. W. G., *Values in the Comprehensive School* (Oliver and Boyd, 1961): a classic study which endeavours to plot the overall aims of the school.

MILES, MARGARET, *Comprehensive Schooling* (Longman 1968): the Headmistress of Mayfield School, London, describes her approaches in a readable account.

MONKS, T. G., *Comprehensive Education in England and Wales* (NFER, 1968).
Comprehensive Education in Action (NFER, 1970): a statistical research survey with an excellent section on pastoral care.

PEDLEY, ROBIN, *The Comprehensive School*, Revised Edition (Penguin, 1969): the best general theory and survey.

*ROSS, J. M., *et al.*, *A Critical Appraisal of Comprehensive Education* (NFER, 1972): the last of the main NFER research reports, this looked at twelve schools and usefully compares each aspect. Important.

ROWE, ALBERT, *The School, as a Guidance Community* (Pearson Press, 1971): a personal and forceful account of the writer's Hull school.

RUBINSTEIN, DAVID, and SIMON, BRIAN, *The Evolution of the Comprehensive School* (Routledge and Kegan Paul, 1969): such a historical survey, which charts clearly the steps to comprehensive schools via 'multi-lateral' ones, may seem academic. In fact this book is essential reading if the problems and possibilities of today's schools are to be fully understood by the teachers.

Bibliography

BURTON, W. J., *Comprehensive Education, A Select Annotated Bibliography* (NFER, 1971).

Studies of Youth

This important section is of surveys to portray the school's clients. Neither statistics nor speculation can do so fully, but the insights are a vital addition to a teacher's personal experience.

BAZALGETTE, JOHN, *Freedom, Authority and the Young Adult* (Pitman, 1971): a provocative research report on the interaction between adults and young people, 'in particular examining how the resources of adults are used by young people as they take up full adult roles in society'. Important.

DANIEL, R., BUTLER, N. and GOLDSTEIN, H., *From Birth to Seven*, (Longman, 1972): the first report of the National Child Development's cohort study has implications for the whole of schooling.

DOUGLAS, J. W. B., *The Home and the School*, a study of ability and attainment in primary schools, (MacGibbon and Kee, 1964): a study of a large nation-wide sample of children from birth through primary school. Among the findings is a new assessment of the importance of homes.

DOUGLAS, J. W. B., ROSS, J. M., and SIMPSON, H. R., *All our Future*, a longitudinal study of secondary education (Peter Davies, 1968): a nation-wide sample of pupils studied from birth; their secondary experience is reported on here.

ERIKSON, ERIK H., *Identity, Youth, and Crisis* (Faber, 1968): an important psychological study of the 'identity crisis' of adolescence.

MILLER, DEREK, *The Age Between: Adolescents in a Disturbed Society* (Hutchinson, 1969).

MITCHELL, JOHN J., *Adolescence, Some Critical Issues* (Holt, Rinehart and Winston, Toronto 1971): although written from a North American standpoint, this is a thought-provoking and useful study.

MORTON-WILLIAMS, R., *et al.*, *Sixth Form Pupils and Teachers*, Volume I (Books for Schools Ltd for the Schools Council, 1970): a massive statistical survey with sections on 'The Pupils and Their Backgrounds, 'Pupils' Attitudes', and 'The Teachers'. It is most valuable in exploring the reality of assumptions commonly held.

MUSGROVE, FRANK, *Youth and the Social Order* (Routledge and Kegan Paul, 1964): this witty, deep, and well-researched book is a personal exploration of the 'status of youth', its determinants and consequences. Well worth reading.

*SCHOOLS COUNCIL, *Enquiry 1: Young School Leavers* (HMSO, 1968): report of an extensive survey of young people, parents, and teachers. Essential reading, though it needs interpreting with care.

SHIPMAN, MARTIN, *Childhood – a sociological perspective* (NFER, 1972).

SUMNER, R. and WARBURTON, F. W., *Achievement in Secondary School* (NFER, 1972): a fascinating attempt to survey the characteristics that go with school success and 'allergy'.

*WALL, W. D., *Adolescents in School and Society* (NFER, 1968): an outstanding analysis of young people, drawing on a wide range of mainly psychological but also sociological research.

Internal Organization

GUNN, S. E., 'Teaching Groups in Secondary Schools', *Trends in Education* (July 1970): a good introductory survey to the possible grouping methods in secondary schools.

*HARGREAVES, DAVID H., *Social Relations in a Secondary School* (Routledge and Kegan Paul: 1967): an interesting sociological study with implications on grouping and organization.

HEYCOCK, CLAYTON, *Internal Organisation and Management*, (Sceptre Publishing, 1970): a report on a survey of a number of comprehensive schools. The chapter on responsibilities is good, and the diagrams very valuable.

D.E.S., *Slow Learners in Secondary Schools* (HMSO, 1971).

MARLAND, MICHAEL, *Head of Department* (Heinemann, 1970): although written for potential Heads of Department, this gives a detailed account of how a secondary subject-department might be organized and therefore discusses many organizational aspects of comprehensive schools.

*MOORE, B. M., *Guidance in Comprehensive Schools* (NFER, 1970): compares the organization of different types of comprehensive school. Excellent.

*RICHARDSON, ELIZABETH. *The Teacher, The School, and The Task of Management* (Heinemann, 1973): a very important book that examines a school in change, and especially the role relationships, in great detail.

SHIPMAN, M. D., *Sociology of the School* (Longman, 1968): a helpful book to get one thinking about the school as a community.

YATES, A., *Organising Schooling* (Routledge and Kegan Paul, 1971): Yates edited a mammoth international survey of grouping practices for UNESCO. This more recent book is a shorter, more readable account.

Counselling

BLOCHER, DONALD, H., *Developmental Counseling* (Ronald, New York, 1966).

CRAFT, M. and LYTTON, H. (eds.), *Guidance and Counselling in British Schools* (Arnold, 1969).

DAWS, P. P., *A Good Start in Life* (Careers Research Advisory Centre, 1968).

HALMOS, P., *The Faith of the Counsellors* (Constable, 1965).

HOLDEN, A., *Teachers as Counsellors* (Constable, 1969).
Counselling in Secondary Schools (Constable, 1971).

JONES, ANNE, *Counselling in Practice* (Ward Lock, 1970).

SCHOOLS COUNCIL, *Counselling in Schools*, Working Paper No. 15 (HMSO, 1967).

*TYLER, LEONA E., *The Work of the Counselor*, 3rd edition (Appleton-Century – Crofts, New York 1969).

VENABLES, ETHEL, *Counselling* (The National Marriage Guidance Council, 1971).

Relationships with Homes

CAVE, R. G., *Partnership for Change: Parents and Schools*, (Ward Lock Educational, 1970).

*CRAFT, M., RAYNOR, J., and COHEN, L., (eds.), *Linking Home and School*, revised and enlarged edition (Longman, 1971).

FRASER, E., *The Home Environment and the School* (University of London Press, 1959).

LINDSAY, C., *School and Community* (Pergamon Press, Oxford 1970): two Scottish comprehensive schools are studied and reported on in detail 'to discover the role of the school in the community'.

MCGEENEY, PATRICK, *Parents are Welcome* (Longman, 1969): as well as arguing the general case, this gives case-histories of particular schools, including secondary schools.

MIDWINTER, ERIC, *Home and School Relations in Educational Priority Areas* (Liverpool EPA Project, 1970): brings out the *educational* needs in a school's relationship with home.

SHARROCK, ANN, *Home/School Relations: Their Importance in Education* (Macmillan, 1970).

Bibliography

SHARROCK, ANNE, *Home and School*, a select and annotated bibliography (NFER, 1971): a very useful survey of the whole field.

Miscellaneous

Obviously, the pastoral aspect of education is so central, that
very many books on education are worth reading in this
context. This is a sample, including some on aspects of the
curriculum, which are especially relevant to pastoral questions.

CLEGG, ALEC, and MEGSON, BARBARA, *Children in Distress*
(Penguin, 1968).

DEPARTMENT OF EDUCATION AND SCIENCE, *Careers Education in Secondary Schools* (HMSO, 1973).

HARDY, MAUREEN: (ed.), *At Classroom Level* (Forum Publications, 1971). See especially Part II.

HAYES, J., and HOPSON, B., *Careers Guidance, the role of the
school in vocational development* (Heinemann, 1971): a thorough
survey of the whole field from psychological testing to careers
in the curriculum.

LYONS, K. H., *Social Work and the School* (HMSO, 1973): a
study of the role of an Educational Social Worker.

MARLAND, MICHAEL, *Towards the New Fifth* (Longman, 1969):
a discussion of the part to be played by English and the
Humanities with older pupils after the raising of the school
leaving age, with some possible schemes for linking subjects.

RICHARDSON, ELIZABETH, *The Environment of Learning*
(Heinemann, 1973): this classic book on relationships within
a school is now re-issued in the Organization in Schools series.

RUBINSTEIN, DAVID, and STONEMAN, COLIN (eds.), *Education
for Democracy* (Penguin, 1970; revised edition, 1972): an
uneven collection of essays claiming to be a 'radical mani-
festo' on British education. A number of contributors have
important points about comprehensive schools and their
underlying thoughts.

SCHOOLS COUNCIL, *Cross'd with Adversity*, Working Paper No.
27 (Evans/Methuen, 1970).

STROUD, JOHN, *An Introduction to the Child Care Service* (Longman, 1965): a helpful brief survey.

TAYLOR, L. C., *Resources for Learning* (Penguin, 1971).

TIBBLE, J. W. (ed.), *The Extra Year* (Routledge and Kegan Paul,
1970).

TURNER, BARRY (ed.), *Discipline in Schools* (Ward Lock Educational, 1973): a well contrasted and down-to-earth series of essays.

WALTON, JACK (ed.), *The Secondary School Timetable* (Ward Lock Educational, 1972).

YOUNG, MICHAEL, *The Rise of the Meritocracy* (Thames and Hudson, 1958, and Penguin Books, 1961): a brilliant satire that postulates the ultimate situation if selection were to be extended and refined.

Periodicals

Forum – a thrice-yearly journal 'for the discussion of new trends in education', published from 71 Clarendon Park Road, Leicester. Has specialized in the comprehensive school, and in ways of working with mixed-ability groups.

Comprehensive Education – the journal of the Comprehensive Schools Committee.

Trends in Education (HMSO, quarterly). A combination of theoretical consideration, comparative survey, and practical suggestion, edited from the Department of Education and Science. There is a strong tradition of excellent articles on school-organization policy.

The Contributors

C. JAMES GILL

Mr Gill taught in the Isle of Man and London for sixteen years, and was headmaster of Salford Grammar School for a short time before joining H.M. Inspectorate of Schools. After twenty years in the Inspectorate he retired in 1965 from the position of Chief Inspector (Teacher Training) and was awarded the C.B. In the same year he was appointed Gulbenkian Lecturer in Education in the Institute of Education, University of Keele, to take charge of the course leading to a Diploma in the Advanced Study of Education with Special Reference to Counselling. This was one of the first university courses in counselling in this country.

Mr Gill retired from a senior lectureship in 1971. Among his interests, apart from education, he includes fell walking, gardening, photography and the theatre.

BOB GROVE

After graduating in English and Education at York University, Bob Grove taught English and Drama and was a tutor at a large comprehensive school in London. He is now a member of staff at the Park House Therapeutic Community, Godalming.

DENIS E. INCE

After varied experience in child-guidance work and secondary-school teaching, Denis Ince moved for seven years in colleges of education before becoming Head of Department of Social Sciences at Edge Hill College of Education, well known for its practical emphasis on the place of a social understanding in education. He also lectures part-time at the University of Liverpool; is Chairman of the Youth and Community Work Training Association; is a Marriage Guidance Counsellor; and has recently written a book with the title *Contact* – an account of three-year research project on work with socially deprived young people in Liverpool.

PATRICK MCGEENEY

After thirteen years' teaching in secondary school and in further education, Patrick McGeeney did five years' research with the

Institute of Community Studies. He was a lecturer in Education at the Exeter University Department of Education, and is now in teacher-training at Manchester University.

With Michael Young he has written *Learning Begins at Home* (Routledge and Kegan Paul, 1968) and on his own wrote *Parents are Welcome* (Longman, 1969). He is a frequent contributor to *Where*.

MICHAEL MARLAND

After reading English and History at Cambridge, Michael Marland taught at a German Oberschule and then at Simon Langton Grammar school for boys in Canterbury. From there he went as Head of the English Department to Abbey Wood, a mixed comprehensive school for 1,200 in South-East London. Then for five years he was Head of English at Crown Woods School, a comprehensive school of 2,000 pupils, where he later became Director of Studies. He is now Headmaster of Woodberry Down Comprehensive School in North London.

He is on the committee of the York/Nuffield enquiry into the preparation of teachers for working with socially deprived children, the Independent Television Authority's School's Committee, the Schools Council's English Committee, its Working Party on the Whole Curriculum, and the Council's Drama Sub-Committee, of which he is Chairman. He is also on the Bullock Committee on the Teaching of Reading and the Uses of English.

CHARLES STUART-JERVIS

Charles Stuart-Jervis is Headmaster of Abbey Wood School, an eight-form-entry mixed comprehensive school in South-East London. Among other things he is a novelist, writer, and lecturer. Although he did not come into teaching until his early thirties, he has had wide experience as a year master, sixth-form master, and Head of English in comprehensive schools. He has also been Head of Aristotle Secondary School and Samuel Pepys Comprehensive School, both in London.

He reviews regularly for *The Teacher* and *Times Educational Supplement*, and in the past four years has been involved in developing management courses for secondary schools. He has lectured widely on management and the teaching of English and Drama.

Index

BIBLIOTHÈQUE CHAMPLAIN

3 9365 00175037 3